D0282897

THE FIFTH ALFRED I. duPONT-COLUMBIA UNIVERSITY

SURVEY OF BROADCAST JOURNALISM

THE ALFRED I. DUPONT–COLUMBIA UNIVERSITY SURVEY AND AWARDS IN BROADCAST JOURNALISM

THE JURORS

Richard T. Baker
Edward W. Barrett
Dorothy Height

John Houseman
Sig Mickelson
Michael Novak

Elie Abel, chairman

Marvin Barrett, director

Barbara Eddings, assistant director

Louis G. Cowan, director of special projects,
Columbia University Graduate School of Journalism

JURORS EMERITUS

Arthur Morse, 1968–1969
Sir William Haley, 1968–1969
Michael Arlen, 1968–1970
Marya Mannes, 1968–1970

DUPONT FELLOWS

William Seifert, 1968–1969
Thomas Goldstein, 1968–1969
Michael Hanson, 1969–1970
Helen Epstein, 1970–1971
Michael Meadvin, 1971–1972
Steven Petrou, 1971–1972
Zachary Sklar, 1973–1974

THE FIFTH ALFRED I. duPONT-
COLUMBIA UNIVERSITY
SURVEY OF
BROADCAST JOURNALISM

Moments of Truth?

EDITED BY MARVIN BARRETT

Thomas Y. Crowell Company
Established 1834 • New York

743333

Copyright © 1975 by The Trustees of Columbia University
in the City of New York

All rights reserved. Except for use in a review, the reproduction or
utilization of this work in any form or by any electronic, mechanical,
or other means, now known or hereafter invented, including xerogra-
phy, photocopying, and recording, and in any information storage and
retrieval system is forbidden without the written permission of the
publisher. Published simultaneously in Canada by Fitzhenry & White-
side Limited, Toronto.

L. C. Card 74–32575

Manufactured in the United States of America

Library of Congress Cataloging in Publication Data

Barrett, Marvin.
    Moments of truth?

    (The Fifth Alfred I. du Pont-Columbia University sur-
vey of broadcast journalism)
    Includes index.
    1. Television broadcasting of news--United States.
I. Title. II. Series: Alfred I. Du Pont Foundation.
The Alfred I. Du Pont-Columbia University survey of
broadcast journalism ; 1972/73.
FN4784.T4A43 1972/73   384.55'4
    ISBN 0–690–00680–2   74–34201
      0–8152–0370–5 (Apollo edition)

1   2   3   4   5   6   7   8   9   10

Foreword

LITTLE DID Jessie Ball duPont realize when in 1942 she established the Alfred I. duPont Foundation to honor the memory of her husband by encouraging broadcasting in the public service what was in store, over thirty years later, for her devoted servants at the Alfred I. duPont–Columbia University Survey and Awards in Broadcast Journalism.

We of the staff have been through the most exciting and excruciating eighteen months in the history of the media. The following pages, which attempt to tell part of the tale, are dedicated to the brave men and women who came through with flying colors, and others no less brave who didn't.

—MARVIN BARRETT

Contents

GREAT TRUTHS do not take hold of the hearts of the masses. And now as all the world is in error, how shall I, though I know the true path, how shall I guide? If I know that I cannot succeed and yet try to force success, this would be but another source of error. Better then to desist and strive no more. But if I do not strive, who will?

—CHUANG TZU
Chinese sage, 369–286 B.C.

IF WE SHOULD ever fail in our responsibility, to whom could the people turn for the truth?

—Elton Rule
President,
American Broadcasting Company, Inc.
May 23, 1973

THE FIFTH ALFRED I. duPONT-
COLUMBIA UNIVERSITY

SURVEY OF
BROADCAST
JOURNALISM

1 • The Truth Confounded:
Watergate I

THE GUT QUESTION before this committee is not one of individual guilt or innocence. The gut question for committee and country alike is and was, how much truth do we want?

A few men gambled that Americans wanted the quiet of efficiency rather than the turbulence of truth. They were stopped a yard short of the goal by another few who believed in America as advertised.

So the story to come has its significance not in the acts of men breaking, entering, and bugging the Watergate but in the acts of men who almost stole America.

The date was May 17, 1973; the place, the Senate Caucus Room, which mature TV viewers remembered from the Army-McCarthy hearings held in the same chamber two decades before. The occasion was the first session of the seven-man Senate Select Committee on Presidential Campaign Activities. The speaker was Lowell Weicker, a large, deceptively bland-looking man, the panel's youngest member, the junior senator from Connecticut, and a Republican whose stripe had, in recent months, become uncertain.

His remarks had been preceded by those of two fellow senators: the venerable Sam Ervin, from North Carolina, who as chairman had gaveled the Watergate hearings to order at precisely ten that morning, and Vice Chairman Howard Baker, from Tennessee.

Ervin and Baker were the undoubted stars of the show, which was to dominate the nation's TV sets for eleven weeks, outranking its predecessor on the premises in both durability and impact.

At first hearing, Weicker's words might have seemed senatorial hyperbole. As things developed, they were, if anything, an understatement.

The remarks were heard by more than seventeen million Americans on the four TV networks and millions more on radio stations across the land.

By the end of the first five days of hearings A. C. Nielsen

estimated that 47.4 million households, or 73.2 percent of all
television households in America, had tuned in to at least one of
the Watergate sessions. The audience continued to grow as star
witnesses began testifying. CBS estimated that at the end of
thirty-seven days of hearings viewers had spent 1.6 billion home-
hours watching daytime coverage on the three networks, or 24.4
hours of viewing per television home. Four hundred million
home-hours more were spent watching Watergate on public
television stations—equivalent to another six hours per home.

The cost to the broadcasting industry for production, lost time,
and advertising was estimated to be $7 million to $10 million.

Watergate was, according to Richard Salant, president of CBS
News:

> . . . the major peacetime story of this generation and quite
> possibly in the entire history of the United States. It certainly
> will be more than a footnote to history, more than a chapter; it
> will be whole history books—and quite a lot of them. It
> involves allegations concerning actions and non-actions of the
> incumbent of the highest office of the land, of the most
> powerful office in the world—and those whom he had chosen
> to work immediately with him. It involves issues relating to the
> fundamentals of our governmental structure, of the demo-
> cratic process, of the relationship between the governors and
> the governed, of the basics of the election process itself.

Actually, as far as the press was concerned, the major digging
was all but done. It had been eleven months since the bungled early
morning break-in of the Democratic headquarters in the mammoth
Washington, D.C., complex known as Watergate had led to the
arrest of the perpetrators.

Since then, thanks mainly to the persistence of two young
reporters on the Washington *Post*, the ripples caused by what
presidential Press Secretary Ron Ziegler dismissed as "a third-rate
burglary attempt" had become waves that threatened to capsize the
ship of state.

In less than a year the process of patient revelation had brought
about the resignation, discharge, and indictment of more than a
dozen men from the staffs of the White House and the Committee
to Re-elect the President, not counting the seven hirelings directly
involved in the act. And, as Senator Weicker implied, this was only
the beginning.

But if the investigative work was mainly completed as far as the press was concerned, the media's part in the larger drama was far from played out.

Already the Watergate story had been given credit for restoring the morale and credibility of a badly shaken profession, and if Senator Weicker were to be believed, for saving America itself from being ripped off. In addition to the indefatigable gumshoeing of reporters Bob Woodward and Carl Bernstein, prodigious professional risks had been taken, mainly by editor Ben Bradlee and publisher Katharine Graham, of the Washington *Post*, who had persisted in backing the story when few others in the business of informing America chose to be interested.*

Former attorney general John Mitchell had used a brutally vulgar expression to describe Mrs. Graham's uncomfortable position. Ron Ziegler had denounced her reporters' work as "shabby journalism, based on hearsay, character assassination, innuendo or guilt by association." But the risk had paid off. By spring 1973 Mrs. Graham's team had seen Mitchell's hubris wilt and had won apologies from Ziegler. The president himself had indicated some remorse. In his April 30 address to the nation, two and a half weeks before the hearings began, the president announced the resignations of his two top staff members, H. R. Haldeman and John Ehrlichman, and his current attorney general, Richard Kleindienst, and fired his legal counsel, John Dean, before a nationwide TV audience of 66.5 million Americans. Minutes later in the White House press briefing room the president told a group of reporters and photographers: "Ladies and gentlemen of the press, we have had our differences in the past, and I hope you give me hell every time you think I'm wrong. I hope I'm worthy of your trust."

This victory, or armistice, as it turned out, reflected little credit on broadcasters. As so often before, they had been late and light on the story. It wasn't until October 1972 that Walter Cronkite anchored a two-part report totaling twenty-three minutes on "The CBS Evening News" which for the first time put the Watergate story clearly and substantially before millions of Americans. In

---

* How great the risks were was confirmed sometime later by the leaking of corrected versions of tapes of White House conversations held in September 1972, during which Nixon, referring to the special attention the *Post* was giving Watergate, commented, "The main thing is the *Post* is going to have damnable, damnable problems out of this one. They have a television station and they're going to have to get it renewed. The game has to be played awfully rough." In January 1973 the license of WJXT, the Post-owned station in Jacksonville, was challenged by three groups, with Nixon cronies prominent in two. In the same month WPLG Miami, another Post-owned station up for license renewal, had gotten the same treatment from another group of pro-Nixonites. In November 1974 the WPLG challenge was suddenly withdrawn without explanation.

broadcast terms it was an act of considerable courage. For *Post* editor Bradlee, who at that moment, after four months of virtually solitary and highly visible digging, was wondering if he would ever get reinforcements on his heavily bombarded beachhead, Cronkite's arrival was a lifesaver. "Editors throughout the country really downplayed the Watergate story and dismissed it as a vagary of the Washington *Post*," said Bradlee. "The editors began to move these stories up only after Cronkite did the two segments on Watergate— they were blessed by the great white father." His ironic words were an impressive acknowledgment by one medium of another's prodigious impact.

Nevertheless, once CBS had taken the leap (there had been reports of pressure from the highest quarters to tone down the second installment) there was no comparable follow-up on the other networks.

The story sputtered along through the election and inauguration with NBC, ABC, and PBS (the Public Broadcasting Service) still to give it any comprehensive attention.* The first extended ABC report came in April 1973; NBC and PBS waited until early May.

Although Senator Ervin's committee was established in February, it was not until March, nine months after the break-in, that James McCord, an ex-CIA employee and one of the five men caught in the act, wrote a letter to Judge John Sirica, chief judge in the Watergate break-in trial, alleging perjury and involvement in high places. All at once, and together, the most reluctant editors and news directors came to attention.

Quickly, the TV press became the principal purveyor of the story to the nation. Not because TV had more inclination or talent for conveying it, but because the principals and the American public chose to have it that way.

Following McCord's letter to Sirica the story spilled out in

---

* Members of the Network News Study Group in the department of political science at Massachusetts Institute of Technology surveyed network television coverage of Watergate during the 1972 campaign. Their conclusion: "Early evening news watchers by and large received . . . a fairly straight serving of headlines from the *Post* and other newspapers. There was little original reporting by any network and almost nothing that could be called investigative reporting." In the seven weeks before the election, CBS devoted 71 minutes 9 seconds to Watergate. ABC devoted 42 minutes 26 seconds, NBC, 41 minutes 21 seconds. CBS did minute-or-less items only five times. More than half of NBC's stories were less than a minute long; slightly less than half of ABC's were. Two shocking examples of important items given short shrift: NBC gave only 34 seconds to the decision of Representative Wright Patman's banking committee not to investigate Watergate. ABC gave only 12 seconds to the Washington *Post* story that named H. R. Haldeman for the first time in connection with Watergate.

multiple versions. The procession to the talk and panel shows began. Between mid-March and the opening week of the hearings, Watergate-related guests appeared on "Meet the Press," "Issues and Answers," "Face the Nation," "60 Minutes," "The CBS Morning News," "Today," the Dick Cavett and Johnny Carson shows, "First Tuesday," "The Reasoner Report," Elizabeth Drew's "Thirty Minutes With . . ." and an unspecified number of local radio and TV shows.

In the months that followed, the number of guests increased, as did the seriousness of the talk. Both John Dean and John Ehrlichman were heard prior to their Senate appearances in trial runs before national TV cameras.*

Of those presidential spokesmen who remained loyal and were not under indictment the most conspicuous undoubtedly was Patrick Buchanan, who seldom missed an opportunity to bad-mouth the press. Only Vice-President Spiro Agnew seemed to make less use than usual of the air—Agnew and the president himself, who after one last attempt to explain Watergate five days after the hearings began, lapsed into a three-month silence.

If there was any doubt that TV had made the story its own, the next eleven weeks in the Senate Caucus Room dispelled it.

It was a proprietorship that commercial TV networks seemed not completely happy to have. After the first five days, with all four networks in attendance, across-the-board coverage of the hearings lapsed. The reasons given varied. The viewers objected. The ratings had declined. It cost too much. It was against the public interest. One or two networks could do it as well as four.

---

* How much TV was taken for granted by the White House was demonstrated by the following conversation taped in the Oval Office March 27, 1973.
The participants: the president, Haldeman, and Ehrlichman.
The subject: Jeb Stuart Magruder.

> *H.* If Magruder goes public on this, then you know—
> *P.* Incidentally, if Magruder does that, let's see what it does to Magruder.
> *E.* It depends on how he does it. If he does it under immunity, it doesn't do anything to him.
> *P.* All right—except ruin him.
> *H.* Well, yeah. It ruins in a way. He becomes a folk hero to the guys.
> *P.* He becomes an immediate hero with the media . . .
> *E.* Mike Wallace will get him and he will go on "60 Minutes," and he will come across as the All-American Boy . . . who was serving his president, his attorney general, and they misled him.

Actually, it was Ehrlichman who went on with Wallace three months later. Magruder waited until June 1974, when his autobiography was published on the eve of his departure for prison. At that time he appeared with Barbara Walters on the "Today" show, Dick Cavett, and Paul Duke on PBS' "The Washington Connection."

In self-justification the networks leaned heavily on half-truths. Many viewers did object at first to being deprived of their soap operas and games, but the publicizing of their objections brought a large and enthusiastic flow of mail supporting network coverage of the hearings. The final mail count at two of the three networks was substantially in favor: at ABC 64 percent for, 36 percent against; at CBS 61 percent for, 39 percent against. At NBC the score was tied.

For public TV, which gave some of its viewers a double dose of the hearings, live during the day, replayed on tape at night, they brought in the largest audience and greatest inflow of cash contributions ($1.5 million) in its history. In the first fortnight of the coverage the National Public Affairs Center for Television (NPACT) received 66,000 letters, 99 percent favorable.

Although, mysteriously, daytime viewing in New York diminished 30 percent, thanks to across-the-board coverage of the hearings, the Television Information Office reported that the average audience for Watergate coast to coast ran 12 percent higher than the entertainment programming it replaced.

Gross advertising revenues lost to the commercial networks were unquestionably high, being estimated at as much as $600,000 a day on those days when the hearings were carried by all three. A small part of this figure was made up by slipping commercials in before and after the proceedings and by "make good" ads, which were rescheduled at another time and place in the broadcast day.

However, there were some unacknowledged benefits to the networks. As the investigations proceeded, evidence accumulated that broadcasters had been under uncomfortable pressure from the subjects of the hearings. One fallout of the hearings was that such behind-the-scenes pressure became less and less likely. Also, the network news and public affairs departments, the people directly concerned with Watergate coverage, had been since 1969 engaged in a desperate struggle with the White House to preserve their credibility and good name (DuPont-Columbia Surveys 1969–70, 1970–71, 1971–72). The Watergate hearings were a crucial engagement in that struggle.

The White House had badly misjudged the networks' behavior.

According to tapes released later, the president had not expected live coverage because of the enormous cost. President Nixon had estimated that the networks would give the hearings at most "five or ten minutes on the evening news."

As for public interest, the reasoning was that the TV audience deserved a choice and this could be provided by rotating coverage among the three commercial networks with public TV bringing up the rear. For the sake of their millions of addicted fans and to reduce network costs, the games and soap operas should be permitted to return on two out of three of the systems every day.

Rotation was instituted on June 5, the first time that networks had ever entered into an agreement to take turns covering an extended major news event. The decision was a possible trial balloon for rotating coverage of future party conventions and some presidential speeches.

Such rotation assumed that the entire country would still have access to live coverage of the hearings on at least one TV channel in every market. Although rotation in the large markets did give the viewer such an option, in smaller markets with fewer than three channels the Watergate hearings were regularly unavailable.

In spite of their reluctance and rationalizations, the four networks were all back in the hearing room on June 25 after a week's recess that was called to spare Soviet Communist party leader Leonid Brezhnev any unpleasantness during his visit. The chief attraction was John Dean, the president's counsel, who promised to be the first witness to implicate his former boss directly in the affair. The interest in Dean's testimony and his negotiating power for immunity had both been built up by a TV appearance and a torrent of leaks concerning what Dean was telling in preliminary talks with the committee staff.

The Dean leaks, which were ascribed to both sides (Dean's attorneys said the White House was using this means to discredit Dean before he had a chance to be heard in public), were the most conspicuous to date in an investigation in which, before it ended, the practice of using unnamed sources would be a major issue.

The buildup of Dean's appearance was more than justified. The testimony, delivered by the dapper, unflappable young man over five days, in an unhesitating monotone and with apparently total recall, was in many ways the climax of the TV coverage of Watergate.

No one could estimate how many millions listened to the president's former counsel finger the boss, since it was a non-report week for ratings on the networks. The vast number who did tune in heard for the first time of the cover-up, the enemies list, the political use of the IRS, hush money, and offers of clemency in exchange for witness silence.

The truthfulness of Dean's testimony remained at issue from the first day he gave it, but accurate or not, for many Americans what led up to and followed the Watergate break-in was never again quite so clearly focused and logically explained. Nor was there the slightest question as far as Dean's testimony was concerned as to where the primary responsibility lay.

Following Dean's appearance, approval of the president by the American people dropped to 40 percent, a 28 percent decline since the previous January and the sharpest six-month drop in popularity ever recorded for a chief executive.

The publishers' and broadcasters' communication of unadulterated John Dean, however innocent of bias it may have been, was undoubtedly the single most provoking thing that had happened to the president in all the pages and hours of Watergate coverage thus far.

Prior to Dean's appearance on the witness stand there had been some pretense of the president's leading the search for the true miscreants, of his being on the senators' side in the pursuit of truth. Now, as in a Hitchcock film, the supposed leader of the hunt was revealed as the quarry. The pack, which had already been loudly sniffing, turned, senators and press, Republican and Democrat alike. The question changed from "Who was responsible for the act?" to, in the words of one of the president's staunchest backers, "What did the president know? When did he know it? And what did he do about it?"

As the hearings proceeded, they trooped on and off camera, the earnest, clean-cut, frequently shaken young men and their less obviously accommodating elders. The parade went on for thirty-seven days, was interrupted for seven weeks, returned again for sixteen days in the fall, and then went off the air forever.

In those few months the American people had a great deal to assimilate. As chief majority counsel Samuel Dash said, "With television every citizen could sit in his living room and hear the evidence."

In addition to Dean, Americans had heard Herbert Porter, assistant to Maurice Stans in the Committee to Re-elect the President, another well-groomed young man although considerably less sure of himself. Porter said wistfully, after admitting to lying to both the FBI and the grand jury,

> I kind of drifted along. . . . In all honesty [I did nothing] probably because of the fear of group pressure that would ensue, of not being a team player. . . . I first met Mr. Nixon when I was eight years old in 1946, when he ran for Congress

in my home district. . . . I felt as if I had known this man all my life—not personally perhaps, but in spirit. I felt a deep sense of loyalty to him. . . . I had been told by others in the campaign that this kind of thing was a normal activity in a campaign. . . . I had never been involved in a political campaign before. . . . These things were all news to me and I accepted them for what they were.

TV viewers had seen and heard the All-American boy Jeb Magruder, who had urged Porter to lie, say in justification of his own illegal acts:

We saw continuing violations of the law by men like William Sloane Coffin [Magruder's professor of ethics at Williams College]. He tells me my ethics are bad. Yet he was indicted for criminal charges. He recommended on the Washington Monument grounds that students burn their draft cards and that we have mass demonstrations and shut down the city of Washington . . . . We had become somewhat inured to using some activities that would help us in accomplishing what we thought was a cause, a legitimate cause.

The TV audience heard Magruder's superior, John Mitchell, formerly the attorney general, the top law enforcement officer in the land, say in answer to Senator Baker's query: Didn't he now think it was a mistake not to tell the president the full details of the break-in?

"Senator, I am not certain that that was the case, because we were talking about the weeks of June in 1972, where I still believed that the most important thing to this country was the reelection of Richard Nixon. And I was not about to countenance anything that would stand in the way of the reelection."

Apparently unfazed by Mitchell's frankness, Baker asserted a moment later, "Well, we still do get along fine and I am delighted that I have this opportunity to probe into the great mentality of a great man."

This courtliness, which prevailed through the interrogation of John Mitchell and Maurice Stans, did not prevent the ex-cabinet members' attorneys in the Vesco case from basing a motion for dismissal of charges in part on "the carnival atmosphere of Watergate precipitated as it has been by the Senate hearings and the grand jury leaks."

Although, according to the committee's rules of procedure, "A witness may request, on ground of distraction, harassment, or physical discomfort that, during his testimony, television, motion picture, and other cameras and lights shall not be directed at him," none of the thirty-five witnesses called was granted this opportunity to escape the public eye.*

The most surprising and ultimately devastating testimony did not, however, come from John Dean's five days nor from the extended interrogations of Mitchell and Stans, but from a brief appearance by one Alexander Butterfield, an obscure former deputy assistant to the president, since appointed head of the Federal Aviation Administration. Butterfield, with some diffidence, informed the senators that it was likely that all the presidential conversations referred to by Dean and denied or forgotten or remembered differently by the other parties could be easily verified, since he knew for a fact that the president had had an elaborate and secret recording system installed throughout the White House offices to record for posterity whatever the chief executive and his companions might say.

In an interview with James J. Kilpatrick published in the Washington *Star-News* ten months later, the president explained:

> They [the tapes] were made, curiously enough, in a very offhand decision. We had no tapes, as you know, up until 1971. I think one day . . . Haldeman walked in and said, "The library believes it is essential that we have tapes," and I said why? He said, "Well, Johnson had tapes—they're in his library at Austin—and these are invaluable records. Kennedy also had tapes," and he said, "You ought to have some record that can be used years later for historical purposes."
>
> I said all right. I must say that after the system was put in, as the transcribed conversations clearly indicated, I wasn't talking with knowledge or with the feeling that the tapes were there. Otherwise I might have talked differently.
>
> My own view is that taping of conversations for historical purposes was a bad decision on the part of all the presidents: I don't think Kennedy should have done it. I don't think Johnson should have done it, and I don't think we should have done it.

---

* Several witnesses, including Gordon Liddy, were not called to testify in public because committee lawyers expected them to take the Fifth Amendment or remain silent. Of those who actually did testify, only John Dean and Maurice Stans requested not to be televised. Both requests were turned down by the committee.

This staggering piece of information from Butterfield froze the proceedings momentarily with its possibility of easily confirming or refuting what everyone so far had been at such pains to remember, forget, assert, or deny.

Things turned out, however, to be not quite that simple.

Nixon's counsel, Fred Buzhardt, acknowledged the presence of the taping equipment in the White House and confirmed that it was still in use. (The White House announced July 24 that it was finally turned off for all time.) However, there was no offer to relinquish any of the hundreds of tapes that were known to exist. Eventually the attempt to get the tapes became, thanks to White House claims of executive privilege and other delaying tactics, as difficult as the uncovering of the truth itself.

Meanwhile the hearings continued.

John Ehrlichman, Nixon's top domestic adviser and the number two man on the White House staff, had already told Mike Wallace, on "60 Minutes" in late June, that he knew nothing about an enemies list and that he had never directed or okayed any secret wiretaps on newsmen or men in government.

Ehrlichman denied any prior knowledge of the plumbers' break-in at the office of Daniel Ellsberg's psychiatrist, Dr. Lewis Fielding. In any event he refused to agree that this was an illegal act since it was done as "a national security undertaking of the highest priority."

Before the senators, Ehrlichman admitted that he had approved a "covert investigation" to obtain information about Daniel Ellsberg, but denied approving any illegal "breaking and entering." Aside from this refinement and an intensified attack on John Dean, Ehrlichman repeated at greater length and with more legal embellishment what he had told "60 Minutes" viewers.

Haldeman, the president's right-hand who had been accused by Dean of leading the cover-up, was one of the few witnesses who arrived on camera without first having volunteered something to the press. He testified for three days, saying that neither he nor the president had any knowledge of the Watergate break-in. Haldeman claimed that John Dean had misled him and the president into believing that no one in the White House was involved. And he disputed Dean's recollection of various conversations between himself and the president. Haldeman asserted that Nixon had rejected the idea of clemency and that he had said that paying hush money to Watergate defendants would be wrong.

The strongest voice to be heard in the president's favor,

according to many, was Patrick Buchanan. Buchanan, the man responsible for the president's daily media reports, also had been credited with ghosting the harshest anti-media speeches of Vice-President Agnew, Office of Telecommunications Policy chief Clay Whitehead, and assorted other surrogates.

In September, during the second phase of the hearings dealing with questionable practices other than the Watergate break-in, Buchanan, never at a loss for words, came on like gangbusters.

> For a variety of reasons I appreciate the opportunity to appear before your select committee. But in candor I cannot speak with the same enthusiasm of the manner in which the invitation was delivered. . . .
>
> . . . The surprise announcement that I was to be called as a public witness before these hearings was made over national television before even the elementary courtesy of a telephone call of notification had been extended.
>
> Of greater concern to me, however, has been an apparent campaign orchestrated from within the committee staff to malign my reputation in the public press prior to my appearance. In the hours immediately following my well-publicized invitation there appeared in the Washington *Post*, *The New York Times*, the Baltimore *Sun*, the Chicago *Tribune*, and on the national networks, separate stories all attributed to committee sources alleging that I was the architect of a campaign of political espionage or dirty tricks.
>
> . . . Mr. Chairman, this covert campaign of vilification, carried on by staff members of your committee, is in direct violation of Rule 40 of the rules of procedure for the select committee. That rule strictly prohibits staff members from leaking substantive materials. . . . It seems fair to me to ask, how can this select committee set itself up as the ultimate arbiter of American political ethics if it cannot even control the character assassins within its own ranks.

The rest of Buchanan's testimony, dealing mainly with campaign strategy, was somewhat less emphatic.* But Buchanan had made

---

* More interesting were the thirty-four documents and memos released on the day of Buchanan's testimony. Among them were suggestions as to how network presidents could be threatened with legislation if there was not equal time given the White House candidate in news coverage; how to manipulate the press; a sinister aside on PBS commentator Sander Vanocur: "Incidentally, given his performance the other night, Vanocur is a positive disaster for us and McGovern's most effective campaigner. He may have to be fired or discredited if we are to get anything approaching an even shake out of that left-wing taxpayer-subsidized network"

his principal point in his opening statement, a point which was to be made by him and other representatives of the Administration over and over throughout the ensuing weeks. It implied, one way or another, that what was happening in the nation's press was no less than a vast conspiracy including not only newspapers, newsmagazines, and networks but senators and representatives, judges and grand jurors, and prosecutors as well. The conspiracy was supposed to deny the president the mandate he had won from an overwhelming majority of the electorate. It was a petty personal action by a handful of people in the media who were dictating to the public what it should think and feel.

Persistence and patience, or just handing the bad news along, was labeled vindictiveness. For a journalist to insist on a simple explanation was another proof that he was not only biased but a bad loser. There was no reference by White House critics to the broadcasters and newspaper publishers who had been overwhelmingly on the president's side in the 1972 campaign. Or how, thanks to the circumstances of the conventions and the campaigns, print and broadcast coverage inevitably gave the advantage to the Republican presidential candidate. (See DuPont-Columbia Survey 1971–72.)

Nor was what was being painfully revealed day by day on the nation's TV screens ever admitted, that the real tarnishing of Nixon's image was being effected by those who had been and, in most instances, continued to be his most enthusiastic and devoted admirers.

Actually Buchanan's sharp words were among the last to come from the Senate Caucus Room over the three commercial networks.

It was late September, and since the fall TV season was beginning and advertising losses would increase, the pressure at the networks against coverage built up. The fact that the Gallup poll indicated after the August recess that the majority of the public wanted the broadcasting of the hearings to continue and that the ratings* confirmed the wish did not keep the hearings on the air.

(PBS). And an even more sinister aside on punishment for Chet Huntley, who had been reported critical of the president. Said one of Buchanan's associates to another, "The point behind this whole thing is that we don't care about Huntley—he's going to leave anyway. What we are trying to do here is tear down the institution. . . ." (see Appendices I and II).

  * CBS said that rotated Watergate coverage earned an average rating of 8.2. Entertainment programs on each of the other two networks averaged a 7.4 rating. Nielsen ratings showed that when Watergate was rotated, daytime television viewing overall increased by 10 percent.

On September 26 the three networks met and voted two to one against continued rotating coverage. When CBS revealed the vote to the press, an angry NBC executive complained to *Variety*:

> Salant is casting us and ABC as heavies, making it seem that we sabotaged daily coverage of the hearings, when in fact CBS is free to cover them by itself every day or any time it wishes because we're all still maintaining the electronic pool. If Salant thinks we're wrong in choosing to exercise our own journalistic judgment for the duration of the hearings, he's not prohibited by our decision from going it alone.

Salant obviously felt this suggestion was unfair. "We're talking about $750,000 a week on a three-day schedule, and meanwhile the Senate committee seems disorganized and we have no idea how the hearings will go from this point. I couldn't recommend full live coverage every day, not at those prices."

Other anti-coverage voices had been heard, including Senator Barry Goldwater's, who wrote in *The New York Times* of September 11, 1973:

> . . . there is little doubt in my mind that we can at this same time sacrifice further televised hearings—with their monotonous repetition. I am not proposing an end to the Senate investigation and to matters related to Watergate. But I am suggesting that we call a halt to the daily television spectacle that, by its very nature, holds the United States Government up to criticism and ridicule.

On August 15, in his first speech since the opening week of the hearings, President Nixon had pointed out that "During the past three months the three major networks have devoted an average of over twenty-two hours of television time each week to this subject. . . . We have reached a point at which a continued backward-looking obsession with Watergate is causing this nation to neglect matters of far greater importance to all of the American people. We must not stay so mired in Watergate that we fail to respond to challenges of surpassing importance to America and the world."

During October and November only public TV covered the hearings in full in the evening and only WNYC-TV New York kept them on live during the day.

In January, when Senator Ervin alerted the networks for the absolutely last round of hearings, all three affirmed their readiness to resume live rotating coverage. At the last minute, in deference to the Mitchell-Stans trial about to start in New York, the hearings were canceled.*

When what turned out to be the last day of televised Watergate hearings, November 15, was finally gaveled to an end, the question remained, as it had been stated by Weicker at the outset: "How much truth do we want?"

There were, of course, other questions, conspicuous among them: How much exactly had been accomplished by the on-camera interrogation of thirty-five witnesses and more than 2 million words of testimony?

Patrick Buchanan, still fuming months after his own appearance, said that "no congressional committee staff in history has managed a more deplorable record of violating its own rules of confidentiality and systematically savaging the reputations of its witnesses than the majority staff of Sam Dash."

On the other hand, there was the estimate of the nation's news directors, most of whom saw Watergate in a more optimistic light. Their remarks, received by the Survey before the affair had run its full and tragic course, reveal some of the problems and opportunities with which Watergate confronted the broadcast journalist.

A news director in Charleston, West Virginia, wrote:

> Watergate came at a time when journalism was being threatened by a seemingly planned assault by government. It vindicated journalism of all charges made by an Administration that was intent on, I believe, breaking down the credibility of the press and subduing it.

From Minneapolis, Minnesota:

> There is less public hostility toward the media in general and toward television specifically. It [Watergate] has boosted our credibility locally, and has created a better atmosphere for acceptance of local investigative reporting. And viewer comments about biased news coverage have decreased. . . . Investigative reporting is suddenly fashionable.

---

* Judge Gerhard A. Gesell had refused the committee access to the White House tapes, commenting later: ". . . surely the time has come to question whether it is in the public interest for the criminal investigative aspects of its work to go forward in the blazing atmosphere of *ex parte* publicity directed to issues that are immediately and intimately related to pending criminal proceedings."

From Lubbock, Texas:

I am amazed by those members of the public, the government, and even the media, who fault the media for hammering away at the fact that our leadership has found itself in a position of being exposed for corruption, power brokering, and outright criminality. Those who want the media to "hush up" about Watergate and related matters do not in my mind deserve a free nation. I am frankly appalled.

From Albuquerque, New Mexico:

I feel the national and particularly Washington Press Corps has done two jobs on this one: one very excellent and the other deplorable. First, the uncovering of the Watergate mess was and is first-class investigative journalism of the highest order. Second, the personal interjection of contempt and obvious bias in reporting on the part of some in the continuing story of Watergate is not only showing the individual reporters to be grinding a personal axe with the Administration and Nixon, but is reflecting on all journalists as being much less than the objective people we claim to be and ought to be. For this reason our operation will not use much of the material supplied by the network concerning Watergate.

From New Orleans, Louisiana:

Our mail tells us, our phones tell us: people are tired of hearing about Watergate, and they regard it as some kind of newsman's paranoia against Richard Nixon. Naturally, we keep this in mind in building our news programs, not as an excuse to curtail this kind of coverage, but rather as a reminder of our responsibility not to be guilty as charged.

From Harrisonburg, Virginia:

Good reporting demands not only the accurate depiction of events, but the placing of those events in their proper context. The depiction of Watergate as a cataclysm has raised serious doubts among the American people about the judgments of journalists, and about their willingness to follow themes in reporting rather than search out perspective. They wonder whether Watergate was as big as it looks because of the absence of war and other cataclysms to cover, and they wonder why events unfavorable to the president invariably get headlines and show leads, while events favorable to the president tend to get buried. Their doubts are legitimate and should be faced by serious journalists everywhere.

From Miami, Florida:

> I think in general that Watergate has helped all news
> operations. The Nixon administration was tampering with the
> First Amendment. We are not out of the woods yet. But the
> exposure of Watergate restored credibility to the media and
> strengthened its defenses against what appeared to be a telling
> brutal assault upon freedom of information. For the moment,
> the tide has turned.

In the wake of Watergate, Senator Lawton Chiles of Florida had
introduced an act for national "government in the sunshine" to
parallel the open state legislature of Florida* and twenty-four other
states and based, as Florida governor Reuben Askew put it, "on
the simple premise that the public has the right to know when, how,
and why its business is being conducted." A ten-member Joint
Committee on Congressional Operations recommended in October
1974 that both the House and Senate introduce live television and
radio coverage of floor proceedings.

Although the Watergate hearings were over, it was not likely that
the doors of any branch of government would ever again be so
tightly closed to the public or the media. Watergate was seen by an
estimated 21 million people on its biggest day, July 11, the second
day of John Mitchell's testimony. The networks had worked out a
way of sharing coverage which, although not perfect, served the
public reasonably well and would be employed again in the
summer of 1974 to carry the House Judiciary Committee deliberations on impeachment to the American people.

Perhaps the most eloquent summing up of the impact and
importance of the network treatment of Watergate was made by
Richard Salant in justifying his performance to a group of hostile
and skeptical affiliates in the spring of 1974:

> Sure I'm tired of it too; as a citizen, I am not edified when it
> looms so large in so many broadcasts. I'd much rather see

* Jacksonville's public broadcasting station, WJCT, after eight years of experi-
mentation in broadcasting city government meetings, began in 1973 to televise
proceedings of the Florida state legislature. "Today in the Legislature," an hour of
highlights and interviews from the day's proceedings, was fed by WJCT to seven
other public stations in Florida with remarkable results. A Corporation for Public
Broadcasting survey found that 67 percent of regular viewers felt the coverage
increased their understanding of the legislative process. Ninety-three percent of the
legislators themselves said the cameras had not bothered them and 80 percent
detected no difference in their conduct on the floor. Seventy-nine percent of the
viewers questioned detected no bias in the coverage. Only 6 percent of the legislators
themselves saw bias in the editors' judgment.

more of Charlie Kuralt on the road. I'd far, far rather see the discovery of a cure for cancer as the lead story on one week, a cure for the common cold on the second week, and solid peace in the Mideast on the third week.

But Watergate *has* happened and it *is* with us. We didn't invent it—nor do I think we have overplayed it. . . .

The real magic of radio and television, as Dr. Stanton* so often used to say, is that, by live broadcast, they can bring the entire nation directly to history. The American public need not rely on the filter of what a reporter s..ys happened or an editor's compression. If these proceedings are open to us, every American viewer and listener can be there, witnessing with his own eyes and ears one of the major historic events of this nation—making up his or her own mind on the basis of firsthand impressions. And that is what democracy and television are both all about.

What Salant seemed to be saying was that TV's highest vocation was not to uncover or investigate or comment on the news in the traditional journalistic sense but to stand witness at the great and crucial moments of history, to record and transmit them to the nation. If one accepted this evaluation, the coverage of Watergate undoubtedly contained some of television's finest hours.

* Dr. Frank Stanton, former president of CBS.

2 • Tijuana on Sunday Afternoon
Watergate II

THE MAIN STRETCH of the Senate Watergate hearings in the spring and summer of 1973 was accompanied by an extended TV silence on the part of President Nixon. However, the months preceding and following were studded with presidential appearances and pronouncements of particular significance to the broadcaster—not only because they were so frequently made on camera, and were carried on all four TV networks simultaneously, but because they represented important engagements in the continuing battle between the Administration and the press, and particularly the broadcast press.

The earlier phases of that battle have been described in other volumes in this series and in the preceding chapter.

Now that the warfare is over, it is difficult to recall just how bitter and uncertain of outcome the conflict once appeared to be—difficult because subsequent events have blurred the outlines of what went before, but also because now that the danger has passed Americans prefer to forget that it could happen again, that vigilance is still the price of freedom for the press as for the citizen.

In one of President Nixon's early public statements on Watergate he had said:

> It was the system that has brought the facts to light and that will bring those guilty to justice—a system that in this case has included a determined grand jury, honest prosecutors, a courageous judge, John Sirica, and a vigorous free press.

Here, it turned out, was simply another enemies list. In the months that followed, no one in that catalogue was spared the contempt of the president or his associates. The villains chosen to be discredited might change from day to day. They could be former White House aides, senators, representatives, judges, prosecutors, or juries, depending on the ground where the confrontation of the moment was taking place. But the one constant adversary appeared to be "a vigorous free press."

The consistent White House emphasis on this threat from outside of government could have been explained by the unflattering and damaging material the press communicated daily. But calculation, not just blind rage and a need to strike back, played an important part in these repeated attacks on the sources of public information. To challenge the facts as revealed one by one by the courts and Congress, to discredit a growing army of witnesses seemed a far more difficult task than to discredit the instrument by which the facts and witnesses were reaching the people, thus casting doubt on facts and witnesses alike.

It was not remarkable that a generation raised on, and conditioned by, television entertainment should have found the secondary phase of Watergate both fascinating and believable. From March 1973, when James McCord, a recognizable action-adventure type, made his startling claims, to the first weeks of the Senate hearings in May and June, the public's acceptance of bad Watergate news palpably grew. As long as the media as investigator was uppermost, the Administration's counterattacks were relatively ineffectual. The media as juggernaut and judge, the apparent instruments of retribution, was something else again.

As the balance of power began to shift away from a White House convinced that if it was clever and tough enough it could simultaneously use and control the nation's sources of information,* to publishers and broadcasters who had only to report what had happened during the previous twenty-four hours to mortally wound, a stubborn public resistance seemed to emerge.

This resistance, no doubt, was always there. It was in great part the predisposition of most Americans to favor the president, any president—an unwillingness to damage the dignity of the nation's highest office. There was also the majority's loyalty to its own judgment, its reluctance to admit a mistake. But beyond both of these factors, a basic suspicion of the press had become part of the common experience of Americans, Republican or Democrat, black or white, male or female, young or old, rich or poor. A suspicion

---

* As late as June 1973 William Paley, head of CBS, whose network was the most persistent in its coverage of Watergate, had issued an edict which forbade network newsmen to give instant analysis following presidential addresses (see Appendices III and IV). This was interpreted by some as a conciliatory gesture toward the Administration prompted by threats of regulatory or legislative discipline (see Appendix V).

which had been carefully nurtured by those in power and which was sometimes justified.

The broadcasters, however much their newsmen might seem to disapprove of the president, could not escape a bias in his favor. If Nixon demanded time he got it, on all four networks. If coverage of the House and Senate committees could be rotated or ignored, that of the president could not. As long as he kept moving and speaking there was no possibility of ignoring him, the ultimate weapon of the media against those whom they disapprove of or despise.

He was an irresistible force, at least until his term was over, or he resigned, or was impeached and convicted and removed from office—all, for the moment, apparently remote possibilities. And the media, whether they wished it or not, frequently served his purpose just by being there.

This ambivalence on both sides characterized one of the remarkable standoffs in modern history. In the Middle Ages, the last time a comparable encounter of power with equal but disparate power occurred, the adversary who instructed and disciplined the temporal authority was the church, subject in its turn to instruction and discipline by such rulers as could muster the strength and shrewdness.

In twentieth-century America the press seemed to be assuming the role of the medieval papacy. Both the military, in Vietnam, and industry, in the environmental and the energy crises (see Chapter 4), had felt its power. Now it was the politicians', specifically the president's, turn. His treatment at the hands of the media, as it turned out, would be even more quickly and decisively effective.

On August 22, 1973, the president had his first encounter with the press since the beginning of the Senate Watergate hearings, which had gone into recess two weeks before.

The news conference was held on the lawn at San Clemente on a single hour's notice. It was broadcast on all four networks to a daytime audience. The president was generally conceded to have acquitted himself extremely well, although the questions were unusually direct, from a group of newsmen whose eagerness for contact with the chief executive had been exacerbated by his long unavailability.

He answered the questions he wished to and used the others to reach the public directly. Midway through the meeting he described his grievances in some detail. When asked to specify who, as he had charged earlier, was exploiting Watergate to keep him from doing his job, Nixon said:

> I would suggest that where the shoe fits, people should wear it. I would think that some political figures, some members of the press perhaps, some members of the television perhaps would exploit it. . . . There are a great number of people in this country who didn't accept the mandate of '72. After all, I know that most of the members of the press corps were not enthusiastic. And I understood that about either my election in '68 or '72. That's not unusual. Frankly, if I had always followed what the press predicted or the polls predicted, I would have never been elected president.

When asked about how much his capacity to govern had been weakened by Watergate, Nixon replied:

> . . . to be under a constant barrage—12 to 15 minutes a night on each of the three major networks for four months— tends to raise some questions in the people's minds with regard to the president; and it may raise some questions with regard to the capacity to govern. . . . We've had 30 minutes of this press conference. I have yet to have, for example, one question on the business of the people. Which shows you are—how we're consumed with it.

Peter Lisagor, White House correspondent for the Chicago *Daily News* and a regular on public TV's "Washington Week in Review," summed it up: "The president outscored us on points." His remark defined the meeting's peculiar character. It was a fight, an engagement, a scouting expedition with scattered fire.

The president followed up his ostensible advantage with another press conference on September 5 which dealt mainly with the impending energy crisis and was generally playful in its attitude toward the press except for one sharp thrust. In answer to a question from NBC's Richard Valeriani about rebuilding confidence in his leadership, Nixon said:

> . . . It's rather difficult to have the president of the United States on prime-time television—not prime time—although I would suppose the newscasters would say that the news programs are really the prime time—but for four months to have the president of the United States by innuendo, by leak, by frankly, leers and sneers of commentators, which is their

perfect right, attacked in every way without having some of that confidence being worn away. . . . We have tried to do things. The country hasn't paid a great deal of attention to it. And I may say the media hasn't paid a great deal of attention to it; because your attention, quite understandably, is in the more fascinating area of Watergate. . . . What the president says will not restore it [confidence]. And what you ladies and gentlemen say will certainly not restore it.

His next air appearance was a radio address on September 9 which dwelt on his legislative goals and the need for getting on with "the people's business." The broadcast came five days after the grand jury had returned indictments on four of the White House staff (including John Ehrlichman) involved in the break-in of Daniel Ellsberg's psychiatrist's office.

There followed a period of presidential unavailability which carried through the outbreak of hostilities in the Middle East and the swift decline and fall of Vice-President Spiro Agnew.

Although Vice-President Agnew had been uncharacteristically moderate in his public pronouncements for some time prior to the summer of 1973, he remained the single most effective member of the president's team in the fight against the broadcast press. His precipitate resignation in October 1973, under threat of indictment on multiple counts of extortion, bribery, conspiracy, and tax evasion, could be considered by the vindictive as a victory for the media over the Administration. In fact it inaugurated a new stage in their warfare.

The circumstances leading up to the vice-president's resignation, his plea of *nolo contendere* to a charge of tax evasion, and his light sentence* were read by some anti-Nixonians as a possible preview of what was in store for the president himself. Although this was, at the moment, considered an extreme view, the parallels were striking enough to encourage James Reston of *The New York Times* to write a column on an Agnew television press conference in which the vice-president had effectively protested his innocence just weeks before judgment. Reston wrote:

He [Agnew] didn't hide for weeks or months behind "executive privilege" or issue proclamations about his "legal rights." After a short but unfortunate delay, he saw the reality. The headlines in the newspapers made him look like a crook,

* Three years of unsupervised probation and a $10,000 fine.

so he came out fighting. . . . He didn't ask but told the President he was going to call a press conference at 3 o'clock the next afternoon. He didn't have a few "friends" in the press around to hear his story, but invited everybody. TV cameras and all. He asked for the tough questions, and he got them. Even without knowing the facts in Agnew's case, the feeling after his press conference was very much in his favor—in fact, that finally in this town somebody in power had talked up with candor and passion, and taken the risk of telling the truth.

Agnew, as soon became apparent, was standing up to the press and fooling a roomful of avowed skeptics. His show of bravado, however, offered no clue to the president's own behavior.

The press had been much more dangerously misused in the Agnew affair than in this one deliberately misleading press conference—most notably in the leaks of the Baltimore grand jury proceedings to newsmen—by all sides, for there were more than two sides in the matter of proving Agnew's guilt or innocence. The obvious purpose of these leaks was to somehow affect the outcome of Agnew's ordeal and they were yet another evidence of the prodigious and treacherous power of the press. The power, in this instance, was like an open hose in the hands of unruly youngsters, each spraying and getting sprayed in turn, or perhaps, more accurately, considering the outcome, a gun with the safety catch off.

One party wanted to hasten the time of decision, another would have liked the investigation to proceed with all deliberate speed, yet another preferred to delay judgment indefinitely. The press served all three at one time or another and with little or no acknowledgment that it was being used, if indeed it was aware of the fact.

Most conspicuous among the critics of such leaks had been the president himself, who in his August 22 press conference reported he had ordered Attorney General Elliot Richardson to investigate the Justice Department and immediately dismiss anyone found to be involved in leaking information about the investigation in Maryland to the press. The president's words:

> . . . the leak of information with regard to charges that have been made against the vice-president and leaking them all in the press, convicting an individual, not only trying him but convicting him in the headlines and on television before he's even had a chance to present his case in court is completely contrary to the American tradition.

A single concentrated example of the inexact and yet deadly way the press allowed itself to be manipulated was in the airing of Assistant Attorney General Henry Petersen's alleged statement about the vice-president, "We've got the evidence. We've got it cold," broadcast by correspondent Fred Graham on CBS Radio's "World News Roundup," September 22. The two-hundred-word item, a classic example of source reporting (see Appendix VI), with its intransitive verbs and anonymous informants, became the occasion for an outpouring of indignation and self-justification from both sides.

The subsequent wholesale subpoenaing of the press by Agnew's lawyers, which was justified in terms of this and other leaks, brought up questions of the First versus the Sixth Amendments (see Appendix VII), which were increasing in urgency. Those who received subpoenas included employees of *Time, Newsweek, The New York Times*, the New York *Daily News*, the Washington *Post*, the Washington *Star News*, CBS, and NBC, as well as Attorney General Richardson and his two top assistants, William Ruckelshaus and Henry Petersen.

Richardson agreed to the interrogations, although the Justice Department labeled the subpoenas "frivolous" and added, "We strongly object to the subpoenas issued to newsmen. We have never supported incursions into this sensitive area for the mere purpose of conducting fishing expeditions and it is plain that this is all that is involved here."

The statement could be weighed against the remarks of Federal Judge Walter E. Hoffman when he granted the subpoenas. "I have learned, over a period of twenty years as a judge and an additional twenty-three as an attorney, that the news media frequently are wholly or partially inaccurate. . . . We are rapidly approaching the day when the perpetual conflict between the news media . . . and the judicial system . . . must be resolved."

Vermont Royster commented in *The Wall Street Journal*: "The obligation of police authorities and of lawyers is to due process, to do or say nothing extralegal however deserved they think it may be. The obligation of the press is to both honesty and justice, the one no less than the other. Words may break no bones but they can do men grievous injury."

It was a sentiment agreed with and ignored by both sides. Theories as to who was responsible for the Agnew leaks included the White House and the vice-president as well as the Justice Department and the Maryland officials involved.

On September 22, ABC, in yet another source story, reported that the principal origin of news leaks about the Agnew case were Leonard Garment, the White House counsel, and Melvin Laird, the former secretary of defense who now had replaced John Ehrlichman as President Nixon's top domestic adviser.

The real justification for leaks, according to a *Newsweek* column on the subject, was the search for truth. "When official statements are found to be deceitful, the press can hardly be blamed for turning to unofficial ones in order to try to get at the truth." Leaking also gave an opportunity to small individuals in large organizations, military and industrial as well as political, to speak out anonymously with some hope of escaping reprisals from their all-powerful superiors.

In the Agnew and Watergate cases, however, the sources of leaks were not always small or powerless, and, in many instances, their purpose had not been to reveal dangerous truths but to manipulate the press and, through it, the public and the judicial and legislative branches of government as well. Nor was the press all that fastidious. Closed sessions, whether of grand juries or congressional hearings, were considered fair game for reporters in search of a scoop. Long before the Senate Watergate hearings the amount of significant information concerning the affair reaching the press via leaks far exceeded that which came from legitimate and identifiable sources.

Leaks could be used, and were, by the strong as well as the weak. Even when true, as they frequently turned out to be, their ultimate purpose could be to subvert or prevent a larger truth from coming to light. They were one more flattering and intimidating acknowledgment of the power of the press.

Almost as common and just as suspect as the leak was the arranged interview or panel show appearance where the guest delivered a preconceived message and got away without revealing any more than he had planned.*

Throughout the Watergate affair the traffic in such experts with axes to grind was continuous.

Perhaps the ultimate word on leaks came from a man who had

---

* The White House was not only generous in providing such guests but accommodating in times of crisis. When General Alexander Haig taped an interview with Mike Wallace for the July 28, 1974, edition of "60 Minutes" at San Clemente before the first article of impeachment was approved by the House Judiciary Committee, he "choppered up" to San Francisco to do a second version which would take into account the drastic new developments.

been both perpetrator and victim. In his statement following his surprising plea of guilty to obstruction of justice in the Ellsberg break-in case, presidential counsel Charles Colson said:

> During the pretrial motions, I listened very intently to many of the arguments related to the national security justification of the Ellsberg break-in. Judge Gesell's words from the bench—to the effect that if this is to be a government of laws and not of men, then those men entrusted with enforcing the law must be held to account for the natural consequences of their own actions—had a profound effect on me. Whether at the time certain actions seemed totally justified and indeed essential to the national interest is not the issue. If the overriding national interest requires extraordinary action, then every possible legal sanction must be observed, every right to individual due process respected. We cannot accept the principle that men in high government office can act in disregard of the rights of even one individual citizen.
>
> My plea acknowledges that I endeavored to disseminate derogatory information about Dr. Ellsberg and his attorney at a time when he was under indictment by the same government of which I was an officer. Judge Gesell's words had particular impact upon me because I have either been under indictment or been the target of serious accusations for the past two years. I know what it feels like—what it must have felt like to Dr. Ellsberg—to have the government which is prosecuting me also try me in the public press. I know how it feels to be subjected to repeated and in some cases deliberate leaks from various Congressional committees. In fact, there are records showing that the C.I.A. deliberately planted stories with several major news organizations accusing me of involvement in criminal activities.
>
> I regret what I attempted to do to Dr. Ellsberg. It is wrong whether it is done to him, to me, or to others. Not only is it morally right therefore that I plead to this charge, but I fervently hope that this case will serve to prevent similar abuses in the future.

After he resigned, Agnew had his final say in a prime-time farewell protesting his innocence and containing a virulent parting shot at the press.

> Late this summer my fitness to continue in office came under attack when accusations against me made in the course of a grand jury investigation were improperly and uncon-

scionably leaked in detail to the news media. I might add that
the attacks were increased by daily publication of the wildest
rumor and speculation, much of it bearing no resemblance to
the information being given the prosecutors. All this was done
with full knowledge that it was prejudicial to my civil rights.
The news media editorially deplored these violations of the
traditional secrecy of such investigations but at the same time
many of the most prestigious of them were ignoring their own
counsel by publishing every leak they could get their hands on.
From time to time I made public denials of those scurrilous
and inaccurate reports and challenged the credibility of their
sources. . . . Notwithstanding that the government's case for
extortion, bribery and conspiracy rested entirely on the
testimony of individuals who had already confessed to criminal acts and who had been granted total or partial immunity in
exchange for their testimony against me, their accusations
which are not independently corroborated or tested by cross-
examination have been published and broadcast as indisput-
able fact. . . . What is it that makes my accusers, self-con-
fessed bribe-brokers, extortionists and conspirators, believable? And I point out that their stories have been treated as
gospel by most of the media.

Then hard upon the outbreak of a new war in the Middle East
came the single most provocative domestic action of the Nixon
presidency—at least so far as the press was concerned—the firing
of special Watergate prosecutor Archibald Cox for insubordinate
behavior in insisting that the White House relinquish nine of the
controversial tapes in its custody.

In the process Nixon had been presented with the resignation of
Elliot Richardson, the attorney general who at his confirmation in
the earlier days of the Watergate affair had pledged to the Senate
he would "pursue the truth wherever it may lead." Richardson, a
Nixonian of impressive adaptability, had served the president first
as undersecretary of state, then as secretary of health, education,
and welfare and as secretary of defense before replacing Attorney
General Richard Kleindienst, who in turn had replaced John
Mitchell. Departing with Richardson was another long-term Nixon
man, William Ruckelshaus, one-time environmental chief and
currently deputy attorney general.

The affair, which took place on Saturday, October 20, and was
immediately labeled "the Saturday night massacre," created a great
public outcry, followed by no fewer than eighty-four Congressional
resolutions for impeachment of the president.

Although the Watergate hearings were off the air, the chief
Democratic counsel, Samuel Dash, felt that the hearings had
"readied the public" to object to the firing of Cox and the refusal of
the tapes and also to recognize highly questionable behavior where
before they would have seen "just another Washington shenani-
gan."

The Cox affair would have been difficult under any circumstances for the public to ignore.

The TV coverage was massive. In the afternoon, a few hours
before his official dismissal, Cox had held a lengthy press conference explaining his position. The hour-long meeting was carried
live on three national TV networks. The same evening, following
his firing, both CBS and NBC carried special broadcasts giving
background and commentary on the event. An aura of indignation
hung over both.

Although it was too late to change the guests on the Sunday
panel shows, Melvin Laird had already been scheduled on NBC's
"Meet the Press." Senators Edmund Muskie and Charles Mathias
were on ABC's "Issues and Answers." On both networks a large
proportion of the questions dealt with Watergate and the Cox
firing.

On Monday the network newscasts carried a total of twenty-two
news spots about the Cox affair. And "the fire storm," fanned by
the press, kept on roaring.*

Tuesday morning, former Attorney General Richardson, flanked
by his wife and Ruckelshaus, held his own press conference, being
greeted at the outset by a two-minute standing ovation from the
five hundred Justice Department employees who had gathered,
with the cameramen and reporters, to hear his departing remarks.
The press conference was carried live and in full for an hour and
five minutes on the national TV networks. ABC, CBS, NBC, and
PBS all did follow-up specials, which included consideration of the
ironic fact that three hours after Attorney General Richardson's
farewell appearance Nixon agreed to relinquish the crucial tapes.

And there was still more. On Wednesday Walter Cronkite did
one of his infrequent "CBS Evening News" interviews with

---

* Before the week was over NBC had racked up a total of 4 hours and 37 minutes
of bulletins, inserts, interviews, and special programs on the incident; CBS, 4 hours
and 11 minutes; ABC, 2 hours and 37 minutes. PBS had 2½ hours of preemptions
plus four 30-minute wrap-ups during the week. "Today's" guests from Monday to
Friday included William Ruckelshaus, Jerome Waldie, Charles Wiggins, Charles
Alan Wright, Barry Goldwater, Birch Bayh, and Peter Dominick.

Archibald Cox. It was a highly sympathetic ten minutes. In it Cronkite alluded to a news story alleging that $1 million of 1972 campaign funds had been siphoned off to create a private trust fund for the president. It was also implied that Cox's firing came not from his demand for the tapes but as a result of his knowledge of this unwholesome secret and campaign-funding abuses.

The Florida banking activities of the president's friend, Charles "Bebe" Rebozo, had already been the subject of a three-part inquiry by CBS reporter Robert Pierpoint the preceding week, and ABC's William Gill had given the private investment fund story its first airing.

If the press seemed to be victimizing the president, there was plenty of evidence of press harassment from the other side. Week after week there had been revelations of break-ins and wiretaps in newsmen's homes and offices; of an enemies list which contained prominent mention of several journalists; of attempts to get specific newsmen fired. There was confirmation of the suspicion that the IRS and the FCC, among other government agencies, had been solicited to help in punitive measures against newsmen and news organizations, the most conspicuous of these being the FBI investigation of Daniel Schorr (this had been falsely justified as a preliminary to the White House hiring of one of its most outspoken critics).

In addition, there was a never-ending barrage of anti-media remarks from Administration spokesmen. William Small, the head of the CBS News Washington Bureau and soon to be promoted to senior vice-president of CBS News, told the Radio and Television News Directors Association meeting in Seattle on October 10, the day of Agnew's resignation:

> I am disturbed because the press of this country, and most particularly broadcast journalism, has been maligned constantly and consistently by the national Administration and its friends. I am bothered because despite the lessons of this year and the revelations of Watergate and all the rest, the maligning of the press has not stopped.
> The attacks on us this very year range from last month's news conference where the president of the United States claimed he was being victimized "by innuendo, by leak, by frankly leers and sneers of commentators," and all the way down to Donald Segretti, that pious mouse, who testified last week before the Watergate committee and complained that his reputation had been damaged by press reports of his activities.

There are some things that we ought to say about the wonderful folks who brought us Watergate. We ought to say it was not the press, it was not broadcast journalism that broke into the Watergate complex and Larry O'Brien's office.

Small followed with a frontal attack on Patrick Buchanan and his efforts to manipulate the press:

> It is disturbing to find that these people, who have spent these years attacking us and questioning *our* motives, should at the same time be trying so hard to distort the product we put on the air. . . . In the end we have been hurt by this Administration and we have a lot of work to do to restore our own image.

All these grievances were fresh in the minds of both sides on the evening of October 26 when the president walked in to face his tormentors and unwilling accomplices in the East Room of the White House with a jaunty step and a big smile.

He had just muttered to a CBS producer before entering, "Cronkite's not going to like this," adding almost inaudibly, "I hope."

There were two hundred members of the Washington press corps present, and, as with each of the president's announced TV appearances, the conference was broadcast by all three commercial networks and the Public Broadcast Service. It lasted precisely forty minutes and was viewed by an estimated audience of 63.9 million, with 11½ million additional radio listeners tuned in.

Later Patrick Buchanan compared the atmosphere in the room to the bull ring in Tijuana on a Sunday afternoon. Who was matador and bull was for the moment still uncertain.

The first ten minutes were taken up with prepared remarks on the Middle East war. The president announced that delivery of the Watergate tapes requested by Cox would be discussed with Judge John J. Sirica the following Tuesday and that he would soon appoint a new special prosecutor to succeed Cox.

The conference was then opened to questions. After three exchanges on the handling of presidential documents and the appointment and authority of the special prosecutor, CBS' Dan Rather asked, "Mr. President, I wonder if you could share with us your thoughts, tell us what goes through your mind when you hear of people who love this country and people who believe in you say reluctantly that perhaps you should resign or be impeached?"

"Well, I'm glad we don't take the vote of this room, let me say," Nixon said in beginning a long rambling answer, which touched from time to time on media mistakes in the past. However, it was not until two questions later, when the president was asked, in an obvious allusion to Watergate, how many shocks the nation could sustain, that he pointed out that the difference between the old days when the nation was more stouthearted and a less heroic present was "the electronic media. I have never heard or seen such outrageous, vicious, distorted reporting in twenty-seven years of public life. I'm not blaming anybody for that. Perhaps what happened is that what we did brought it about, and therefore the media decided that they would have to take that particular line.

"But when people are pounded night after night with that kind of frantic, hysterical reporting, it naturally shakes their confidence."

The president had never been more succinct in expressing his feelings about the press nor more specific as to what segment of it he found particularly repellent.

From then on the president's hostility to the broadcasters took over. Another question about his emotional condition under the stress of recent events brought another angry answer:

> The tougher it gets the cooler I get. Of course, it isn't pleasant to get criticism; some of it is justified, of course. It isn't pleasant to find your honesty questioned, it isn't pleasant to find for example that speaking of my friend Mr. Rebozo, that despite the fact that those who printed it and those who said it knew it was untrue, said that he had a million-dollar trust fund for me that he was handling. It was nevertheless put on one of the networks—knowing it was untrue. It isn't pleasant, for example, to hear or read that a million dollars in campaign funds went into my San Clemente property, and even after we have a complete audit, to have it repeated. . . .

Asked about the impact of Watergate on negotiations with the Soviet Union, Nixon came back to the same subject:

> What he [Brezhnev] also knows is that the president of the United States, when he was under unmerciful assault at the time of Cambodia, at the time of May 8, when I ordered the bombing and the mining of North Vietnam, at the time of Dec. 18, still went ahead and did what he thought was right. The fact that Mr. Brezhnev knew that regardless of the pressures at home, regardless of what people see and hear on

television night after night, he would do what was right. That's what made Mr. Brezhnev act as he did.

Robert Pierpoint, the CBS newsman responsible for the three-part report on Rebozo, and a native, like the president, of Whittier, California, stood up and asked the question which brought into focus what the press conference was actually about.

> Mr. President, you've lambasted the television networks pretty well. Could I ask you, at the risk of reopening an obvious wound—you say after you've put on a lot of heat, that you don't blame anyone. I find that a little puzzling. What is it about the television coverage of you in these past weeks and months that has so aroused your anger?
> *President*: Don't get the impression that you arouse my anger.
> *Pierpoint*: I have that impression.
> *President*: You see, one can only be angry with those he respects.

Toward the end of the answer to the next question the president had recovered himself sufficiently to add:

> Let me say too I didn't want to leave an impression with my good friends from CBS over here that I don't respect the reporters. What I was simply saying was this: that when a commentator takes a bit of news and then with the knowledge of what the facts are distorts it viciously, I have no respect for that individual.

After a brief, bitter interchange with former White House aide Clark Mollenhoff, now a working newsman again, the president withdrew.

Following the press conference, which left more than one newsman deeply shaken, Robert Pierpoint, the individual most directly involved in the president's attack, was quoted as saying he felt "shocked and frightened. Anyone that emotional about anything is inclined to be a little unbalanced—that's what bothered me." Nor was the criticism all directed toward the president. ABC's Tom Jarriel described the hostile atmosphere of the room: "There was too much rudeness, too much aggressiveness, too much loudness."

But despite enough provocation on both sides to explain more than one fit of temper, the suspicion persisted that Nixon's attack on the broadcasters had not been altogether spontaneous, that he had gone into the room intending to show up the journalists as bullies.

If the president was, indeed, asking for public support against the media over their own shoulders and facilities, at least the early response was on his side. Phone calls to the networks ran two to one in Nixon's favor. More than one journalist deplored the lack of respect shown by his colleagues. An editorial in the Chicago *Tribune* said:

> The responsibility for this degeneration in presidential press conferences must be shared between reporters and president. There is too much a willingness to goad the president, a human being after all, with insulting questions.

Still, a Gallup poll taken immediately after the news conference showed that 53 percent of those who watched found the president's Watergate explanations "unconvincing," while only 31 percent remained convinced and the others were uncertain.

Probably the most interesting comment on the conference came from a devoted Nixon partisan, William Safire, a former Nixon speechwriter, now a *New York Times* columnist. Safire wrote in the October 29 edition:

> To be the object of hatred of a despised minority has long been considered a political plus. . . .
> Mr. Nixon's latest display of what is usually a decorously draped hatred of the press was not a stupid blast, however. . . . When he returned the fire of his tormentors he handed them a victory, because he was not playing off a despised minority—he was rubbing his neck against the cutting edge of what had become majority sentiment.
> The element of calculation is gone. We are witnessing honest hatred, gleefully returned, and at the root of the mutual hatred is an irresponsible, self-indulgent and ill-examined attribution of evil motives. . . .

Although Nixon was not to have another press conference for four months, the aftermath of this head-on collision between the president and the media, the most emotional and bitter since Nixon's famous farewell in 1962, was as chaotic and packed with provocation as its prelude.

Examples of the viciousness and distortion in television reporting mentioned by the president were immediately requested from the White House. The National News Council, a body established by the Twentieth Century Fund and other foundations to investigate allegations of misconduct in the printed and broadcast press, took on the president's accusations as its first major assignment and promised to research the matter thoroughly. The White House promised to cooperate.

Other events that came in rapid succession following the conference included a *Time* editorial—the first in its fifty-year history—which called for Nixon's resignation. Even more surprising was an ABC evening newscast commentary by Howard K. Smith, the one TV anchorman generally conceded to be strongly pro-Nixon. Following the announcement on October 31 that two of the nine tapes promised to Judge Sirica in the press conference did not exist, Smith became the first network commentator to call for the president's resignation.

Into this growing uproar Senator Lowell Weicker (appearing on the local Martin Agronsky show over WETA, the public TV station in Washington) released a sheaf of heretofore unpublicized documents which described elaborate attempts by the president's aides to manipulate the media.

Among these memoranda were accounts of meetings with network heads in 1970 in which they were portrayed as knuckling under to White House pressure exerted specifically by presidential counsel Charles W. Colson. The irony of these revelations immediately following President Nixon's all-out attacks on TV journalists was lost in the hard-breathing indignation of broadcasters denying that such things could ever have happened. Colson claimed:

> These meetings had a very salutary effect in letting them know that we are determined to protect the president's position, that we know precisely what is going on from the standpoint of both law and policy, and that we are not going to permit them to get away with anything that interferes with the president's ability to communicate.

The network officials, Colson reported, were "very much afraid of us and are trying hard to prove they are good guys." The harder he pressed NBC and CBS, Colson said, "the more accommodating, cordial, and almost apologetic they became." At CBS, Paley "went out of his way to say how much he supports the President." (See Appendix VIII for complete memorandum.)

Paley responded:

> From time to time members of the White House staff have
> made representations to CBS management criticizing CBS
> News coverage on the ground that the White House had been
> treated unfairly. Similar representations were made by all
> recent Administrations, both Democratic and Republican.
> Under no circumstances have these representations been
> permitted to affect CBS News reporting or the diligent exercise
> of our journalistic responsibility to cover the news fairly and
> accurately. CBS management has always upheld the integrity
> of CBS News, pointing out that our news judgments will never
> yield to outside influences.*

Indeed the record contained examples of network protection
afforded newsmen under attack by government officials, most
notably in the case of Dan Rather, who had been the subject of a
conversation between CBS News President Richard Salant and
White House aide John Ehrlichman as early as the spring of
1971.

A new mood had overtaken the American media, a realization
that if at one time the president seemed to have the upper hand, he
was now admitting by his behavior to an equality with the press
which, if closely examined, was revealed to be something less than
equal.

Nixon, frequently called "the single most powerful man in the
world," was now being outclassed by another power, the power of
the media—an abstraction with a thousand heads, many of which
seemed suddenly indifferent and impervious to his wrath.

The superior power of the press was alluded to with more and
more frequency by presidential partisans, if only to denounce it.
"Who elected Walter Cronkite?" was a favorite question.

Meanwhile, the original presidential contention, delivered and
clung to as dogma—that Watergate was a single isolated incident, a
third-rate crime that sensationalism and prejudice had converted
into a monstrous fantasy—had come unstuck. Furthermore, the
assumptions that the networks and publishers would not, and the
American people could not, focus on a small, significant detail long
enough to draw some meaning from it, went by the boards. The
latter assumption, shared by both president and network execu-

---

* Eleven days later the rule prohibiting instant analysis of presidential talks was
lifted. (See Appendix IX.)

tives, was demonstrated to be false not only by the surprisingly large audiences for the televised Watergate hearings but most recently by the surprising degree of public attention to the firing of Cox and the contradictory explanations for the missing and the interrupted tapes.

The power of the media, and particularly of television, had been formidably demonstrated. And this power did not derive from any desire to "get Nixon"—if such a desire existed. It had nothing to do with disparaging comment, instant analysis, the raised eyebrow, or the smirk, or even the digging out of embarrassing details. It came from the simple fact that the cameras were there, and stayed there, recording, observing, sorting out, remembering and reminding.

This power was hardly new, nor had it always worked to the president's disadvantage. According to TRB, writing from Washington in *The New Republic*:

> Television is the president's medium. It has made the modern president possible. Mr. Nixon can ask and get prime time when he wants it. He is the only man in America who can; he can speak right into your living room at will; the TV mike is more powerful than the monarch's orb and scepter; it is the symbol and instrument of his power. Save at elections it is a monopoly appurtenance. . . .
> But in the Watergate probe television passes out of the president's control, for the time being.

The time being, for the president, turned out to be a very long time indeed.

Meanwhile, in order to effectively abuse TV, Nixon had to use it. In order to effectively use it, he had somehow to defuse it. If this wasn't done the president's very presence on TV contributed to the medium's plausibility and rendered all his accusations of prejudiced treatment and instant corruption finally hollow.

There were those who saw the president's apparently spontaneous rages against the press and TV not as acts of a man harassed and victimized beyond enduring but as a cunningly devised plan to discredit the press under optimum conditions, i.e., with the whole nation looking on. An encounter like the one of October 26 gave Nixon, if it went well (and a remarkable number of his press conferences did go well), a double opportunity: first to put across his ideas and arguments despite the newsmen's questions—thus bolstering his image as an effective president; second, and with increasing frequency, it would seem, to maneuver the press into attitudes where the journalists appeared to be bullying, arrogant, irreverent, hectoring, nit-picking, and unpatriotic.

Even though many viewers were shocked by the harshness and narrowness of Nixon's attack on the press and on Robert Pierpoint specifically, just as many, undoubtedly, were upset by the hostility and disrespect that the newsmen displayed toward the elected leader of the nation.

Whatever the ultimate effect (and polls taken later seemed to indicate that such maneuvers had no lasting impact on press credibility), Ken Clawson, White House director of communications, followed through immediately with a campaign to reinforce the president's negative feelings *about* TV *on* TV.

The Monday following the October 26 press conference, Pat Buchanan was interviewed on "The CBS Morning News" by the two men who had particularly felt the weight of Nixon's anger three days earlier, Dan Rather and Robert Pierpoint.

During the thirty-five minute encounter Rather read a quote from David Wise's *The Politics of Lying*:

> As president, Richard Nixon has unleashed and personally participated in the strongest, most highly coordinated, and ultimately the most dangerous attack on the nation's constitutionally protected press since the Alien and Sedition Acts of 1798.

Buchanan's own assessment of the situation followed:

> What we have—what's come up in this country, in my judgment, is like the railroads at around the turn of the century; the networks in the United States have gained a position of power and dominance over the flow of ideas and information to the American people which I think is excessive; it's injurious to the democratic process, in my judgment, and every legal and Constitutional means ought to be considered in order to break up that dominance, in order to spread— spread it out so that you decentralize power in this area. Now, the networks and the newspapers, the dominant newspapers— The Washington Post Company, *The New York Times*—have a tremendous power in this society to influence opinion. In our judgment, just as the First Amendment gives you the right of a free press, the right of freedom of speech to criticize us, to say that the president of the United States is not doing a good job,

so we can exercise the same freedom to say that the networks are not doing a good job. *The New York Times*, for example, might not be doing a good job, and the Washington *Post* might not be doing a good job. I think the First Amendment is a two-way street, as applies to us as well as to you. . . . In my judgment, it would be a better situation in this country if, instead of controlling, say, five major markets, the three network news organizations had to compete in those major markets . . . you control and own five stations, and they have—have no other choice but to take your news. In my judgment, if there were a competitive situation, and you had, say, eight networks working . . . if there were competing voices, I think you would have far less criticism on the part of government. . . . Our concern is not with the exercise of your freedoms; it's with the power of the networks.

As if to underscore Buchanan's judgment, the following week the White House Office of Telecommunications Policy presented a scheme to drop an additional sixty-seven VHF stations into the nation's TV grid, a suggestion greeted with indignation and horror by the networks, which saw in it not only a deliberate threat to the profits of their owned and operated stations and their affiliates but a step toward the possible foundation of a fourth commercial network. (See page 119.)

Clawson had already scheduled White House Chief of Staff General Alexander Haig to be on "Face the Nation" that Sunday. David Eisenhower was booked onto the NBC "Today" show for Tuesday morning. His wife, Julie Nixon Eisenhower, followed three mornings later.

In the next fortnight some specifics were brought forward to support the · president's original contention that the press in its reporting was, if not "outrageous, vicious, distorted, frantic and hysterical," at least unfriendly and unkind.

These instances went back as far as the coverage of the renewed bombing in North Vietnam at Christmastime 1972, in which the president was referred to unflatteringly in quotes as "a tyrant" and "having taken leave of his senses." There were claims of alleged disproportion in the time allotted to presidential spokesmen on the air, particularly on the Walter Cronkite show, where the White House claimed the only Watergate-related interviews had been with Daniel Ellsberg, John Dean, and Archibald Cox. Furthermore, of the twenty-two spots on network news on the Monday following Cox's firing, nineteen were considered unfavorable, two favorable, and one neutral.

"Were those nineteen television news spots reporting, or were they creating an impeachment atmosphere?" Clawson asked. "That day on television was probably the last straw for the president—the outcries for impeachment on television in the wake of the Cox firing."

Although NBC and CBS carried Cox, and all three networks carried the Richardson press conference in its entirety, only CBS, the president's men complained, had paid Secretary of State Kissinger the same courtesy at his news conference about the Middle East crisis. They saw the same disproportion in the fact that all three networks had covered turncoat Dean's five days of testimony in the Watergate hearings but only one looked on when the president's men, Haldeman and Ehrlichman, testified.

The networks had logical justifications for all these alleged inequities, except, perhaps, for their neglect of the Kissinger press conference.* CBS News said it had issued standing invitations to Haldeman and Ehrlichman that were not taken up. The source of the derogatory 1972 quotes about bombing North Vietnam was clearly labeled Radio Hanoi. As for lighter coverage of pro-Nixon testimony, it grew out of the network rotation policy which affected pro and con witnesses alike.

When more specific examples of distorted reporting were asked for, the White House seemed unwilling or unable to provide them, claiming insufficient time and staff. In late January the National News Council put together a fifteen-page report, which, after a description of its attempts to get specifics from the Administration, concluded:

> It would be difficult, if not futile, however, for the Council
> to attempt to deduce, from broad and non-specific charges, the
> particular actions of the television networks that inspired the

---

* Hanging over the Kissinger press conference had been the shadow cast by the newsmen's suspicion that the international military alert called by the president the preceding night might have had its *raison d'être* in domestic turmoil rather than Russian brinkmanship.

The use of a carefully chosen media event to dilute or divert attention from an inadvertent one was an old suspicion in Washington, where the timing of each moonshot was closely examined for possible ulterior Vietnam motives, and where, once Watergate broke, all Nixon acts and movements, whether to Cairo or Nashville, Moscow or Houston, were assumed to be carefully thought out distractions from the "big story." Even the energy crisis had been suspect. This time, when the question, usually suppressed, was put at a major media event, the secretary of state's press conference, Kissinger replied firmly, "It is a symptom of what is happening to our country that it could even be suggested that the United States would alert its forces for domestic reasons."

president's remarks at his news conference on October 26, 1973. Under the circumstances, the National News Council cannot proceed with the type of study and analysis it contemplated.

We believe it is seriously detrimental to the public interest for the president to leave his harsh criticism of the television networks unsupported by specific details that could then be evaluated objectively by an impartial body.*

After the holidays the president went into a period of high visibility, and the press had no choice but to follow him.

In February in Huntsville, Alabama, the president, welcomed by George Wallace, told a flag-waving Honor America Day rally that the media had created "a distorted view of America."

A week later, at what was to be the first of three news conferences—plus a televised question-and-answer session—in less than a month (a Nixon record), the president announced the end of the energy crisis and defined what he considered necessary grounds for impeachment.

On March 6 he held another press conference. In the course of answering a question about the Administration's proposed campaign reform bill, he said, "Among the matters that I think are of particular interest to all of the members of the press is the fact that we believe that candidates should have a right to defend themselves against false charges that are made during a campaign, whether by their opponents or by the press." Of his top aides Haldeman, Ehrlichman, and Colson he said bitterly, "While they have been convicted in the press—over and over again—while they have been convicted before committees—over and over again—they are now before a court."

On March 15 the president began a cross-country tour which took him to Chicago to meet a gathering of sympathetic business executives, whom he told:

> As far as Watergate is concerned, it has been carried on, it has been, I believe, overpublicized and a lot of charges have been made that frankly have proved to be false. I'm sure that many people in the audience have read at one time or other, either in our news magazines, possibly in a newspaper, certainly heard on television and radio such charges as this: that the president helped to plan the Watergate thing before and had knowledge of it; that the president was informed that

_____

* For the entire statement, see Appendix X.

payments were being made on March 13, and that a blackmail attempt was being made on the White House on March 13, rather than on March 21 when I said was the first time those matters were brought to my attention. That the president had authorized the issuance of clemency or a promise of clemency to some of the defendants, and that the president had ordered the burglarizing—again, a very stupid act, apart from the fact that it's wrong and illegal—of Dr. Ellsberg's psychiatrist's office in California. Now all of those charges have been made. Many Americans—perhaps a majority—believe them. They are all totally false and the investigation will prove it, whatever the Congress does—the tapes, etc., when they all come out, will establish that they are false.

From Chicago, the president went to the opening of the new Grand Ole Opry in Nashville, where a hero's welcome was staged in the hangar of the Tennessee Air National Guard especially refurbished for the occasion. Enthusiasts waving American flags sang to the tune of "Okie from Muskogee" a song entitled "Stand Up and Cheer for Richard Nixon." It went in part:

> I'm sick of what I'm reading in the papers
> I'm tired of all that trash on TV
> Stand up and cheer for Richard Nixon
> I've been hearing talk about impeaching
> The man we chose to lead us through these times.
> But talk like this could weaken and defeat us.
> Let's show the world we're not the quitting kind.

Later, on the Opry stage, the president played the piano—"Happy Birthday," "My Wild Irish Rose," and "God Bless America"—in honor of his wife's sixty-second birthday, and dropped Yo-Yo with Roy Acuff. Then he moved on to Houston and the annual convention of the National Association of Broadcasters.

The paradox in the situation was that in the broadcasters, the employers of his supposed arch enemies, the TV journalists, he found some of his staunchest supporters. Their enthusiasm seemed undiminished by the fact that in 1973 he had declined their invitation and sent a 180-word telegram instead.

In 1974 he came in person, spoke less than five minutes, and then opened himself to questions from reporters especially imported for the occasion, among their number Nixon's nemesis, Dan Rather. The president launched a few mild barbs against the press, including such examples as "The President should treat the press just as fairly as the press treats him" and "Maybe one of the reasons that 80 percent of the American people believe that the country is already in a recession is that almost 80 percent of them watch television news or listen to radio news."

However, the most significant exchange was short and sour. It had been preceded by mixed applause and boos from the floor when reporter Rather rose to put a question.

"Are you running for something?" the president asked acidly.

"No sir, Mr. President," Rather responded. "Are you?"

The television cameras had caught in this petty exchange what was unquestionably a low point in the deteriorating relationship between the chief executive and the press.

Demands for Rather's resignation came from a dozen CBS network affiliates and criticism of his pertness was widespread in the media. However, CBS News President Richard Salant stood by him, saying, "I think that Mr. Nixon is using Rather to personalize his confrontation with the press. That diverts the issue at hand." *

By June, the Phillips-Sindlinger Survey reported that Dan Rather, although he was still only number seven on the "very high in trust" list, was the newscaster experiencing the greatest increase in public confidence. "The tremendous impact of the Watergate scandals," the survey reported, "is boosting public faith in CBS liberal newscasters and eroding the credibility of ABC's more friendly to the Administration team."

And so it had gone: Advantage gained, advantage lost. In April in New York City John Mitchell and Maurice Stans were judged innocent after they and their lawyers had insisted that they would never be able to get a fair trial anywhere thanks to Watergate exposure in the media.

---

* There had been an interchange between Nixon and Rather during the August 22 press conference in San Clemente which in retrospect seemed to have set the stage for the Houston encounter.

Rather had said, "Mr. President, I want to state this question with due respect to your office but also as directly as . . . .

Nixon interrupted, "That would be unusual."

Rather: "I'd like to think not. It concerns the events surrounding Mr. Ehrlichman's contact and on one occasion your own contact with the judge in the Pentagon papers case, Judge Byrne . . . ." Rather went on to outline the events as they had been reported in the press.

Nixon: "Well, I would say the only point of your statement that is perhaps accurate is that I'm a lawyer . . . ."

After giving a corrected version of the events as he saw them, the president concluded: ". . . this is the explanation of what happened, and obviously you in your commentary tonight can attach anything you want to it. I hope you will be just as fair and objective as I try to be in giving you the answer."

The next night Nixon appeared on the networks to announce that finally he was going to release the transcripts of thirty-one tapes piled up in fifty loose-leaf binders in a huge stack on the table beside him.

Again an attempt was made to use the media and denigrate them at the same time. In the course of his address Nixon said:

> During the past year, the wildest accusations have been given banner headlines and ready credence as well. Rumor, gossip, innuendo, accounts from unnamed sources of what a prospective witness might testify have filled the morning newspapers and then are repeated on the evening newscasts. Day after day, time and again, a familiar pattern repeated itself. A charge would be reported the first day. That's what it was—just an allegation. But it would then be referred back to the next day and thereafter as if it were true. The distinction between fact and speculation grew blurred. Eventually, all seeped into the public consciousness as a vague, general impression of massive wrongdoing, implicating everybody, gaining credibility by its endless repetition.

Later he added:

> I realize that these transcripts will provide grist for many sensational stories in the press . . . I've been reluctant to release these tapes not just because they will embarrass me and those with whom I have talked—which they will—and not just because they will become the subject of speculation and ridicule—which they will—and not just because certain parts of them will be seized upon by political and journalistic opponents—which they will. I have been reluctant because the principle of confidentiality is absolutely essential to the conduct of the presidency.

Beside him as he talked were the notebooks which on the nation's TV screens looked like a veritable Everest stacked there, apparently to convince the public of the court's excessive demands and the president's generosity in meeting them.

Nor could the network cameras keep their eyes off this pyramid of paper, zooming in on it time and time again during the thirty-five minutes the President was on the air. (The next day all fifty were consolidated into one document which was eventually issued as a single $2.50 paperback.)

A further attempt to manipulate the press was made by

presidential lawyer James St. Clair, who had delayed distribution of the tape transcripts for five hours and substituted a highly selective digest of them which was intended to form the basis for the first news reports both in print and on the air. During this period he himself appeared on the network newscasts explaining the true significance of the tapes.*

Ken Clawson was busy too. As many as possible of the panel and talk shows had been booked in advance by the White House press aide for the express purpose of giving the American public a favorable interpretation of the tapes. Dean Burch, ex-head of the FCC, now the president's counsel, was on "Face the Nation" the Sunday before the tapes were released. Alexander Haig appeared on ABC's "Issues and Answers" the following Sunday. Haig's message:

> I think we, as the American people, as a society have got to understand that never in the history of this Republic has any subject been investigated so thoroughly, have so many thousands and indeed millions of words of testimony been taken, so much evidence scrutinized, both publicly and privately, by various forums, grand juries, special prosecutors, Senate committees, and now judiciary committees. The time has come, in my view, for the facts that have resulted from this excessive introspection to be assessed by the House committee, to make their judgments and to get on with the business of the American people. . . .
>
> Now I am not endorsing whatever alleged wrongdoing may have occurred in the Watergate affair, but I think the time has come for all of us—and I include the media as well as the members of the Congress and, indeed, our own White House people—to bring this matter to a conclusion.

James St. Clair, on NBC's "Meet the Press," was of approximately the same mind. But Representatives Tom Railsback and Paul Sarbanes from the House Judiciary Committee preparing for an impeachment inquiry felt differently and said so on CBS's "Face the Nation," labeling the president's action "partial compliance. . . . If the tapes are available . . . those should be provided to the committee."

* One presidential assistant told David Wise, the author of *The Politics of Lying*, "Everyone assumed the tapes would be leaked and leaked selectively in the way most harmful to the president. So the best thing was to go ahead and dump them. They were going to be broadcast willy-nilly. So it was best to put them out and let the president take the credit. And put a White House twist on what the tapes showed."

In the end the president's contention that here was the truth, the whole truth (with a few unintelligibles and expletives deleted), and nothing but the truth, and that further questions and demands were unnecessary harassment, did not prevail.

The edited tapes were scrutinized by all the media with devastating effect. There were special selective readings on CBS and NBC as well as PBS, and the transcript was given marathon readings on Pacifica stations in New York, Berkeley, Los Angeles, and Houston, and on National Public Radio, with at least forty-one stations plugged in carrying the full text over an entire weekend.*

Eventually transcripts of the unedited tapes were made available, and the disparities, many giving evidence of attempts to deceive, were examined once more by the media.†

And then, miraculously, the advantage seemed to shift. Following the release of the tapes there were widespread reports that the president was benefiting from a public revulsion against the press and its undue concentration on Watergate. As usual the reports came from the press itself.

Time magazine, in a cover story entitled "Covering Watergate: Success and Backlash," reported that in April 1974 a California poll indicated that a majority of those interviewed since the preceding October believed the Watergate coverage to be excessive, while those who found the coverage unbiased had dropped from a clear majority to 44 percent. A Gallup poll in July 1974 reported that 48 percent of the people queried thought Watergate was a "serious" matter, while an almost equal number, 43 percent, dismissed it as "just politics." In a DuPont–American Association

---

* KVII-TV, Amarillo, Texas, wrote the Survey: "When it became obvious no one was going to print the presidential transcripts in a manner where everyone who wanted to read them could, we printed 15,000 copies in a newspaper format and sold them at fifty cents a copy. Our newspapers had not even serialized the transcripts. We went to press with the first 10,000 on May 13. They were gone in one week and so we had 5,000 more printed. It is our first and probably last newspaper."

† Lee Frischknecht of NPR sent a letter to Representative Peter Rodino, chairman of the House Judiciary Committee, saying: "Those of us in the broadcasting media believe you could accomplish your aim of informing the public even better if you also released copies of the tapes themselves. What better way for the public to get an accurate version of the discussions?

"I appeal to you and your committee to release copies of the tapes. We at National Public Radio have broadcast readings of the complete White House transcripts of the tapes and will be doing the same for the transcripts of the eight tapes your committee has released. We would be doing even a greater service if we were able to broadcast the tapes themselves." The tapes themselves, however, were not to be released until 1975.

of University Women survey, more than 55 percent of the answers concerning the amount of Watergate coverage in the respondent communities were negative. Newsmen themselves complained that Watergate-related stories dominated the front pages and tops of newscasts, taking space and time away from equally important national and international stories.

A TV news director in Montana wrote the Survey:

> Although it is certainly a significant chapter in our history, it is apparent national news reporters have become so wrapped up in it they've forgotten about the rest of the world and for that matter the rest of the nation. Much of the detailed coverage and exhaustive amount of time spent has resulted in public distrust of news reporters as well as politicians. That is a lesson perhaps difficult for the working press to swallow.

As early as September 1973 Herbert Klein, former director of communications for President Nixon and currently a vice-president for corporate relations of Metromedia, the proprietor of eighteen major-market TV and radio stations, told a Kansas City audience gathered for "TV Day at the Advertising and Sales Executives Club":

> Television has overplayed it [Watergate] to the exclusion of more current and interesting news, in some cases is still doing so. It's to the point where that obsession has taken our eye off the ball. There is no simple answer to what happened at Watergate, but we need to pull back, recognize that there will be such incidents, regroup and forge ahead.

There were other, more serious, criticisms than overexposure. Such strange bedfellows as Barry Goldwater, Spiro Agnew, Archibald Cox, and Senator William Proxmire all had seen a common danger in the concentration on Watergate.

Agnew was first, telling students at the University of Virginia in May 1973, on the eve of the hearings and before his own long hot summer, that the media's reporting techniques were "a very short jump to McCarthyism."

Proxmire on the Senate floor said of news stories on the Watergate cover-up that the president was:

> . . . being tried, sentenced and executed by rumor and allegation.

My point is this: It is unfair, unjust and unwise to the president and to the country to rush into print with such a flat charge that certain unidentified investigators for the grand jury have elicited certain information from a witness. The witness has not told this to the press. Some anonymous investigators allegedly have done so. But the story is partial. It is wholly unconfirmed. It may or may not be confirmed or refuted later. There is simply no way of knowing now whether it is true or not. But it may very well have gone a long way toward destroying the president of the United States.

I succeeded the late Senator McCarthy in the Senate. I was very much opposed to his motives and his tactics, which were to make severely damaging charges, such as accusing a person of being a Communist, knowing that they would be denied; but no matter how strongly they were denied, the charges still remained. I find this kind of persecution and condemnation without trial McCarthyism at its worst.

Cox, speaking to the Harvard Chapter of Phi Beta Kappa the spring following his peremptory dismissal, said:

In the heyday of Joseph McCarthy the intellectual world, including the press, was properly outspoken about the danger of *ex parte* accusation, the unfairness of planting of charges in the press without adequate opportunity for denial, and the lack of true adversary proceedings. Should not the same objections be raised when the staff or possibly some member of the Ervin committee leaks the results of incomplete investigation, gives out the accusatory inferences it draws from secret testimony, and even releases proposed findings of guilt upon men under indictment and awaiting trial? Procedural fairness does not depend upon whose ox is being gored.

Surely, there is also need for voices to stress the importance of constraints upon the means by which we pursue even the worthiest objectives. "The people in the White House," one of them recalls, "believed they were entitled to do things differently, to suspend the rules, because they were fulfilling a mission. That was the only important thing—the mission." Of course the White House aides were not the first so to justify physical aggression, lying and cheating, and disregard for the rights of speech, privacy, dignity and other fundamental liberties. Disregard of the constraints by some breeds further disregard upon the part of others. Brute power becomes the determinant of what is falsely labeled "justice." Only the spirit that is not too sure it is right speaks for the values of civility and reason.

McCarthyism was not, of course, limited to one side. Pro-communist leanings were ascribed to the press by a number of Nixon supporters, most notably by Rabbi Baruch Korff of the National Citizens' Committee for Fairness to the Presidency, Inc. A typical sample of this sort of attack was contained in a speech delivered in April 1974 by Bruce Herschensohn, a deputy special assistant to the president, in the keynote address to the Seventh Conference of the World Anti-Communist League in Washington. After castigating the press for its handling of the Vietnam War, Herschensohn summed it up:

> But the majority of this nation overrode the morning and nightly bombardments given by those who were irresponsible within the national media, and our commitment was not surrendered. Our history of that decade should be recorded that while the weak yelled for peace at any price, the strong were dying for the cause of freedom and the great majority of this nation knew the cause was worthy.
>
> . . . In a nation whose memory is often short, it is worth remembering what we were told as those same newscasters and analysts go on to other puusuits—it is worth remembering so we can better evaluate what we are told today, and tomorrow. They themselves will not remind us, as it would reduce their credibility to shambles.
>
> There are today continuations of yesterday along with new plateaus to be reached. The pursuits of good men are difficult enough. . . . It is my hope and prayer that President Nixon will be successful in bringing about a generation of peace—not peace of surrender that was advocated by so many in the media, but the kind of peace that can lead future generations to their ultimate destiny—a world of peace within freedom without hunger.

Nor was there any reticence about employing holy scripture. If Senator Sam Ervin quoted the Bible extensively during the opening phases of the Watergate hearings, a year later the Reverend Billy James Hargis, a clergyman of conservative bent, was encouraging his co-religionists to send stones to Congress to be cast first by those who were without sin.

Nixon, who claimed 68 percent approval in the polls at the time of his inauguration in 1973 and had dropped to an all-time low of 25 percent approval in March 1974, had slowly climbed back to 28 percent by June. In the same month the Gallup poll reported that sentiment for his removal had declined from 48 percent to 44 percent.

An episode in June seemed to epitomize the low estate to which the press had fallen. Leaks from the House Judiciary Committee hearings concerning Secretary of State Kissinger's possible implication in illegal wiretapping had caused the Secretary to threaten— before the cameras—to resign unless totally absolved of any misbehavior, an action seemingly aimed as much at the media as at whoever had leaked the information to them.

Senator Barry Goldwater told the Senate:

> It is time that we decide once and for all whether it is more important to protect secret information relative to our government or more important to provide more circulation for newspapers, more viewers and listeners to the electronic media, and more money and adulation for people willing to turn against their government.

From a totally different and unexpected direction, press critic Edward Jay Epstein relieved the press of either responsibility or credit in matters relating to Watergate. Writing in *Commentary* magazine, Epstein ended his exercise in disparagement:

> The fact remains that it was not the press which exposed Watergate, it was agencies of government itself. So long as journalists maintain their usual professional blind spot toward the inner conflicts and workings of government, they will no doubt continue to speak of Watergate in terms of the David and Goliath myth, with Bernstein and Woodward as David and the government as Goliath.

During this period of presidential resurgence a series of apparent bombshells had been dropped on Nixon's camp. They included the disclosure that the Watergate grand jury had voted unanimously to name Nixon as "unindicted co-conspirator" in the Watergate cover-up; the pleading of guilty to an obstruction of justice by Charles W. Colson, reputedly the toughest and nastiest man ever employed by the White House; and multiple subpoenas sent to the White House by the courts and Congress.

The public was becoming "anesthetized," one White House aide was quoted as saying. "We are seeing the beginning of a counterreaction by the public to the initial overreaction to accusations against the president."

Press aide Ken Clawson added, "The impact isn't there any more. Last fall we used to talk about what the next bombshell would be. But now there aren't any more bombshells and there won't be any more in the future."

It was mid-June.

3 • The Blip That Burst
Watergate III

AMERICANS TIRED OF WATERGATE COVERAGE, BUT
READY FOR IMPEACHMENT TELEVISION

THIS HEADLINE appeared in the July 15, 1974, issue of *Broadcasting* magazine, followed by an article that included the figures from one of the last of twenty-five Gallup polls on the subject of Watergate. The numbers were not spectacular: 53 percent sated with Watergate, 53 percent willing to see impeachment proceedings televised. But they reflected a mood that Congress was about to act upon. If the TV public was fed up with Watergate, the majority of Americans wanted to see justice done.

Two months earlier, on the afternoon of May 9, Chairman Peter Rodino, Jr., had opened the House of Representatives Judiciary Committee hearings on the possible impeachment of President Nixon. With four TV networks and twenty million Americans looking on, the congressman had explained the ground rules.

> For some time, we have known that the real security of this nation lies in the integrity of its institutions and the trust and informed confidence of its people. We conduct our deliberations in that spirit.
>
> We shall begin our hearings by considering materials relevant to the question of Presidential responsibility for the Watergate break-in and its investigation by law enforcement agencies.
>
> This is one of six areas of our inquiry. We expect to continue our inquiries until each area has been thoroughly examined.*

* The other five areas of inquiry taken up by the Judiciary Committee were allegations concerning: (1) domestic surveillance directed by the White House, (2) intelligence activities directed by the White House during the presidential campaign of 1972, (3) the personal finances of the president, (4) efforts by the White House to

Then, eighteen minutes after Rodino had gaveled the meeting to order, the committee went into executive session. The TV networks, the press, and the public were invited to leave hearings that, in the opinion of the chairman, might "tend to defame, degrade or incriminate."

Outsiders would not be permitted back for two and a half months.

During those eleven weeks the Administration-media struggle entered its final phase, as did the Nixon presidency.

There were signs of desperation on both sides. Officially, the hearings in which counsel was presenting evidence to the committee concerning the six areas of possibly impeachable offenses were held in secret, with only a brief daily statement issued to the press. As a result the congressmen at the beginning and end of each session had to run the gauntlet of more than a hundred information hungry reporters. The hallway outside the committee's chambers soon was being compared to the heavily bombarded Slot between Guadalcanal and Bougainville Island in the Solomons in World War II.

If little substantive information was gained by pinning congressmen against corridor walls, the committee itself had sprung a hundred leaks, most of them, according to the White House, prejudicial to the president's cause.

The White House earlier had deplored the Senate hearings as a circus creating an atmosphere in which any sort of fair judgment was impossible. Now the president and his supporters urged that the House hearings be opened to the public and that many of the same witnesses whose appearance before the senators had so upset them should be called.

Full exposure of the hearings, the president's spokesmen contended, was the only possible way to determine the truth. For once, the president and the broadcasters seemed to agree. An editorial in *Broadcasting* magazine stated:

> There are influential members of the House who still oppose the admission of live broadcast coverage—asserting that the presence of camera and microphone would somehow corrupt the legislative process. It is a specious fear. Indeed the denial

---

use agencies of the executive branch for political purposes and White House involvement with illegal campaign contributions, and (5) other misconduct not falling in the previous categories, such as the secret bombing of Cambodia and impoundment of funds.

of public attendance through the media of radio and television will only raise more doubts about an impeachment process that is already open to considerable question.

In retrospect, the wiser members of the Judiciary Committee must be questioning their decision to keep the first phase of hearings closed. As could have been expected, the testimony that was supposed to be adduced in privacy has been profusely leaked. There have been few days without their juicy revelations that may, or may not, reflect what was actually said.

To open the sessions to pad-and-pencil reporting would of course enormously improve the coverage. Journalists could get the testimony at first hand instead of through third parties whose bias dictates the extent and accuracy of their accounts.

But pad-and-pencil reporting is not enough when the question is as important as the impeachment of a President and when the incomparable reporting instruments of radio and television are at hand. To deny the use of modern communication is to deny the electorate a service it is owed. The House leadership would be well advised to consider how the public would react to a prohibition against broadcast coverage.

Most conspicuous among the "juicy revelations" had been the House version of a 16-minute tape of a March 22, 1973, conversation with John Mitchell and John Dean that the president had omitted from his own edited version released ten weeks before. In other tapes—especially those of March 13 and March 21—the Judiciary Committee had picked up a great deal the president's transcribers had not put on the record, filling in gaps that seemed to indicate clear presidential knowledge of the Watergate cover-up.

The White House did not take these damaging revelations lying down. It launched an elaborate counteroffensive, enlisting a number of the most outspoken of the remaining Nixon loyalists.

Their targets included both the press and the personnel of the House committee, which was variously described as "a kangaroo court," a "lynch mob," "character assassins," "radicals," and "partisans," as well as "an impeachment lobby" that utilized leaks to put "malicious and pernicious interpretations" on the evidence.

When Chairman Rodino was reported in the press as having said that all twenty-one Democrats on the committee were prepared to vote for impeachment, a statement Rodino denied ever having made, Ken W. Clawson, White House director of communications, responded indignantly:

Chairman Rodino's partisanship and the bias of other Democrats on the House Judiciary Committee was confirmed today out of Mr. Rodino's own mouth. Mr. Rodino's abuse of the impeachment process clearly requires that he be discharged as chairman and replaced by a fair-minded Democrat. Although Mr. Rodino's comments constitute foot and mouth disease, it nevertheless obviously reflects his personal views.

The Reverend John J. McLaughlin, who had received major media exposure as "Nixon's priest," demanded at a news conference covered by Boston TV that Rodino, "a crude political tactician," disqualify himself from the impeachment deliberations. In Pittsburgh, for a TV appearance a week earlier, he had remarked concerning his fellow Jesuit Reverend Robert F. Drinan, a representative from Massachusetts, that "if he did do this leaking or if he condones such leaking by his personal staff, he should be disqualified from the House Judiciary Committee, censured by the House of Representatives, and brought to trial by law-enforcement authorities." *

Although the focus seemed to have shifted to the Judiciary Committee members, the press was not spared. White House aide Bruce Herschensohn hit the lecture circuit. As he put it in a letter to CBS News vice-president Gordon Manning, part of an exchange concerning White House access to tapes of CBS News stories, "I have been traveling around the country making speeches in which I attack CBS News and, as you know, that is vitally important, so I am sure you will forgive my delay in responding."

Patrick Buchanan swung wildly. "The networks and the national news media," he said on National Public Radio, distort their coverage of the news by giving "enormous, positive, and favorable publicity to movements associated with the far left." These movements, Buchanan explained, included "the anti-war movement, the consumer movement, the civil rights movement."

The president himself discussed the press with Rabbi Baruch M. Korff, head of the National Citizens Committee for Fairness to the Presidency, Inc., in an interview released in mid-July:

There are some, putting it in the vernacular, who hate my guts with a passion. But I don't hate them, none of them.

* Father Drinan, along with Elizabeth Holtzman, Jerome Waldie, John Conyers, and other committee liberals had been accused of springing several important leaks.

Individually I understand. Their philosophies are different.
They don't agree with my positions and after all, they want to
write and take me on.

They are consumed by this issue, and I can see, not all, but I
can see in the eyes of them, not only their hatred but their
frustration, and I, as a matter of fact, I really feel sorry for
them in a way, because . . . they should recognize that to the
extent that they allow their own hatreds to consume them,
they will lose the rationality which is the mark of a civilized
man. . . .

I have seen men as a result of Congressional hearings, as a
result of inspired leaks, and as a result of source stories, et
cetera, men who were not guilty be badly damaged in terms of
their reputations. . . . I have seen them tried and convicted in
the press and on television, so that the chance for them to get a
fair trial any place is almost impossible. . . .

I would only suggest that an historical assessment would be
that it was probably, to use the word scandal, the broadest but
thinnest scandal in American history. . . .

I would suggest in terms of Watergate, it has caught the
imagination of the press, for another reason and I do not say
this with any bitterness at all, but I am not the press' favorite
pin-up boy. If it hadn't been Watergate, there would probably
have been something else. So now they have this. But I will
survive it and I just hope they will survive it with, shall we say,
as much serenity as I have.

. . . If I were basically a liberal by their standards, if I had
bugged out of Vietnam, which they wanted, Watergate would
have been a blip. They wouldn't have cared but it is because I
have not gone down the line with them that they care.

In spite of the president's low opinion, the press gave his trip to
the Soviet Union in early July front-page and top-of-the-evening-
news treatment. All four networks plugged in to the Loring Air
Force hangar in Limestone, Maine, when on his return the
president made a report to the nation on the less than sensational
accomplishments of his latest Moscow visit.

Three weeks after the president's return, the House of Representatives voted 346 to 40 to open the final debates of the House
Judiciary Committee over articles of impeachment to the public
and the full panoply of the press. For the first time in history live
microphones and cameras were permitted into a deliberative
session of a House Committee, and this time they would stay to the
end. It was a landmark decision, which could herald the opening of
full-floor sessions of the Senate and the House to broadcasters.

This possibility had been the subject of extended discussion both among legislators and the press. Senate majority leader Mike Mansfield had expressed his approval:

> It is my personal view at this time that the use of television would recognize the historic significance of an event of this kind as well as television's essential role in the direct informing of the American public. Its use would reflect a Senate judgment that the people have, in this case, not only a right but a need to know.

The national TV critic who calls himself "Cyclops" wrote in *The New York Times*:

> In recent years, what is "real" has come to seem what has happened on television. Our elections, our assassinations, our moon landings, our wars become realities because we have seen them with our own eyes, on TV. We haven't had much to celebrate lately, but at least our grief has achieved a form. In the same way, justice must be served, and we must experience it in the only national community we have, which is the airwaves. This event belongs to us; the cameras are an extension of us; TV represents us as much as the men and women we will be watching.

In the same newspaper, columnist James Reston took the opposite position:

> The emotional tension on all the actors on this world stage would almost forbid careful and precise discussion. The pressure on the President would be almost unbearable. The reaction of members of the television audience is fairly predictable. They would be sending telegrams, expressing their views for and against the President, by the millions, threatening House and Senate members with defeat at the next election if they voted this way or that. . . .
> But to do all this before the red eye of the camera, to sift the evidence and condemn the President on the floor of the House or Senate, knowing that you will be seen on Soviet, Chinese and European television tomorrow, is a complicated nightmare for every man who rises to speak.
> It is a troubling question and we had better be careful about it—and careful in time.

Republican Representative Delbert Latta of Ohio had other reasons for objecting to TV's presence in the House: ". . . you can't tell me that the networks are going to give all that costly time to the Judiciary Committee. They are going to cut out some portions and give the American people what they [the networks] want."

Fred Friendly, former head of CBS News, offered some specific recommendations: no anchormen in the House or Senate chambers, no rear-screen projection to give the effect of reportorial presence, no editorial commentary or interpretative reporting while the sessions were in progress, no commercials.

> In 1974, television's credentials for admittance will be the justified claim that it can provide a reserve ticket for every American who wants a front row seat in the spectators gallery. . . . The citizen with such a seat is entitled to his privacy, even his solitude, without some well-meaning sightseeing guide or expert whispering in his ear.

Most enthusiastic of all was undoubtedly NBC News president Richard C. Wald, who sent an excited memo to his executives in May before the Judiciary Committee hearings began.

> We are about to embark on the most important story this division has ever covered. It may be the most important story of the century.
>
> Before us there stretches the certainty of a redistribution of Presidential power, no matter what the outcome of the process that begins with the deliberations of the Judiciary Committee. The Imperial Presidency is over, for a time at least. No President has given up so much, so visibly, ever. And no period of our history has ever involved so many of us in the fabric of how we are governed.
>
> It is the biggest event of our times and we were drawn into news because we wanted to deal with history, with events greater than ourselves, with the issues and the men that are important.
>
> But therein lies a problem that worries me. We tend at times like this to get manic, to fall into that form of excitement that sustains us in the small hours of an election morning and makes the problems seem worthwhile. The deadline pressure and the story carry us along, unthinking, on a crest of activity.
>
> I do not want us to become part of the story. We are not hounds chasing the hare. The excitement is in the event, not in

us. What begins in journalistic energy must not end in predicting, or reaching or guessing.

This is an awful time, and I mean that it should fill us with awe. A great, wheeling tragedy is being played out before us and I do not want to anticipate its movements. I want to report each day as it happens, record each significant moment, but I do not want to push it along. There is no specific remedy I can give you. There is no set of rules handy for contingencies such as this. Just be aware of the problems, be aware of your own tendencies. There is no glee in this. It will bring good to none.

And if we do not get caught up in the moment, history will hold us better.

Wald had sent a crew of thirty, including Barbara Walters, John Chancellor, Douglas Kiker, Ray Scherer, Carl Stern, and "Today" producer Stuart Schulberg, to cover the hearings on May 9, only to be asked to leave a few minutes after they began.

On July 24, when "the most important story of the century" was once more available to the TV cameras, Wald's network was giving its viewers a full evening of entertainment, as was Friendly's former employer, CBS. Thanks to a three-network decision announced July 22 that the Judiciary Committee hearings would be covered in rotation, ABC was the only commercial network on hand to carry the proceedings.

Once again, public television's NPACT was the only TV facility to be present in the committee chambers from beginning to end for what NPACT president James Karayn agreed was "the most important assignment we've ever had. Involved in the coverage of these hearings are matters concerning the Constitution, the Presidency, and Congressional processes. Ninety percent deals with things that have never been dealt with before. We learned a lot from our Watergate coverage and realize that it was just preliminary to this event."

As in the Senate Watergate hearings, NPACT took first place in assuring Americans access to an event of enormous importance, offering public TV affiliates both live coverage and prime-time replays, a service that, thanks to the length of individual sessions, kept some public TV stations on the air as late as 4:25 A.M. and for a total of fourteen and a half hours of the twenty-four.

Despite the buildup, the initial reaction to the hearings as a TV event was something less than enthusiastic. Howard K. Smith on ABC, the network that had the privilege of covering the first night,

commented that the proceedings needed a professional TV director. Kevin Phillips, writing in *TV Guide*, said:

> For the first 45 minutes or so, the action unfolded like wet
> cardboard, and as the boys in the control room candidly
> admitted, it took a bomb hoax [the first of three during the
> coverage] to bail them out. . . . Chairman Peter Rodino had
> performed with the elan of a second-string Newark bookie;
> ranking Republican Edward Hutchinson with the verve of a
> small-town mortician. . . .

The best thing, according to Phillips, was the performance of
Republican Representative Charles Sandman of New Jersey, the
only congressman of the thirty-eight participating to make a frontal
attack on the press during the committee's five days on the air.
Sandman blasted his fellow congressmen as well as the media:

> We started in closed session and we swore by everything
> that was holy that we would uphold the rules of confidential-
> ity. That has been the joke of the century. There has been
> nothing confidential in this committee. Members of the other
> side have reported to the media every hour on the hour, some
> every hour on the half hour. We have become the first forum
> in the history of man to release to the public every shred of
> information we have before a single decision was ever made.
> When did that ever happen before—never. . . . Now, it is not
> the purpose and objective of any media [sic] to make the news.
> It is the purpose and the objective of the media to fairly report
> the news.

Sandman was undoubtedly the most irascible of the representatives lined up at the double tier of desks swept by the TV cameras.
But one by one his less outspoken colleagues came into focus, and
if the sum total of their remarks was not box office, they impressed
the attentive viewer with their intelligence, their probity, and
frequently with their passion.
Shana Alexander wrote in *Newsweek*:

> By the end of the week the parade of 38 speakers, each
> striving in his or her own way to do honor to himself, the
> system, and to history, had done much to restore one's faith in
> this nation's moral tone. There was nothing heroic about these
> 38 people save their common humanity. That turned out to be
> more than enough.

The public response was mixed. Although the ratings for the debates were respectable, entertainment on at least one of the other networks won out every night the House proceedings were in prime time.

Total viewership for the six days the debates were on the air was estimated at 70 million. At any one time 6.8 million households were tuned in, and those tuned in averaged 88 minutes out of the sessions, which averaged 194 minutes in length, a high percentage of the total offered considering the demands put on the viewers' intelligence and attention.

Thanks to prime-time preemptions, the cost to the networks, despite the fact that they were on one at a time, ran more than $2 million for the first three days of the debates. When the final bill was in, it was estimated that the forty-six hours of coverage cost the networks a total of $5 million in billings, more than half the cost estimated for the thirty-seven days of the Senate Watergate hearings.

Besides recommending that the congressmen employ professional assistance, Howard K. Smith had said before he went off the air at 10:46 P.M. July 24 that it had been "an undramatic ending to a very dramatic day." Contributing to the day's drama had been another stunning blow to the president's cause, the Supreme Court's decision that Nixon would have to relinquish the sixty-four tapes subpoenaed by Special Watergate Counsel Leon Jaworski.

The next day some attention was diverted from the events in the House of Representatives by the president's speech on the economy, delivered in Los Angeles' Century Plaza Hotel to 1700 business men and women. Scheduled for 7:30 P.M., EDT, the speech was carried by all four networks, and the Judiciary Committee debates were delayed to accommodate the president.* In thirty-five minutes he still managed to get the same number of viewers that the debates accumulated over three hours of prime time. However, the winner for the evening remained the "Streets of San Francisco" on ABC.

* Earlier that week a significant demonstration of growing network resistance to White House demands for TV time came in the handling of two major statements delivered by presidential counsel James St. Clair. On Monday St. Clair's press conference to answer questions on his view of the Judiciary Committee inquiry, scheduled for prime time, was taped and highlights replayed later by NBC. Two evenings later when St. Clair chose 7 P.M as the hour to read the president's response to the Supreme Court decision on the sixty-four tapes, an obvious effort to get the top of the news, CBS taped his announcement and placed it at a more appropriate place later in its newscast.

If the hearings could not compete with the kind of second-class entertainment that the network decision to rotate coverage put them up against (mainly reruns and summer replacements), they still rewarded the consistent viewer with a reassuring glimpse of how and how well the U.S. government worked, and also how little negative effect the presence of television cameras seemed to have on the behavior of the congressmen participating.

Representative James Mann of South Carolina contended, "I realize that the arguments made here in front of these cameras would not be made for the benefit of me as a member of this committee. I don't think Mr. Sandman would be so strident or even so partisan if these proceedings were not being conducted to influence the opinions of the American people."

But few of the thirty-eight representatives present, whatever messages they might be sending to their constituents, sounded unduly strident or partisan.

The American people, Congress, and the press had all come a long way in the past twelve months. In the Senate Watergate hearings the summer before, the story (who was telling the truth, who was lying) was everything. In the House, the evidence had been ordered and refined and the main concern was to work out how it could or should be used in the awesome process of impeachment. It was a demanding process unfamiliar to everyone, including the thirty-eight principals who during the six days they were on the air became remarkably distinct in their personalities and capabilities to any attentive TV viewer. As the country looked on they hammered out, debated, and finally voted out three of the proposed five articles of impeachment. In the process they proved to the American people that they were something considerably more than political hacks or "435 orators in search of an idea."

For this R. W. Apple, Jr., of *The New York Times* gave credit to television:

> Television clearly had much to do with the tone of the debate. There were complaints about the lights, and Hungate of Missouri finally took to wearing sunglasses. There were complaints last night [July 30] from the Republicans that the Democrats had deliberately delayed discussion of the tax article so it would be seen during prime time.
>
> But the presence of the cameras held the members to a reasonable standard of relevance and decorum and guaranteed that all would be in their seats. It also gave those who

feared that they were voting against the grain of their constituents a better chance to explain themselves than could a whole year of speeches, newsletters and news conferences. If television is permitted to cover future Congressional debates on momentous questions it could work a profound change in Congressional politics—in some ways as profound as its impact on Presidential politics since 1960. Through a means the Founding Fathers never dreamed of, the Representative could truly become the Federal office-holder closest to the people.

Indeed, the impeachment debates had gone a considerable distance in demonstrating a corrective to what had for several years been perceived as a dangerous inequity in television's service to the executive and legislative branches of the government.

Not everyone, of course, was equally enthusiastic. Representative Charles Wiggins of California, the leading pro-Nixon spokesman, was quoted as saying:

> Its [television's] impact on the Committee was to inhibit the kind of robust, free debate that characterizes Congressional committees. It's a fact that during our debate there was grandstanding—because TV was there. And because TV was there, every member took his full allotted time for speaking, and what we ended up with instead of a debate was a series of speeches. In my own personal scale of values, a full and free debate is infinitely preferable.

Jack Brooks, a liberal Democrat from Texas, seemed to agree:

> A serious effect that would not be noticed by nonparticipants was the tendency to force the actual give-and-take of political negotiation out of the committee room and into the back room.

Broadcasting magazine had its own view:

> Never has a committee been more conscious of its deportment. Suits were pressed, linen was fresh, hair was combed, and members stayed awake. The last, by itself, would justify the continued presence of live cameras in the Congress.
> More than appearances were changed by broadcast coverage. Debate was unusually sharp, debaters unusually well prepared. If all committee deliberations were conducted with

equal competence, the performance of Congress would be significantly elevated.

There is no reasonable excuse that can now be offered to deny broadcast journalism admission to such ensuing proceedings on impeachment as may be held in House and Senate. (Indeed there is no reason to exclude it from any public sessions on the Hill.)

The coverage, according to Apple, accomplished one even more important thing. It destroyed for all time the much used White House argument that the whole Watergate case was "the illegitimate product of the news media."

The White House needed all the arguments it could muster.

Besides the Supreme Court's ruling on the tapes, there had been John Ehrlichman's conviction two weeks earlier, the indictment of ex-Treasury Secretary John Connally on bribery charges, and the defection of a Nixon supporter, Representative Lawrence Hogan of Maryland, who had announced at a press conference televised in Maryland and Washington, D.C., the day before the Judiciary Committee began its debates that he would vote to impeach the president.

Seven days later on July 30 the last of the three articles of impeachment was voted against the president, and August 19 was set as the date to present them to the full House.

On August 7 the House voted clearance for full press coverage of the floor debate in the House, and indications were clear that the Senate would follow suit. For the first time in history, deliberations of the House and Senate would be seen on TV.

The clearance was never used. On August 5 the president was persuaded by his aides to release transcripts of three crucial tapes of the sixty-four he had been ordered to deliver to Judge John Sirica, with an accompanying statement that acknowledged his complicity in the Watergate cover-up.

Three days later Nixon made his thirty-seventh scheduled appearance on TV as president. It was seen by 110 million people, more than had ever tuned in to a presidential speech before, more indeed than had witnessed any event on TV since man landed on the moon. In a 16-minute speech, which seemed as free of rancor as it was of any sense of guilt or responsibility, Richard M. Nixon announced that he was resigning.

The struggle between the thirty-seventh president of the United States, the Republican who had been elected by the largest popular vote in the history of the nation, and what his vice-president, Spiro Agnew, had called "the men of the media, a tiny, enclosed fraternity of privileged men elected by no one and enjoying a monopoly sanctioned and licensed by government" was at an end.

4 • Oil on Troubled Waters
The Energy Crisis

IN OCTOBER 1973 nine Arab nations representing proprietorship of 60 percent of the world's proven oil supplies moved to cut off all shipments to the United States as a punitive measure for alleged U.S. support of Israel in the Middle East conflict. After years of warnings and threatening symptoms, the "energy crisis" was finally acknowledged to be at hand by both the leadership and citizenry of the United States.*

If Watergate presented American journalists with powers, opportunities, and responsibilities they had never dreamed of, or at least never admitted they possessed, the energy crisis called unpleasantly into question certain reassuring assumptions that most Americans including journalists had held without serious challenge since the founding of the Republic.

Again it was the broadcasters, first and foremost, who brought the bad news.†

In time expended on it by network news departments the energy crisis was second only to Watergate. Between October 1973 and February 1974 NBC devoted 689 reports totaling 17½ hours to the subject on the "NBC Nightly News," the "Today" show, and the NBC News Program Service. This did not include five editions of "Meet the Press" devoted to energy in the same period, nor a full evening three-hour special aired in September 1973, a month before the energy crisis was officially announced. The jumbo NBC special, along with two one-hour follow-ups in March 1974, were the work of the network's top documentarian, Fred Freed, who had devoted eight months to putting the series together and died a few days after the last of the three shows was aired.

* As early as 1952, William Paley, head of CBS, chaired the president's Materials Policy Commission, which had warned of the "extraordinarily rapid rate at which we are utilizing our materials and energy resources."

† A study by R. H. Bruskin Associates reported that 75 percent of 2,581 adults polled nationwide got their information on the energy crisis from TV; on air and water pollution it was 68 percent; on consumer news 64 percent.

CBS launched a weekly Sunday afternoon series called "Energy: . . ." "Energy is so important and so dominates the way we live that it cannot be adequately covered within standard broadcast news formats," Richard S. Salant, president of CBS News, explained. "It demands continuing coverage that will let us understand all of the problems and give insight on how we can individually, and as a nation, meet them. That's our objective in this new series." Walter Cronkite had done two substantial sequences on energy in his nightly news show. ABC had done its "Close-Up" on oil policy, the single most controversial program on the subject, in addition to an impressive amount of day-to-day coverage. Even the Public Broadcasting System, which no longer reserved a regular slot for in-depth coverage of important and controversial national issues and did not have a nightly network news show, devoted a total of 19 hours and 40 minutes to energy between July 1973 and July 1974, mostly in continuing programs such as "Washington Straight Talk," "Wall Street Week," "Behind the Lines," "Firing Line," "Washington Connection," "The Advocates," and "Washington Week in Review." In addition, several segments of "Man Builds, Man Destroys," a thirteen-part series on the environment produced by PBS in cooperation with the United Nations, directly addressed the energy situation.

If energy was the networks' number two story, on local newscasts it undoubtedly rated first, always barring sports and the weather.

To most Americans Watergate was the twilight of the gods, an isolated action in the past, capable of interpretation only by participants or journalistic busybodies privileged to be on or near the scene of the crime.

The energy crisis appeared, at least for some distressing weeks, to be the twilight of middle America, no farther away from a great many citizens than their own garage or cellar.

Watergate rubbed America's nose in its leaders' soiled linen and finally seemed to require no more of any citizen than an act of faithful forbearance or angry judgment. The energy crisis and the inescapable threats of deprivation and environmental dilapidation that accompanied it demonstrated to Americans at firsthand how they had squandered their birthright and fouled their own nests. Retribution was nigh—at least until American ingenuity and know-how could be mobilized to prevent the inevitable.

Former Secretary of the Interior Stewart Udall, a man who had observed earlier stages of the decline through two administrations and had failed to prevent it, said Americans considered themselves

> so rich and powerful (and so capable of pulling off quickie "technological miracles") that any serious long-term "energy gap" is unthinkable. Yet the unthinkable has already happened, as a cocksure nation has allowed gargantuan shortages to develop. The hard reality is that the era of abundant, cheap oil has ended—and there have never been any short-cut substitutes in sight for this versatile commodity. . . . The crunch is, in fact, a deepening long-term impasse that is certain to escalate and send shock waves through our economy for at least a decade.

Beyond their involvement as citizens, the broadcasters, and particularly their journalistic arm, became entangled in the energy crisis in a particularly intimate and uncomfortable way.

More so even than Watergate, the energy story became peculiarly theirs.

Beginning with the early signals of environmental distress, which were bound tightly to the problems of energy and waste, the electronic journalists in many striking instances had covered the story of the nation's resources, and how they were being used and abused, well and at length both nationally and locally. Furthermore, they had done it long before the immediacy and extent of the crisis had been generally acknowledged.

Television was particularly suited to conveying the images of fouled air and water and a ravaged countryside, which made the first installment of the environment-energy story so fascinating and so appalling.

However vivid these visualizations, the warnings and solutions proposed by individual broadcasters often won only momentary attention and were soon contradicted or confused by those who had interests more special than the public's good.*

Still, radio and TV had a big part in encouraging what grew into a large and potent environmental-consumerist movement—at the cost of no small number of displeased sponsors and canceled advertising schedules.

---

* An outstanding example of this was "Taconite and the Lake," WDIO-TV, Duluth's first-rate documentary on Reserve Mining's dumping practices, which was broadcast during the season of 1969–70. Anyone viewing that show would have assumed that in a matter of days or weeks the dumping of potentially lethal waste into Lake Superior, "the largest purest fresh-water lake in the world," would have to cease. The tailings laced with asbestos were still being dumped, after multiple court rulings and appeals, in 1974.

When the story as to what might, or was beginning to, happen suddenly turned into gas lines and cold living rooms, the broadcasters were right on top of it.

Pursuing a prime story, which involved and should concern everyone, the broadcasters suddenly found themselves once more, after the first few moments of camaraderie, the adversary. This time the issues of right and wrong were not so clear cut.

The lessons of Watergate were a part of the nation's moral heritage to which Americans had paid lip service since the Republic was founded—"Honesty is the best policy," "All men are created equal," "Power corrupts," "What shall it profit a man if he shall gain the whole world and lose his own soul."

The energy crisis had its morals too—"Waste not, want not," "As you sow, so shall you reap," "God [or nature if you had no faith] is not mocked." But as the story unfolded, it became for the broadcasters, as it had for politicians in Watergate, increasingly a matter of not casting the first stone and not judging to avoid judgment.

The involvement of broadcasting in the crisis, beyond the simple reporting of it, was quickly apparent.

First and least, there was an uncomfortable moment early on when zealots looking for ways to save kilowatts turned to the closest objects in sight, the radio and TV sets that had originally brought and continued to harp on the unpleasant news.

The suggestion that TV and radio hours ought to be rationed no doubt had some merit, particularly considering the quality and repetitiveness of much that was being transmitted and received.

Secretary of the Interior Rogers C. B. Morton suggested that perhaps Americans might turn off their sets during the peak energy-demand hours of 4 to 7 P.M. Mark Evans, a vice-president for public affairs of Metromedia, suggested an industry-wide 7 A.M. sign on and 12 midnight sign off.*

Some stations voluntarily cut back their schedules, among them WTEN-TV, Albany, which shaved 6½ hours a week by eliminating a daily cartoon strip and a regular telecast of "Roller Derby."

However, before a ground swell could get started, "symbolizing," as Evans put it, "our industry's commitment to the nation's good," the FCC reported that broadcast transmission and reception used only 3 percent of the nation's electricity. Although if the plug were

* Beginning in December 1973 TV viewing ceased at 10:30 P.M. in Italy and Britain thanks to a fuel crisis ruling.

pulled on every radio and TV set in the nation the energy saving would have made up for more than 10 percent of the oil actually lost through the Arab embargo (an estimated 2 million to 3 million barrels a day), any fractional cutback such as that suggested by Evans or Secretary Morton would have had negligible results. The "Late, Late Show," the sign-on sermonettes, and the early evening news were spared.

Other effects of the energy crisis on broadcasting also turned out to be negligible, at least those deriving from the midwinter imposition of daylight saving time and the reduced use of automobiles. A few radio stations suffered serious losses of audience and revenues when the time change deprived them of important early morning broadcast hours. Reduction of drive-time radio listening, according to statisticians retained by the broadcasters, was compensated for by the increased number of passengers in individual cars and the lower speeds at which they traveled.

As for TV, daytime viewing dropped for a while, but thanks to energy crisis stay-at-homes, overall TV usage climbed to an all-time high.

Although Secretary Morton's suggestion that viewers turn off their sets from 4 to 7 each afternoon would undoubtedly have had a drastic effect on local broadcast journalism across the country, few felt any inclination to follow it.

A much more serious threat to broadcast journalism seemed that of advertiser defections and a business recession growing out of the energy shortage. Traditionally, any falling-off of broadcast business was first felt in news and public affairs programming. In this instance, however, it wasn't just a matter of decreased income, therefore decreased news and public affairs. Some of broadcast journalism's best-heeled friends, including the oil and power companies and the automobile manufacturers, seemed bound to be drastically affected.

As early as July 1973, *Advertising Age* was predicting that no less than 35 percent of all national (as well as local and sectional) advertising would be affected in varying degrees, for no less than fifteen years, by the energy shortage. That would involve $2 billion of the $4.5 billion annual national advertising budget. . . .

Never in the history of advertising—national, sectional, or local—have advertising and marketing faced compulsory, legislated, as well as moral, change on such a vast scale and with such abruptness. Certainly consumerism has not even remotely approached the enormous impact of the energy situation in either the immediacy of the time factor (consumerism is now at least eight years old) nor in the dimensions of its impact on advertising and marketing (only a shockingly tiny percentage of advertising and marketing currently reflects the imperatives of consumerism).

In 1973, 3 percent of network revenues came from oil companies, 11 percent from the automotive industry. In spot advertising, which was local broadcast journalism's lifeblood, 2½ percent came from oil companies, 17½ percent from automotive ads. The utilities, which have long used news programs for their messages, in many states were threatened by restrictions on advertising. In a coast-to-coast survey conducted by the Public Utilities Advertising Association in February 1974, 72 out of 136 responding companies reported anti-advertising legislation introduced in their states. Besides these prime advertisers there were all those other products that would be in short supply because of the shortage of energy or the raw materials needed to manufacture them. Considering the list, *Advertising Age*'s percentages seemed conservative.

More specifically, Exxon Corporation gave up a $5 million-a-year sponsorship of Walter Cronkite, and Gulf Oil, a faithful backer of NBC's News Specials as well as political convention coverage, was planning a 20 percent to 25 percent reduction in its ad budget.

However, four months after *Advertising Age*'s dark predictions, shortly after the Arab oil embargo and the president's formal announcement of the crisis, NBC president Herb Schlosser was explaining to *Variety* reporter Larry Michie that broadcasting would be hurt less by energy shortages than most industries. Indeed it might actually be helped. Lack of gasoline would keep people at home, thus providing more viewers for TV. Major advertisers fighting for customers would use what money was left in their depleted budgets on their most effective medium—TV. Detroit would need TV to sell its smaller cars, etc., etc. Any way you cut it, TV couldn't lose—unless, of course, the economy collapsed completely.

Schlosser was right. As far as broadcasters were concerned, the disaster failed to materialize. As in past crises—the radio and TV embargo against cigarette advertising (DuPont Survey, 1968–69) and the imposition of the prime-time access rule—the holes left by defectors were quickly filled, adversity was turned to advantage, and the broadcasters went on to greater prosperity than ever before.

Broadcast revenues for 1973 were the highest in history. For the first time network income broke the $2 billion mark. Spot advertising was reported up 8.6 percent over 1972 and the Department of Commerce was predicting a 10 percent rise in income in 1974. Exxon was back at CBS in March 1974 trying to get reinstated on the Walter Cronkite show with nonproduct ads. In 1973 national automotive advertising increased by 21 percent.

Nor was the prosperity of radio and TV the most surprising result of the energy crisis. If network profits were up 66 percent, the major oil companies, whose announced lack of product was the immediate cause for all the hullabaloo, had, according to Treasury Secretary George Schultz, their best year in over a decade and, according to others, their most profitable ever. Whatever happened, it seemed to benefit the big oilmen as much as the broadcasters. The price of petroleum products went up and stayed up. The number of independent oil companies declined. And perhaps most significant of all, the momentum for environmental improvement, which the energy-producing companies had found so threatening, and fought so bitterly in the past, was diminished and in some instances reversed.

The Alaskan pipeline was approved by Congress with environmental issues still unresolved—its opponents berated for having delayed it so long, thus depriving the nation of the oil it now needed. Not only was the oil depletion allowance, on the verge of being voted out by Congress, saved, but additional investment credits were proposed to encourage the oil companies to increase exploration. Natural gas prices, held down for twenty years, were hiked. Land-use legislation was killed. Strip-mining laws were defanged in the name of the energy shortage. The president suggested the tripling of offshore oil leases and the installation of deepwater ports to accommodate quarter-mile-long tankers. The clean air laws were modified and air pollution requirements for cars delayed.

In fact the darkest shadow (for the oil companies) in this surprisingly bright picture seemed to be the media's and particularly the broadcasters' insistence that all was far from well, that someone besides the environmentalists had made mistakes, and that the situation demanded investigation.

Not that the story was an easy one to report.

The main source of information on energy had always been the industry itself and what little information it offered tended to be sketchy and contradictory. Unlike those involved in Watergate, the oil companies did not leak facts and the political functionaries who might have been more willing to do so seemed not to possess them.

In a remarkable interview with the Capitol Hill News Service at the end of May 1974 John Sawhill, head of the new Federal Energy Office, which was established to bring order out of chaos, admitted that he didn't know whether there was actually more oil available in the United States during the winter embargo by the Arab oil-producing countries than there was during the same period the previous year. When asked whether a price per barrel 250 percent greater than in March 1973 was necessary to encourage new drilling, he replied, "I don't think we have very good information on that."

Sawhill said he had "no evidence either way" to confirm or deny charges by many oil industry critics that the major oil companies had been holding back on the production of natural gas in order to force the federal government to de-regulate its price. "I've heard these rumors. I suspect as we improve on our ability to collect information, we'll be in a better situation to say whether [these charges] are correct or not."

The news media were less reticent than Sawhill. One of the most effective treatments of the subject, and certainly the one that caused the greatest amount of pain to the oil companies, was "ABC News Close-Up—Oil: The Policy Crisis," the sixth in a new series that had finally established ABC as a first-rate maker of prime-time documentaries.

Embedded in the one-hour program were most of the prickly questions being asked oilmen.

Government policy has been aimed at providing a plentiful supply of oil, but today fuel is scarce and its price is skyrocketing. Why? Abundance or scarcity? Is it an energy crisis or an economic or policy crisis? Oil companies have reported record profits since the gas and oil shortage began, yet gas and oil prices continue to rise. Why? Government policy was aimed at strengthening domestic oil production. Yet the rate of oil drilling and refinery construction has declined here at home for the last fifteen years. Why? Has government policy protected the public or has government followed policies more likely to benefit the oil companies at public expense? Why were the import quotas kept so long when they forced the American consumer to pay higher prices for oil?

Why weren't new refineries started two or three or four years ago? How much power do the oil companies have in Washington? Why were oil import quotas so touchy an issue in the White House?

There were also questions raised about competition and monopoly, tax advantages and pro-rationing, and the oilmen's apparently intimate relationship with government and their huge contributions to Nixon's presidential campaigns.

After the program had been aired, Mobil Oil denounced the ABC show as "vicious, inaccurate, irresponsible, biased, and shoddily researched." Herbert Schmertz, Mobil's vice-president for public affairs, demanded satisfaction from both the FCC and the National News Council. The FCC ruled the show within the network's First Amendment rights. The National News Council, in answer to a twenty-two-page list of thirty-two alleged inaccuracies, dismissed Mobil's complaint of bias and distortion saying, "the interests of free expression are best served by allowing full scope to a variety of views, very definitely including those that are one-sided." The council found "no significantly misleading factual misstatements . . ." although the program did "select certain facts that pointed in one direction and omit others that pointed elsewhere. Its organization of the facts presented, moreover, created one specific editorial impression: namely that government policy on oil has been manipulated over the years by the oil industry itself, to the detriment of the public interest and for its own private profit." In a telegram sent by ABC president James Duffy shortly before the documentary was aired to invite executives of thirty-six oil companies to tune in and respond,* the program was described as an introduction "designed to help Americans understand a highly charged and difficult problem . . . researched and executed from every conceivable point of view." Thus, the News Council noted, "ABC was professing adherence to a standard higher than was required of it and higher than it in fact achieved. It is a mistake, in this Council's opinion, for a television network to contend that a documentary on a controversial subject is necessarily 'executed from every conceivable point of view'. . . . But such comprehensiveness is certainly not legally required, and in fact is rarely achieved" (see Appendix XI).

Mobil was having other problems with TV. Its president, Rawleigh Warner, Jr., had objected strongly to the fact that having been interviewed three hours for Walter Cronkite's CBS series on

---

* Nine responded, only one favorably—Apcó.

energy, he had appeared on the air for less than ninety seconds, and that "the basic points I had tried to make died on the cutting-room floor."

More recently, Mobil, in its struggle for what it termed "a fair shake," had tried to buy time to present its message on the networks in up to one-hour lots. It had been unsuccessful even when it had offered to pay double in order that rebuttals of an equal length might be put on the air free of charge. In March, sixteen congressmen, led by New York Representative Benjamin Rosenthal, had counterattacked by asking the networks for equal time to answer existing TV ad campaigns by oil companies, which they considered political advocacy. Another group of congressmen had demanded that the same substantiation required by the FTC for commercial ads be required of the oil companies' "image" ads. Mobil, despite its offer to pay for counter-advertising, invoked the First Amendment in its counter-petition to the FTC, saying, "for every potentially untruthful claim which may be revealed or discouraged by such a rule, the expression of untold numbers of honestly held beliefs will be discouraged." The confrontation between Mobil and the networks soon assumed proportions far beyond those of an advertiser demanding a fair shake or a journalistic subject challenging the objectivity and accuracy of a reporter. In Mobil's encounter with the broadcast industry in both its commercial and reportorial aspects, the oil company as both advocate and advertiser demonstrated, if it didn't unsnarl, the complexities of a very tangled situation indeed. The presence of the government as the sometimes timid regulator of both natural resources and the air waves as well as adjudicator of the First Amendment didn't help matters.

In its eagerness to get on the air, Mobil made common cause with both the conservative Reverend Carl McIntire, who had been fighting the FCC's Fairness Doctrine for years, and the liberal Media Access Project, a public interest organization which boosted counter-advertising and had gone all the way to the Supreme Court in an effort to force CBS to sell time to a group of businessmen opposed to the Vietnam War (DuPont-Columbia Survey, 1971–72).

Mobil's vice-president in charge of public relations was quoted in *Advertising Age* as saying, "The Sierra Club [an old enemy of big oil interests] has even suggested we join in a complaint to the Federal Communications Commission, or even that we try to get on the air by offering to buy joint ads."

Thomas Asher of the Media Access Project explained these odd couplings:

> So long as the [TV] press continues to take the arrogant position that it and it alone knows what the public should view on public issues, we'll be in this perpetual battle—Mobil because they [the networks] won't take their money and us [environmental and consumer groups] because we don't have any money.

On the other hand, Asher took exception to Mobil's haughty attitude toward substantiation of its ads; and as for tax deductions for politically oriented ads, he figured that the public paid for at least half the image ads the oil companies put on the air. In reply to that thrust, the Mobil spokesman denied taking questionable tax deductions for advertising that recommended political action. At the same time he pointed out that some of the groups supporting the drive for counter-oil advertising, equally politically oriented, were backed by tax-free foundations.

But the oil companies' principal fight remained with the broadcasters. Newspapers and magazines regularly cleared the oilman's corporate image ads that promoted their own case and often claimed errors in what was printed elsewhere in the publications.

The networks, with the shadow of the Fairness Doctrine and "equal time" always hanging over them and only recently released from immediate pressure to air controversial ads by the Supreme Court, and with the threat of counter-ads diminishing, were not about to risk their newfound immunity from outside dictates even if they had been willing to be called liars or fools on their own frequencies.

Angered and frustrated by continued media attacks, spokesmen for the oil industry struck back at their tormentors wherever and whenever they got a chance and were, at least in some instances, given coverage in the news.

One of their favorite weapons was, as it had been with the principals of Watergate, the claim that they were not alone in the ranks of the sinners. Answering charges of special government privileges to oilmen, Robert E. Thomas, president of the Mid-America Pipeline Company in Tulsa, told a meeting of the Cincinnati Industrial Advertisers in May 1974, "I would hazard the guess that many publications such as *The New York Times*, Washington *Post*, *Time*, and *Newsweek*, to name a few, might see a sharp drop in their circulation—and their profits—if prices had to be raised to provide for the real cost of mail service so vital to their operations." Of broadcasters he added, "I don't believe [they] pay a penny for their use of our air waves," while, Thomas pointed out, the oil industry paid billions to drill on government lands and in offshore waters and paid a royalty on production.

J. K. Jamieson, chairman of the board of Exxon Corporation, when confronted with his company's 59½ percent increase in earnings over the previous year said he didn't "feel embarrassed" and gave as one reason that, although according to some sources Exxon's income for 1973 was the largest ever earned by an industrial company ($2.4 billion after taxes), Exxon's rate of return on investment in 1972 was only 12½ percent. Six news companies including *The New York Times*, Dow-Jones, and CBS averaged 14½ percent. According to Jamieson, the credibility gap beset not only the oil companies, but the news media and the government as well.

Jamieson's vice-president for marketing, DuVal F. Dickey, was more pointed in his remarks, adding a thinly veiled threat of economic reprisal. After making the same comparison of news media and oil company profits, he said that if the journalists didn't correct what he also referred to as a "credibility gap" about the oil companies' windfall profits "it will play heck with our media schedules."

John E. Swearingen, chairman of the board of Standard Oil of Indiana, speaking to the National Press Club in July 1973, pointed out some other contradictions in the broadcasters' position:

> These growing expressions of concern over future supplies within the energy industries were accompanied by business-as-usual advertising designed to increase demand for cars, most fuels, air conditioning, gas and electric-powered appliances, and all other hallmarks of the good life in affluent America. . . . The whole economy has been geared to providing even larger and more luxurious vehicles, more heat in winter and more air conditioning in the summer, and a range of power-consuming appliances that staggers even sophisticated Europeans.

Swearingen blamed the media for emphasizing the environmental peril while going light on the energy side. If they watched or listened to their own ads they would have thought nothing was wrong.

He also objected to suggestions of monopoly and conspiracy in the oil industry. Pointing out that no company accounts for as much as 10 percent of U.S. crude production refining capacity or gasoline sales, he said:

> Moreover, the allegations are coming to us through the courtesy of an industry in which three companies dominate network television and a press which is totally without direct competition in all but some thirty-seven cities in which there are still two or more competing daily newspapers.

But it was left to Rawleigh Warner, Jr., of Mobil, in a speech to the Edison Electric Institute in June 1974, to give the "he who is without sin" theme its most eloquent expression. Protesting the oil companies' eagerness to get the facts before the public, an eagerness belied by Federal Energy Administrator Sawhill's statements shortly before, Warner referred to "the biggest roadblock we have encountered—the refusal of national television networks to sell us time in which to state our viewpoints on matters of great public import." He went on:

> When the energy crisis hit full-blown last October, there were very few reporters in any media anywhere in the country, outside of oil-producing areas and the oil trade press, who knew much about oil. This was particularly true of commercial television and seems still to be true. As a result, we have a very difficult communications problem and we recognize that. The energy crisis is complex, both in its origins and in its manifestations. The TV networks, by their very nature, seldom seem able to do justice to such a complex issue. There appear to be at least five major elements that account for the structure deficiency of network television news programs.

Warner then proceeded to give one of the most thorough and negative public rundowns on TV news since Vice-President Spiro Agnew's Des Moines speech. The five deficiencies according to Warner were: First, time limitations. "The biggest stories may consume close to two minutes each . . . a good many stories being handled in well *under* a minute each. Also, if the newsrooms are to have time to develop and edit film and to add the requisite dramatic elements, topical stories for the evening news show usually have to be filmed in the morning. . . ." Second, economic limitations. "Keeping camera crews in many different locations could be prohibitive." Third, the tendency of "the networks" to personalize the news. "By this I mean their ever-present need for the highest ratings. They sometimes tend more toward showmanship than toward balanced presentation of the news." Fourth, lack of qualified specialists. The "fifth element of weakness," according to Warner, was "TV is by its very nature an entertainment medium." In support of this he quoted ex-NBC News president Reuven Frank. "Every news story should, without any sacrifice of probity or responsibility, display the attributes of fiction, of drama. It should have structure and conflict, problem and denouement, rising action and falling action, a beginning, a middle, and an end.

"While we are not accusing the networks of bias in their reporting," Warner went on, "we nevertheless feel that their structural deficiencies have combined to make much of their coverage of oil news inaccurate and misleading."

Then, explaining the difficulties and complexities within the oil companies' message, he said:

> We therefore start out with an almost insurmountable problem, which is bad enough in and of itself. But when we then have to cope with television reporters and commentators who usually know next to nothing about the business and seldom seem to have the time or the desire to learn, and when we have to try to impart some understanding in the very limited time allotted—that really is impossible.

Quoting the CBS policy "to sell time only for the promotion of goods and services, not for the presentation of points of view on controversial issues of public importance . . . because it believes that the public will best be served if important public issues are presented in formats determined by broadcast journalists," Warner arrived at the familiar Agnew complaint, "In simple terms, that means that what the people of this country are to see and hear on commercial television is to be decided largely by two or three people at each of two or three TV networks—an extraordinary concentration of decision making."

Then Warner broadened his attack still further:

> First, this country was founded in controversy—hard, openly expressed controversy—and it has remained free and democratic through the continuing clash of opinion and of value patterns. Second, if the networks dedicate themselves almost exclusively to merchandising products, via the enter-

tainment route, they may raise serious questions as to whether what they merchandise as news is actually just entertainment. Third, today's energy crisis is controversial largely because the media have helped make it controversial by printing and broadcasting material so inaccurate that anyone with any knowledge of our industry would have to disagree with it. . . . The real issue seems to be whether the commercial networks should have total control over what is broadcast to the American people. Since network broadcasting is among the most concentrated of U.S. profit-making industries, it would appear that our country may be facing a danger of monopoly censorship. . . . What we're battling for is something at least approaching fair treatment in a medium that seems to be the main source of news for the vast majority of the public, yet one that seemingly has decided that in order to be successful it must concentrate more heavily on showmanship than on presenting news in any depth.

As the coup de grace, Warner delivered his figures on comparative profits between the media and the oil companies:

> The net earnings of Texaco, one of the more profitable oil companies, increased 57 percent between 1970 and 1973. During this same period, the net income of the Washington Post Company increased about 160 percent. . . . Last year Mobil's worldwide earnings were up 48 percent over 1972. Those of *The New York Times* were up 58 percent . . . The pre-tax profits of the three television networks combined—excluding earnings of the stations they own—were up 66.7 percent over 1972.

As with Agnew before him, some of Warner's points were well-taken, others appeared self-serving and deliberately obfuscating. Their main purpose, however, seemed to be to discredit the oil companies' critics, and those critics were of course identical with the ones cited time and time again by the embattled Nixon administration. Mobil's words, "vicious and distorted," were identical with those chosen by President Nixon to blast the media.

The most remarkable paradox, which the oil companies were quick to point out, was that the enemy in both instances was not a group of hairy, undernourished revolutionaries crouched at field transmitters or handpresses but a collection of the fattest media cats in the business.

Eventually the middleman, the advertising agencies—who had been ignored through most of these cosmic salvos—spoke up.

John O'Toole, president of Foote, Cone & Belding, which counted among its clients Braniff International Airways and a substantial list of appliance manufacturers, announced a method for counteracting what he saw as "advocacy journalism's" attacks on the system. He called it "advocacy advertising."

O'Toole said, after a few harsh words about the shortcomings of the press:

> Only advertising can provide sufficient control of the message and the audience reached. Only advertising can supply a reservoir of talent trained and experienced in simplifying complex concepts and relating them to an individual's life in an involving way. . . . Unfortunately, these messages, however forthright . . . may have come too late. At this stage they're like stones being tossed from the parapets of a seriously besieged castle. But they presage, I believe, an era in which companies are going to speak up and speak out in high dudgeon.

An editorial in *Advertising Age* immediately took exception to O'Toole's proposals, saying:

> It's the same old chestnut: Blame the bearer of bad news—in this case, the press—for the bad news. The press, we are being told, is what is wrong with this country. Dammit, the free press is what is right with this country. Mr. O'Toole's contrary viewpoint has no place in a serious discussion of the advocacy advertising concept, which can stand on its own.
> Let's have advocacy advertising because it makes sense for companies to use advertising to tell their side of a controversial story in their own words. But let's not perpetuate shallow, anti-media generalizations in order to make the sale.

In reply, O'Toole clarified his position and intensified his attack on the press:

> I did indeed contend the press has become an advocate of the adversary culture. And I further contended the concept of objective reporting was largely fictional.
> But I didn't, as you assert, base these contentions solely on the highly subjective activities of Tom Wolfe, Gail Sheehy, *et al.* Rather, I said the adversary culture, which deals in crisis and confrontation, provides those commodities which are the stuff that news is made of. The system, when working

smoothly, has little inherent newsworthiness . . . I think subjectivity to one degree or another is implicit in the reporting process and the editorial function. Individuals are, by nature, subjective.

Objectivity is collective. It is many human minds, exposed to several and varied accounts and points of view, forming their rational and, perhaps, irrational opinions. Because advertising can provide different information and different points of view than the traditional news-gathering function, I named this special form of our craft "advocacy advertising" and got on the stump for it. And I must point out that there has been information in recent oil company advertising, information critical to the complex problem of energy shortage that was hard to come by in the news columns, to say nothing of broadcast journalism.

I'm for more information, more opinions, more points of view to help people arrive at some understanding of the complicated issues facing them. And frankly, I'm increasingly concerned about the adequacy of traditional newsgathering and news-dissemination techniques to provide it.

To infer from this position some sort of neo-Agnewism, to paraphrase it into "the press is what is wrong with this country" is, if not bizarre interpretation, certainly a mite hysterical.

Presidential adviser Pat Buchanan, speaking at the Wharton School of Finance, suggested a more direct approach to even things up.

The question that then emerges for conservatives is how—having exposed the existing prejudice of the national press—to gain greater access to the national communications systems.

One way, assuredly, is for conservatives to use their economic power to buy media—to purchase outright radio stations, newspapers, and television stations; and to advance conservative commentators and conservative causes. If advocacy journalism is the wave of the future, conservatives should identify and advance their own advocates.

A second is the employment of the economic weapon of the advertising dollar. Every major communications medium in the country is dependent upon the advertising dollar of Big Business. Yet no institution in our society is more systematically disparaged in the national press than Big Business. If American corporations are so foolish as to pour their millions in advertising dollars into the coffers of networks, newspapers, and newsmagazines that consistently portray them as avaricious and reactionary, then they deserve the shellacking they shall continue to receive. But a politically active and politically angry American business community—with the will to use its economic leverage to win a fair shake—could do as much as a thousand angry addresses to correct the imbalance of the national press.

As for the average individual, confronted with what he views as consistent discrimination against his political interest, the answer may lie in the exercise of his own economic freedom. Not by ceasing to subscribe to the publication in question, but by boycotting the products of the advertisers. Better five thousand letters to the principal advertiser on the NBC Evening News than five thousand into the trash can of the news editor.

Considering the dramatic success of the political left—in boycotting the grapes and lettuce of the California growers—the coordinated use of their economic freedom is not a weapon the people should lightly put aside.

In conclusion, let me only state—should this paper fall into the hands of my friends in the press—the views expressed herein are my own and in no way should be taken to represent the opinions of my sponsor.

The reasoning behind Warner's attack and O'Toole's and Buchanan's suggestions was sometimes obscure. Their intent was not. But the press, certainly not *The New York Times*, was not going to be put off by past failures and inconsistencies. Tom Wicker had already spoken out on the subject of threatened profits. He began his February 19, 1974, column with two quotes:
From page one of *The New York Times* for February 13:

> The Gulf Oil Corporation yesterday announced operating results for 1973. The report indicated a 153 percent gain in fourth-quarter earnings . . . a fourth-quarter profit of $230 million compared with $91 million in the 1972 quarter.

From an advertisement by the Gulf Oil Corporation on page 19 of the same issue of *The Times*:

> There is no digit on earth less pertinent to the solution of the energy crisis than "the pointing finger." If there is blame, there is certainly enough to go around . . . after all, a helping hand is a far more productive tool than any number of pointing fingers. To find energy, find facts, not fault.

"Baloney," was Wicker's comment.

> To begin with, and whatever the effect on newspaper and television profits, I for one, point the finger of fault at pious, self-serving, devious, mealymouth, self-exculpating, holier-than-thou, positively sickening oil company advertisements in which these international behemoths depict themselves as poverty-stricken paragons of virtue embattled against a greedy and ignorant world.

Wicker's indignation was understandable, but although he was willing to forget or ignore newspaper and television profits, that did not eliminate their existence. Nor did it answer the fundamental and very real questions that the oil companies' judging of its judges brought up.

In these gestures of mutual accusation and revelation, as in similar moments during Watergate, truth stood in the wings waiting to be summoned on stage. The dreadful forbidden questions were almost asked. If the oil companies were taking exorbitant profits, and their profits were not as large as the ones taken by those who were accusing them of greed and selfishness, what indeed *were* legitimate profits? And, did profits justify everything, or anything? What was a company's duty to its owners, its stockholders, and to the public? And weren't they all, company, owners, stockholders, members of the same long-suffering aggregate? If the oil companies had ignored this fact and chosen to take excessive profits and neglect the public interest, what were the analogies to this antisocial behavior in the broadcasting industry?

Were broadcasters limiting or ploughing back their profits so that the public might have long-range benefits? Had important programming, including news and public affairs, increased commensurate with earnings? Had broadcast management inquired adequately into the possible long-term negative effects of the programming they did provide on the children, youth, and indeed the adults of the nation? Were what they were selling, the objects and the values which as broadcasters they endorsed through their choice of program content, not to mention advertising, in the best interests of America?

The abyss yawned. The higher realism, with its intimation that the private and public interest just might be identical, threatened. Two great powers in the heat of mutual indignation came close to a truth that applied to both of them—and quickly drew back.

By the summer of 1974 the energy crisis appeared to be over. On February 25 President Nixon had formally de-escalated it to "the energy problem." On March 18 the Arabs lifted the oil embargo. Cadillac announced its biggest May in its seventy-two-year history. "I think there were a lot of people who normally would have bought a Cadillac but were concerned about the energy situation," Robert Lund, the division's general manager explained. "They postponed their purchase and are now coming back into the market. . . . We are going to introduce our 1975 models September 19, a week earlier than the other G.M. divisions, and that will help because we need cars." Appropriately, their TV advertising budget was up.

Talk in Congress of adding to the Emergency Energy Act a provision curbing ads designed to promote the consumption of energy had been abandoned. Gas consumption was rising, as were prices and profits.

By late spring 1974 the networks and local stations had made their major statements on the subject of energy and day-to-day coverage had noticeably dwindled.* CBS' excellent Sunday afternoon half-hour energy reports announced so portentously by Salant in January ran out of gas after nine weeks.

Now and then, with the announcement of such shows as "The Corporation," "The Rockefellers," and a big two-part CBS special on TV news, journalism seemed on the verge of raising the big question. Was Big Business, including Big Broadcasting, doing an adequate and honest job of meeting the needs of the American people?

But each time, considering the magnitude of the real story, the on-air realization was insipid and disappointing. One program, "The Corporation," for the most part a bland and friendly treatment of life at Phillips Petroleum's headquarters in Bartlesville, Oklahoma, touched on two raw nerves—the oil companies' illegal contributions to Nixon's campaign;† and the fact that these vast conglomerates, which demanded unswerving loyalty from their employees, sent their executives as a matter of course to serve without pay in the government agencies responsible for their regulation.

* ABC's evening news coverage devoted 1 hour 22 minutes and 30 seconds to energy items in February 1974. In March, it was down to 37 minutes and 9 seconds. And in June 1974 there was nothing on energy.

† Besides Phillips, Gulf and Ashland oil companies admitted to making illegal contributions.

Even "You and the Commercial," a remarkably brave statement on advertising and the media, didn't get to the heart of the matter. What ultimate purpose did all these lovingly contrived messages serve, and did they in any way accommodate the public interest?

The closest thing to a coherent view of big business accountability was "Close-Up," ABC's admirable series of prime-time investigative reports. In a dozen programs on subjects including fire, food, and coal, as well as the aforementioned "Oil: The Policy Crisis," ABC reporters dug out uncomfortable facts and named names, including dozens of the country's biggest industries and advertisers.

Anthony Harrigan, executive vice-president of the United States Industrial Council, saw industry's treatment at the hands of the media as a "shrill crusade against business . . . absurd and unfair as it is hurtful to the public. . . . The foes of a free economy set out several years ago to create a crisis of confidence in capitalism. That's the meaning of the Nader movement. Using sensational charges against businesses, they have endeavored to create hostility toward the economic system that has enriched our nation. In considerable measure, they have succeeded." *

Conservative commentator Jeffrey St. John, who was regularly heard on CBS' "Spectrum," observed the following:

> During the last few years the media has given full exposure to the environmental movement and its demands for controls on everything from autos to oil exploration. During this period of irrational environmental exposure, responsible dissenting views were almost always excluded. . . . Now important segments of the media are seeking to defend and shield the environmentalists from being made accountable for the consequences of their mistakes—mistakes, not ill-informed judgment. This constitutes just plain intellectual dishonesty on the part of the media and demonstrates their pervasive ignorance about how they are fast becoming the most serious and searing social problem in our society today.

From the other direction, journalist James Ridgeway, writing in *More*, said:

---

* According to figures from the Opinion Research Corporation reported by Mark J. Green in *The New York Times* of June 30, 1974, only 37 percent of the public thought giant corporations should be broken into smaller units in 1965. Nine years later it was up to 53 percent. In 1965 55 percent had "great confidence" in major companies. By 1972 only 27 percent did. Green's explanation for the public's growing disillusionment was a mixture of corruption, immoderate profits and high prices, proved inefficiency and a lack of a sense of social responsibility on the part of many of the nation's biggest businesses.

Underlying the fuel shortage is the fundamental question of how the society is organized. In one way or another, this is sure to be the central issue in this country for the next quarter century, and it cannot be addressed without a ceaseless inquiry by the press at every level into the nature and operation of American industry. The energy crisis is clearly as good a place to start as any.

The late Chet Huntley, both a businessman and a journalist, and the victim of harsh criticism as both, wrote in *The Wall Street Journal* in the summer of 1973, a few months before his death:

One general characteristic of the American press which seems inexplicable is the basic antipathy towards business and industry which I believe exists in our journalism.

The reasons, as Huntley saw them, were that the press itself was not expert enough; that businessmen preferred to talk to the press through public relations counsels, seldom making themselves directly available personally; but most importantly:

American businessmen assert that the purpose of business is to make profit. . . . The businessman who asserts that profit is the sole raison d'être for what he does is creating battalions of Ralph Naders and consumerists. Consumerism, I submit, will destroy business in this country unless we realize that satisfaction of the consumer and not profit is the fundamental purpose of business. A consumer is not begrudging a business profit if the performance is satisfactory. And this means we must cease regarding marketing as a way of looking at the world from a seller's point of view. . . . The degree of ignorance concerning economics in this country is incredible. The business and financial pages of the press have a minute readership. Broadcasting supplies very little basic, fundamental economic information simply because no one wants to listen to it.

The way out of this involves even more creativity and initiative from journalists than they have displayed heretofore. So our press begs for improvement. I would submit, however, that politicians and government are not the people or the institutions to do the improving. The improving will come and it must come from readers and listeners and from journalists themselves.

Whatever the oilmen's complaints,* many broadcast journalists had done a conscientious job of exploring and reporting the energy crisis leading up to and during the comparatively brief period in 1973–74 when the subject occupied the hearts and minds of Americans.

The problem seemed to be that when the public's concern was soothed, the media's attention flagged. Perhaps the dilemma, a continuing one for most journalists on many subjects, was best summed up in the title of a one-hour CBS Report aired in July 1974, "Whatever Happened to the Energy Crisis?"

* By the summer of 1974 Mobil Oil had cut its commercial network TV budget from $10 million to $6 million and issued an ambitious case and point study entitled "The Media and the Energy Crisis."

5 • "The Trojan Horse"
News Consultants

REMEMBER, the vast majority of our viewers hold blue collar jobs. The vast majority of our viewers never went to college. The vast majority of our viewers have never been on an airplane. The vast majority of our viewers have never seen a copy of *The New York Times*. The vast majority of our viewers do not read the same books and magazines that you read. . . . in fact, many of them never read anything. The vast majority of the viewers in this television market currently ignore TV news.

"ACTION NEWS IS EVERYWHERE"

This call to rejoin the lowest common denominator appeared on the wall of the newsroom of Channel 8, the CBS affiliate in San Diego, California, in the fall of 1973, put there by the station's recently arrived "special assistant to the general manager" after a visit from Frank N. Magid Associates of Marion, Iowa. There had been other changes made at Channel 8 following the visit of the Magid organization, the foremost practitioner of the relatively newfound art of TV news consulting. The head of Channel 8's assignment desk had resigned; the station's principal anchorman had been replaced; film budgets and reporter assignments had been doubled; a maximum length of ninety seconds had been suggested for any story put on the air, including feeds from the network, and a Merry Christmas sprightliness and specious ubiquity had overtaken the nightly newscasts. And it was not just at Channel 8. Over at Channel 10, the NBC affiliate, and Channel 39, ABC's local outlet, similar things were happening. Changes even more hectic and drastic had been taking place up the coast in San Francisco, as well as in Minneapolis, Memphis, Winston-Salem, Detroit, Philadelphia, New York, and dozens of other large and middle-sized cities. Action News, or its equivalent, *was* everywhere.

While the networks were nervously backing their news departments in the struggle to meet the momentous events of the day at least part way, and making more money than ever in the process, local broadcasters were electrifying and, in some instances, electrocuting their news departments in the process of making a short circuit through them to the cash. Frank Magid and his associates, among other news consultants, were doing the wiring.

The realization that local news could mean money was an unconscionably long time in coming to many station managements. News and public affairs had up until the late 1960's been assumed to be one of those things you had to do to keep your license. Indeed, as late as June 1973 such an implacable critic of the industry as FCC commissioner Nicholas Johnson in his farewell bombshell, "Broadcasting in America—The Performance of Network Affiliates in the Top 50 Markets," had automatically given top credits for performance of a public service to a station's newscasting (see Appendices XII and XIII). Long before then, astute station owners had realized that they were making money with news and often making more money with it than with anything else on the air. A successful local news operation had other advantages as well. If your TV news team outdrew the local competition it usually meant the viewers were yours for the whole evening. A couple of rating points lead could mean hundreds of thousands of dollars in assorted revenues over a year.

Some learned this lesson earlier than others. As long ago as 1962 Philip McHugh, an ex-radio newsman, and Peter Hoffman, an ex-adman, set up a partnership in Birmingham, Michigan, to advise stations on how they could best increase their news ratings and cut in on the cash.

In 1970 they were joined in news consulting by Frank Magid, a former University of Iowa professor of social psychology, who had been providing market research data to broadcasters for twelve years.

News for the edification of the populace, for information, or for glory was on its way out. News for ratings and money was in.

The technique, to state it in its simplest terms, was to poll the viewers and then tailor the news accordingly. In retaining the consultants the station managers made no bones about their motivation. Profitability, according to a *Television-Radio Age* survey done in 1973, scored second only to "personal satisfaction" as what managers considered "most important to their careers" in broadcasting.

The news consultants were less candid in explaining their

philosophy, which they claimed was essentially humanitarian. Peter Hoffman of McHugh and Hoffman said to the Survey:

> There's no formula of "these are things you must do, these are things you mustn't do." What we do strive for is a greater degree of understanding. We try to achieve the best communication possible—audio and visual—so the viewer has less difficulty. If the viewer has to do all the work, he simply isn't going to do it. We try to put the burden for making news understandable on the presenter, not the receiver.
>
> There are some guys straight out of journalism school who read *The New York Times* every day, and they think everybody reads *The New York Times*. They go out to instruct people and teach them. But television is *not* the New York Times of the air. There are people out there, they've barely finished high school . . . it's not that they're not intelligent . . . they watch a lot of TV. But if you take that instructional approach, everything's going to go right over their heads.

Hoffman's partner, Philip McHugh, says, "The audience has to be treated like human beings. There has to be emphasis on human interest and human beings."

Frank Magid is more belligerent:

> We've been attacked by some news directors and others. They consider us to be an invasion of their sphere of influence. But we can point to fifty top stations across the country who look at us as a source of fresh ideas and a way to develop their product.
>
> Many news directors feel threatened. We find that these are usually the ones who are not as strong, able, or effective. What's getting on the nerves of some of these professional journalists quote, unquote, is that television news is changing so fast that they are being left by the wayside. Some of them had skills that were applicable five or ten years ago. They take comfort in these old ways. But now there's a lot of push for change and this is at the root of all this, but they won't admit it. They say someone is rocking the boat and it's not journalists, it's outsiders. This is the howling of individuals caught in a tremendous revolution. And we think it's a great revolution. We think TV news is better today than it's ever been in this country.

A satisfied news director-client writing to the Survey from the Southwest backs Magid up:

I feel fine with the recommendations and our ratings have increased considerably. However, some members of our staff feel that they have somehow prostituted themselves. They are (amazingly enough) more concerned about having their peers pat them on the back for their great principles than telling the viewing public what is happening in their own area of interest. Some members of the staff think we are here to teach rather than inform and that we should decide what is important for the public to know about rather than finding out what the public is truly concerned about and telling them about that.

And a colleague from the East Coast: "The use of researchers is indeed healthy. Surveying public attitudes brings us down a notch from the mountaintop."

Another opinion came from the West Coast:

In the past year I've spoken with several news directors who are seriously considering other fields of endeavor. . . . there aren't many major markets left where stations don't retain an outside media research and/or consulting service . . . which will screen your shows, critique them, tell you what you're doing wrong, suggest special features to include, etc., etc. Before too many good newsmen leave us, our managers and owners must come to grips with this very real problem . . . otherwise, what television news in the future will be is something none of us in the business will recognize . . . an entertaining half hour or hour with very little of import or significance within it.

Magid's answer to such criticism: "In these offices we have more people who are knowledgeable and who have the credentials to make these decisions than many of those who are in the rank and file of working journalists."

Magid employs a staff of 103 in his self-contained organization, by far the largest news consultancy in the country. Magid Associates does all its own research and includes a department of computer operations and a future-minded think-tank on its 5½-acre site in Marion, Iowa. Eight of the staff are in the news consulting end. Of these, four have television newsroom experience.

McHugh and Hoffman, the second largest consulting firm, has a permanent staff of five men and four women. Three are former news directors in television or radio. Most of the others are from advertising. McHugh and Hoffman hires private market research firms to provide raw data; it then analyzes the data and makes recommendations to client stations.

However bona fide the credentials of the news consultants—and there were those who challenged the validity of their research techniques as well as their journalistic judgment—what they said went in more and more of the nation's newsrooms. The current clients of the ten active consulting firms numbered in the neighborhood of 170. When to that number were added those stations that had used their services in the past, and those that had been subject to the competition of their clients, there remained few if any medium or major market newsrooms unaffected.

The success of their counsel was difficult to gauge. Magid considered it a measure of his success that 95 percent of all the clients who had retained him still subscribed to his service. Hoffman regarded any continual upward movement in the ratings as an indication of his firm's effectiveness.

Magid claimed half of his clients had moved from last place to first in their markets, and that no station had ever lost ground after retaining him. McHugh and Hoffman claimed that, of its clients who were not top in their markets when the consultancy was retained, half had jumped to number one thereafter. The one clear measure used by stations was, as Hoffman put it, "He who is number one in rating book, he make 'em more money."

Although both services said they tailored their advice to the evidence they gathered in any given market, at station after station the results were monotonously similar.

One knowledgeable observer, Ray Miller, news director of KPRC-TV, Houston, who heads a task force to study market researchers for the Radio Television News Directors Association, said, "They can't do anything for you you can't do yourself if you go around the country and see what's working."

A news director in the Northwest wrote:

> They are hired, usually, for one reason. To make a successful news program more successful, or a bad news program into a good one. . . . The terms successful and bad are based only on the ratings of the programs. . . . Naturally, the consultants are going to go just as far as they can in achieving what they feel will be the most successful formula in getting ratings. Many general managers give them carte blanche to do just that, leaving the news director the choice of going along with something he either disagrees with or that he has no control over. . . .

From the South a news director wrote:

> A news operation's business and only business is proper
> news coverage. If a station actually has its finger on the pulse
> of its community and competent personnel to cover the news
> and broadcast it, then no outside consultant is needed.
> Nothing will destroy TV's credibility faster than the trend to
> tailoring the news to a consultant's view of what people want
> to see . . . or simply to generate higher ratings by gimmicks.

Dr. David LeRoy, director of the Communication Research
Center at Florida State University, who has made a careful study
of the methods pursued by market researchers, comments:

> The ploy of the researcher . . . is to overwhelm the staff
> with tables and statistics, and then help them "interpret" the
> findings. Somehow the findings always reflect the bias of the
> research firm. Not meddling with editorial policy, "just fine
> tuning to the station's image." . . . News directors are caught
> in the middle. The front office hires the consulting firm. In
> turn the research findings "suggest" improvements in format
> and personnel. Further, the suggestions for "fine tuning" the
> newscast border on meddling with journalists' decisions.

Dr. LeRoy saw legal difficulties in following such suggestions, a
possible intrusion

> upon the programming responsibility of the licensee in meet-
> ing his obligations and responsibilities under the 1934 Com-
> munications Act and its subsequent amendments. In these
> days of license renewal challenges, any material that suggests a
> delegation of the licensee's programming responsibility to an
> outside contractor should be eschewed. It should be made
> clear at all times that the outside firm's responsibility is to
> advise and inform, and not to dictate personnel, program, or
> other changes. Further, specific comments about how the news
> should be collected, edited, and presented, as well as what
> stories should or should not be covered, *must be avoided by the
> consulting firm.*

There was little evidence that anyone was heeding Dr. LeRoy's
warning, and to date no license challenge had been based on a
station's delegating news authority to any outside agency.

As for the practice of dumping and hiring personnel, it was as much a part of the news consultant's kit as 45-second sound-on-film human interest items and staccato visuals. An example of the sort of advice being bandied about is the following bill of particulars circulated in 1971 at station WTVJ in Miami:

MAGID REPORT
Summary of Recommendations (November 1971)

1. Replace ——.
2. Tandem format on both early and late news.
3. Replace —— with certified meteorologist.
4. Replace ——.
5. Include opinion within sportscast, but not as separate segment.
6. Develop team atmosphere through conversational interchange, perhaps at head of show but certainly in transitions. Develop atmosphere which will produce genuine spontaneity.
7. Change title on both early and late newscast. Same title for both. ("The World Tonight" or something similar.)
8. Use voice-over credits for promotion preceding newscasts (particularly late evening), including at least one headline and standard.
9. Develop production opening for both newscasts. (Similar but not identical.) A production close should also be produced. Audio emphasis in open and close on complete coverage.
10. Lead anchorman should introduce himself at the top of the show.
11. New, distinctive set allowing personalities to be shown sitting together.
12. Participation format, rather than sponsored reports. (Already in effect.)
13. Tease upcoming stories before commercial break.
14. Use bumper slides before commercials. (Already in effect.)
15. Headlines at top of show presented by the personality involved.
16. "Kicker" at conclusion.
17. More stories should be covered; a number of stories should be shortened.
18. More use of voice-over explanation of film stories with background sound from the scene.
19. Use field reporter as extensively as feasible.
20. Use of some national news in early newscast.
21. Make every effort to avoid duplication of early newscast by late newscast.

22. Broward County news should not be reported in great detail.
23. Serialized mini-documentaries should not be used.
24. Minority group stories should be used only when really news; should be presented by a member of the minority group.
25. There should be news *analysis* on a regular basis.
26. Neither editorials nor analyses should last more than 60 seconds.
27. No repetition of editorial. No use of editorial and analysis in same newscast.
28. Both analyst and editorialist must be someone other than the newscaster.
29. Initiate Action Reporter feature.
30. Initiate consumer protection feature—once/week, one minute.
31. Initiate environmental feature—once/week, one minute.
32. Utilize brief, rapid fire newsworthy items on *well-known* people.
33. Utilize stories on new and unusual products.
34. Weather should concentrate on *Miami* area with brief summary of rest of the country.
35. Weathercast should end with understandable forecast for next 24 hours.
36. Long-range forecast is desirable if viewers can be persuaded of accuracy.
37. Weather radar should be promoted heavily.
38. Sports action film should be used frequently, but restricted primarily to major events.
39. Coverage of participation activities (hunting, fishing, boat shows, camping equipment) should be included.
40. Promotion should emphasize the advantages of *WTVJ* news—what is special about it.
41. Promotion should concentrate on "Channel 4" rather than "WTVJ."
42. A slogan emphasizing friendliness and warmth of WTVJ news should be employed.

Richard Townley, who had resigned as news director of KWTV, Oklahoma City, after a dispute with management over control of the newsroom, wrote in the March 16, 1974 issue of *TV Guide*, "It takes a news director with real clout to reject suggestions from a high-priced consultant who has management's ear."

Ralph Renick, vice-president for news, WTVJ, had that kind of clout. The Magid organization finally departed the premises. Renick's comment to the Survey some time after the confrontation:

Within broadcasting itself, there is the question of where we are headed philosophically. And by that I mean the trend in news formats toward more entertainment in the body of a newscast. Call it "happy talk" or "humanized news," by any name the potential for harm to our profession has been vastly increased since its inception.

Change, of course, is desirable within our industry. The technical advances of the last decade allow us to do our job better and faster all the time. But the "happy talk" format is not the kind of change we should be seeking. It can easily lower credibility and does often limit the amount of actual news presented within a news program. It flies in the face of the traditions and standards of journalism, often going against the very fundamentals of our profession. Serious industry leaders should be working to eliminate the injurious elements of the format as it is practiced at many stations. But, unfortunately, the ratings race has prohibited responsible action in many markets.

Coupled to this problem is the rise in recent years of the consultant firm. These agencies have taken hold of many stations and virtually dictated news policy "in absentia," by the use of their research techniques. Too often stations with consultants end up trying to present news only as the research results suggest the people want. But lost in this concept is that a professional journalist should have the ability and news judgment to determine what is important and significant.

Renick added later, "They are really a Trojan horse. They roll it in and suddenly the enemy troops are in your camp. Too often the service is put to political use to permit management to get control of the news when the news director is in conflict with management. What it really is, is franchised news—like McDonald's."

How to live with a news consultant over the years was explained to the Survey by the director of news and public affairs of a prominent and strongly news oriented midwestern station.

The basic recommendation, in late 1967, was to change our old 15, 5, and 10 format (with each segment of news, weather, and sports sponsored by individual sponsor and separated by participating spots) into an expanded 45-minute integrated newscast at 10 P.M., and to an integrated half-hour at 6 P.M., both with participating spots. Since that time, they have provided critiques of our news programs and research studies —with no major recommendations.

The major recommendations of 1967–68 were followed and

many of their subsequent minor recommendations on production techniques, graphics, and assorted other ideas have also been followed. Many others have not. Reaction to the recommendations has depended upon how they fit into our own concept of what our newscasts should be.

I appreciate an honestly motivated, outside critique of our news product, and recommendations on how they can be improved. Our consultants have never dabbled in our editorial decisions, but only in the "cosmetics" of news presentation. Their research has been valuable to us, as have some of their ideas garnered from other markets and news stations they have the opportunity to see, and we do not.

At the time they were retained, we were a strong second in news ratings in our market. We felt we had a better news staff and news product than the competition, but because of long-standing habit and the "sameness" of the shows, we were never able to pull ahead. The changes instituted in part at the recommendation of the consultants turned the market around, and helped make us number one—with no changes in air personalities or news policies.

We are still number one in the market, but the gap between ourselves and the chief competitor has closed in the past year. They also have a consulting firm and have adopted a "formula" type newscast with "Newsreel," "Friends and Neighbors," etc.

I think consultants, if used properly, can be a healthy phenomenon. The problem arises when the consultants try to run a newsroom and make editorial decisions. It is a matter of making the consultants, and your own management, understand the proper role of the consultants in the news operation. In a good station that really cares about covering the news—as well as the ratings—this is no problem. But it is possible, in other operations, for consultants to have an unhealthy influence in news programming.

Just what could happen if a consultant's advice was taken too seriously was demonstrated by one of the liveliest and most frightening segments on CBS' "60 Minutes" during the 1973–74 season. Devoted to local TV news in San Francisco, the sequence began with a look at "News Scene," KGO-TV's eleven o'clock newscast, "one of the highest rated in the country." Excerpts selected from one newscast by "60 Minutes" went:

> And the latest on the little old lady who looked at the nude male fold-outs of Jim Brown and John Davidson, and said— The full story—next—right here, on Channel 7 "News Scene."

(Laughter)

The exorcism craze and scare is spreading all over this country right now. Tonight, a band of young churchgoers (singing "Onward, Christian Soldiers") burned forty books on the occult, plus a Ouija board in Rock Island, Illinois.

Coming up, the mother of a nude talks about her son, barely.

The wife of the ex-mayor of St. Augustine, Florida, was killed in front of her home. She died—screaming for help on her front porch . . . by a man who, police say, may have hacked her to death out of simple pure hate. . . . The congressman still, by the way, would not outlaw massaging hands, arms, and legs, but would prohibit those ladies from tickling your fancy.

(Laughter)

Get out of town, or we'll rub you down! Right?

Come on. Stay tuned now for a Channel 7 report, followed by "The Wide World of Entertainment."

These, according to Mike Wallace, were not isolated examples picked by CBS at random. "That week there was lots more like it." CBS had commissioned a graduate class in journalism at the University of California at Berkeley to monitor the local shows and they had found

55 percent of all the stories on KGO's top rated 11 P.M. news fell into the tabloid category—items on fire, crime, sex, tearjerkers, accidents, and exorcism. The formula is paying off too. At 11 P.M. KGO had more viewers than the other two stations combined. As a result, it makes more money—$900 for a 30-second commercial, while KPIX and KRON can get only a third as much.

Wallace's story of San Francisco TV news became more depressing as it went along. Of the two losers to KGO—locally known as the "Kickers, Guts, Orgasm" station—one, KPIX, had been, as of the preceding June, the leading station in the country in serving the public interest, according to Commissioner Johnson's tabulations. It had also had one of the most professional news staffs of any local station coast to coast, turning out a monthly network-caliber 60-minute documentary.

In a period of ninety days following the end of the 1972–73 season, twenty-nine people had left the KPIX news staff; some were fired, some quit because they disagreed with the station's new news policy. By the time Wallace arrived on the scene the percentage of tabloid items on the monitored 11 P.M. newscasts at KPIX equaled or exceeded those on KGO. The new director of news, Jim Van Messel, hired from Detroit where "he had helped build a winning news organization," confronted by the statistics, said lamely, "You don't save souls in an empty church."

The most painful stretch of the "60 Minutes" essay came at the end when Wallace interviewed Aldo Constant, president of KRON-TV, which seven years earlier had had the top newscast in town.

"KRON's newscast is the most traditional . . . probably the most informative and perhaps the least entertaining," Wallace said in his introduction. Constant's explanation: "Our news director feels that way; that sensationalism in the news is not a proper journalistic standard."

> *Wallace:* And meantime, your ratings don't respond—they don't go up. Your revenues are down and you're willing to stand there like a rock and say "Let the ship go down."
> *Constant:* We're not going to bastardize our news for ratings.
> *Wallace:* In the early days of television, news and documentaries were thought of as loss leaders, public service broadcasts—the kind of programming stations did to satisfy the FCC. Few observers thought that local newscasters would become highly marketable television stars, that local news would become big business. But it has. And that triggers the dilemma: How far do you go to attract an audience?

Although Wallace did not choose to mention it, KGO could attribute its phenomenal success to the arrival of McHugh and Hoffman in 1971 and the changes the firm recommended. KRON had recently retained Frank Magid Associates to help it fight back after its seven-year decline. As for KPIX, it did not have even the market researchers to blame. Although the results were the same, the directives that decimated the KPIX newsroom were drawn up on the premises.*

* What KPIX did have was a new station manager, George Resing, Jr., who had been program director of WLS-TV, Chicago, one of McHugh and Hoffman's biggest winners.

In an earlier, calmer time—mid-season 1972—KPIX had put together a first-rate hour-long documentary, "And Now the News" (see pages 172, 181), an extension of its regular newscast, played in prime time, designed to tell the viewer all about what was going on in the nation's TV newsrooms. The final segment began with newsman Joe Glover (since departed) holding a book up to the camera and saying:

> In one sense, this is what television news all comes down to. This is a rating diary used to measure audiences for all television shows, including newscasts. These diaries are used by both the Nielsen Company and the American Research Bureau. And although they look complicated and are based on how a few hundred people a week fill them out, the ratings are generally trusted by most broadcasters and advertisers.
>
> Television is so expensive that it requires large viewing audiences to turn a profit. . . . Today the major change in TV news style is the introduction of a more relaxed and involved presentation by the newscaster. This has been called "happy talk news" by its detractors, but the label is disputed by some who helped develop the format.

Then Glover introduced a filmed interview with the man responsible for the success of the competition that was at that very moment killing KPIX news. Phil McHugh spoke his familiar piece:

> It's a very, very complex thing because you need to understand what you're dealing with. I use this story so often of . . . somebody in the family dies. Right away, somebody says, well, who's going to tell Mother? Everybody realizes that the communicator of that information is terribly important, and the relationship between the communicator and the person receiving the communication is important. That occurs every day on every newscast in every city between the people who bring the news and the audience. And that relationship is ongoing so it takes somebody that's trusted and understood.

Finally Glover ended the program with the comment:

> Television is a public medium . . . and you are the public. Attempts to control television news programs are attempts to censor the news you see. You are our first line of defense against censorship and repression. . . . And we are yours.

After the show went on the air, KPIX news director Ron Mires had written to the Survey:

> I'm concerned, as are most journalists, about the future of television news based on today's rush to discard journalistic value in favor of entertainment values. Consulting services play an important role for many stations in selecting the content and the people who report and present the news. To make newscasts more "popular," stations cover more spot news, more emotional people-involvement stories, and more consumer reports. While this makes for an interesting program, it does not alert viewers to the "real" social, economic, and political problems of their communities. . . . Stations using this approach have dug deeply into the ratings of the stations broadcasting "conventional" though interesting, well-produced newscasts. . . . The answer would seem to be a compromise. To produce a news program which retains solid content, but includes enough of the entertainment values to attract top ratings. . . . I'm optimistic that the result of the current "revolution" will be positive—that more people will be attracted to television news in the short run, and that stations will find they can reach a balance in the news content they offer over the long run—and still achieve high ratings.

Ron Mires had no opportunity to test his optimism on KPIX. A few weeks later, he and twenty-eight others had departed, replaced by a new, more competitive, news staff. Mires' next assignment was Channel 10, San Diego, where things were different. McHugh-Hoffman was on his side—Magid was with the opposition.

Mires' former boss, William Osterhaus, who had departed before him after twelve years with Westinghouse stations, said:

> I left for a combination of personal and professional reasons. I could see a number of obvious changes going on all over the country which did not appeal to me . . . action news, shorter stories, stacking news according to appeal rather than importance. These were being employed all over by stations seeking to gain impact since they hadn't been able to do it by delivering the news. We had been dominant at KPIX for years by delivering the news and having awfully good people do it. Then the pressure for popularization started mounting. I was willing to examine the public's taste. But I wasn't interested in changing to an inferior news service. And something of the

sort I wasn't interested in seemed to be a route we might have to take.

Less philosophic was Rollin Post who had spent almost a dozen years with KPIX and claimed, "Never, never had anybody outside the news department made the determination on what was news." When the fight with KGO was at its height, according to Post, programmers were making news decisions on KPIX on the same basis as buying reruns of Perry Mason. "The people at KPIX were right out of Watergate—they had no qualms about anything."

Both Post and Osterhaus went to KQED, San Francisco's public TV station whose hour-long "Newsroom" is the oldest and most successful public newscast in the country. "I'm delighted with what I'm doing. I feel refreshed and challenged like I haven't been for the last two years," says Osterhaus. "In 'Newsroom,' we have twenty-five stories in an hour without sports, weather, or commercials. This means we do a lot of 4–7 minute stories."

If the tale of KPIX's fall was one of the saddest in the recent annals of local newscasting, the apparent decline of Group W, its corporate boss, was perhaps even more distressing. Group W was the proprietor of four out of the top five stations on Commissioner Johnson's chart, and at one time rated number one for news in all the markets where its stations operated. Now, in addition to the desperate in-house tinkering at KPIX, McHugh and Hoffman had been invited to see what it could do for KYW-TV, Philadelphia, and the Westinghouse flagship station KDKA-TV, Pittsburgh.

The news director at KDKA was enthusiastic.

> I have found the consultants to be professional and ethical in all dealings. They are very concerned about "localizing" their feelings and remarks, and in no way attempted to "take-over" the station or the news department. I find them valuable because of their objectivity and for their ability to over-view the operation in relation to what is going on in other areas of the nation. I have always been concerned that news managers become isolated in their markets, and do not have time to see what is working elsewhere. Our consultants have given us positive aid in how best to communicate with our viewers and that input was both desired and studied by us.
>
> Unlike many of my colleagues, I feel that the interest in consultants only increases the interest in local news. These people carry out research that no news director is able to do by himself. They are completely separated from the daily

operations and friendships which develop in a newsroom and are able to make truly objective recommendations. They are able to answer questions, or give leads to answers, that "inside" people might simply overlook. Used as a positive tool, I think consultants can only help local news operations.

Even WBZ-TV, the Westinghouse station in Boston, which was still rated first in its market and had a national reputation for top quality news, had retained a news consultant, although one of its competitors had just let another firm go. A report to the Survey from another Boston station read:

> Frank Magid was retained by this station, but dropped in May 1973 on recommendation of the news director. Their recommendations included many ideas tried in other markets (a formula approach) which did not seem to be in keeping with our audience needs and interests. They did suggest we formulize the format to include as many film and audio stories as possible. The news was often measured by the amount of stories and films rather than on the basis of content, importance, or quality. Their recommended length of a film story was a minute and a half at the outside, regardless of the story's importance. They asked we de-emphasize political coverage which seemed out of place in Boston which tradition shows to be THE hottest and most continuing story to cover.
>
> I believe most of the recommendations were made without considering market tradition, competition, innovation, and, most importantly, integrity.

In addition to a failure of nerve in its local newsrooms, after five highly creditable years, Group W had disbanded its Urban America Unit, which had turned out the only first-rate documentary series produced by any of the nation's highly profitable TV station groups.

The reasons given for closing down the unit did little to enhance the reputation of local commercial TV station managers across the country. According to Dick Hubert, executive producer of the award-winning series, Westinghouse's offer to furnish the twenty programs they had produced to the nation's TV stations at bargain prices, and eventually for nothing, had few takers beyond Group W's own five stations. Actually, even for free, out of 246 possible public TV outlets only 13 noncommercial stations put the programs on the air. Among the commercial TV exceptions mentioned by Hubert as taking the shows fairly regularly were WMAL-TV in Washington, WHEC-TV in Rochester, WISN-TV in Milwaukee, and WKBW-TV in Buffalo. The reasons, according to Hubert, why most other stations refused Group W's top quality bargains:

> First, stations are only interested in documentaries in order to win "brownie points" with the Federal Communications Commission, especially before license-renewal time. Furthermore, they believe the Commission will look more favorably on documentaries which they produce themselves, rather than documentaries they might buy from outside producers. The quality of such locally-produced documentaries matters little, for the FCC presumably is satisfied by anything resembling local public affairs programming.
>
> Second, documentaries on social, political, economic, and cultural issues are audience losers. Bigger audiences can be earned with game shows. Besides, documentaries are often controversial, and broadcasters generally don't like getting involved in controversy.
>
> Third, many local stations and for that matter the networks, too, are unwilling to purchase news programming from outside sources because, they say, "We can't vouch for the accuracy or editorial independence of such sources!"

One reason Hubert did not give, and one which might help to explain not only the collapse of the Urban America Unit but the upheaval in the news departments of Westinghouse stations across the land, was the fact that although Westinghouse's broadcasting operation remained highly lucrative, the parent company, Westinghouse Electric Corporation, was experiencing a sharp decline in its profits. This conjunction of corporate trouble and newsroom upheavals might confirm a long-suspected danger to broadcast journalism—that news and public affairs programming, always the first to suffer in broadcasting cutbacks both on network and local levels, could suffer equally from the reverses of non-broadcasting ownership even when the stations themselves remained highly profitable and news budgets held firm.

As a matter of fact, the problems relating to conglomerate ownership were recognized as early as February 1969 when the FCC launched a study of its impact on the quality of broadcast operations. Five years later the commission, after a promising preliminary report, had still not announced its further findings, although thirty-seven conglomerates with broadcasting properties had been canvassed nearly three years ago, and a report had been claimed "almost ready for release" for over two years.

Another theory put forward for the disappearance of the Urban America Unit, a socially concerned group, and for the ratings-oriented doctoring of the local news operations, was the arrival of Frank Shakespeare among the top executives of the Westinghouse "leisure time group," which included Westinghouse Broadcasting. Media adviser to President Nixon during the 1968 campaign and former director of the United States Information Agency, Shakespeare, a onetime vice-president for sales at CBS, had been an outspoken critic of the liberal leanings of broadcast journalism.*

Although TV stations, as well as TV news, were enjoying the greatest boom in their history,† the journalist who went hard after the important story frequently was having a more difficult time than before.

Skimped in the early days of TV because news and public affairs were supposed to be money-losing propositions, the journalist was now being skimped because his sort of news just didn't bring in the ratings or the advertisers. Although news budgets were often increased on consultants' recommendations, in an alarming number of instances where the consultants were retained, documentary activity at the station remained stationary or declined. If mini-documentaries survived within the news format they were usually devoted to sensational subjects. Among the most popular topics for mini-documentaries at stations reporting to the Survey that had

---

* Another recent Westinghouse action ascribed to a change of attitude at the executive level was the refusal of KDKA and KPIX, the two Group W stations on the CBS network, to carry the Democrats' 21-hour telethon in June 1974.

Robert S. Strauss, chairman of the Democratic National Committee, called Group W's action "the worst example of corporate citizenship. . . . Here you have two stations in two major markets having licenses that belong to the people. I think it's an outrage. It's an embarrassment to the television industry."

Donald H. McGannon, president of Group W, replied: "Political telethons create . . . serious problems concerning balance and fairness because of political statements and arguments made during those programs intended to raise campaign funds." These problems were "particularly critical" this time because the decision "involves the third such Democratic telethon in an elapsed period of two years. The Republican party has not had any, hence a very serious problem of fairness has already arisen and will confront stations in the future." Also, McGannon stated, "We are genuinely concerned that the nature of the compensation formula from the network can be construed as a contribution by a corporation licensee being in violation of the federal statutes." CBS was paying its affiliates for only 5½ of the 21 hours. Nevertheless all of CBS' 208 affiliates, with the exception of the two Westinghouse stations, carried the entire telethon.

† A National Association of Broadcasters survey of 382 stations showed that average TV station profits for 1973 were up 19.4 percent over 1972.

retained news consultants were rape, homosexuality, and pornography.

Besides depressing ratings, half-hour and hour-long documentaries at many stations required the time of news personnel already being run ragged answering the requirements of Action News for short, diverse items. And increased film costs for the nightly news further reduced the money available for major film efforts. This lack of opportunity for extended journalism on local TV was particularly painful since finally, after years of earnest trying, local news personnel were getting the equipment and the expertise to turn out first-rate TV essays. But as time devoted to local newscasting and profits increased, space to pursue individual subjects at a decent length, inside or outside of newscasts, shrank.

Archa Knowlton, director of media services for General Foods, one of the few national advertisers who showed any interest in sponsoring substantial local public affairs programming, suggested others join him:

> Advertisers should encourage the kind of broadcasting that seeks to bring the issues of the day to the attention of the viewing public.
>
> People today are concerned about race relations, inflation, education, prison reform, drug addiction, air pollution, housing, fuel shortages and much more. Advertisers, I submit, have an obligation to contribute more to the public than a supply of goods and services at a profit. We can and should foster public understanding of these problems.
>
> In public-service broadcasting, local stations can provide the kind of community service that earns them valuable support at the same time as it spotlights the problems at hand. Almost as varied as the topics that can be covered are the formats available, news specials, one-shot documentaries, weekly panels, rap sessions, and public affairs series. These kinds of programming deserve, and need, advertisers' support.

At the national level, NBC president Julian Goodman had made a direct appeal to the nation's big advertisers. Citing the fact that no advertiser had chosen to participate in NBC's three-hour prime-time program on energy in the fall of 1973, he said:

> I would hope that many businesses who now find themselves caught in the social and governmental pressures of this decade, with a need to explain themselves to a concerned and

influential cross-section of America, might take advantage of the sort of audience news documentaries attract.

Neither call for support seemed to have much effect. Goodman, who found himself in a major fight with his affiliates when he tried to clear a Saturday evening hour for a regular public affairs program,* had very little advertiser response to his challenge.

ABC, which in recent months had made its first big effort toward regularly scheduled documentaries on important subjects, reported that in the last two years, eight of them, four from its highly praised "Close-Up" series, had gone completely unsponsored. Although the practice was a common one, figures on partial sponsorships or bargain pricing for documentaries were unavailable from any of the networks.

Knowlton may have wanted more local public affairs programs than he could find. On the other hand, there were producers of top-quality local TV documentaries whose products went begging. The news director of KGW, Portland, whose grim 90-minute documentary "Death of a Sideshow," aired in prime time in the season of 1972–73, won both domestic (see pages 174, 181) and international awards, wrote to the Survey:

> No prospective sponsor wanted to attach his name to it. Our advertisers, most of whom professed a sincere concern about the community of which they are an important part, shy away from buying programs which are designed to point out and oftentimes offer solutions to troubled areas of that community. It is difficult to continue to do significant documentaries without sponsorship because of the enormous costs involved. We still do them, but at a tremendous loss, and on a far less frequent basis than we would like. These reluctant advertisers will sink thousands of dollars into entertainment and fringe specials.

Thanks to the continued indifference of advertisers, KGW produced no documentaries, grim or otherwise, in 1973–74.

Perhaps the most eloquent rebuttal to all the happy talk about happy talk news came from the president of CBS News, Richard Salant. Addressing a disgruntled group of affiliates at the network's annual meeting in Los Angeles in May 1974, Salant said flatly:

---

* Although Goodman won, the victory was short-lived because the FCC, reversing an earlier ruling at Supreme Court insistence, directed the time returned to local programming. See page 174.

It is a harsh but inevitable fact that news judgments must be unilateral, can't be shared, can't be delegated outside the news organization and can't be put to a committee vote. . . . Sound journalism does not permit substituting a head count for news judgment. In fact, the whole business of journalism is a great deal more than, and is inconsistent with, providing only those stories which people want to hear, giving those stories the treatment most agreeable to a majority of people.

But the support was mainly with the rating winners. At WLS, where an early triumph of news consulting took place, ABC had instituted a series of annual seminars for other affiliates who wanted to find out how to do it too.

In 1974 at its annual affiliates meeting, ABC made another offer to help news departments on scheduling, advertising and promos, visuals and research. Harvey Gersin, director of research and development, pointed out that "if the ratings of one newscast [local] increases, so will the ratings of the other [network]." If the network newscasts themselves had not yet been changed to conform to the new style, their owned and operated stations, particularly those in markets where news consultants seemed triumphant—such as Chicago and New York City—were inevitably affected. At the National Association of Television Program Executives annual conference, the panel scheduled on "how to mount news" included Frank Magid, Philip McHugh, and ABC's Al Primo, who claimed to be the originator of the Eyewitness News concept.

Nor was the impression of triviality and expediency in the news helped by the ever-growing trend to split the 30-second commercial in half, thus increasing the clutter in and around newscasts.

Industry spokesmen inveighed against the practice, promoted by ad agencies and venal station owners, to no avail. Elton H. Rule, president of ABC, made it the central theme of his speech, "Advertiser and Broadcaster—Partners in the New Society," delivered to the Association of National Advertisers in Dorado Beach, Puerto Rico, in November 1972, saying:

> There was a time when the basic unit of commercial time was 60 seconds. Next came the piggyback and split 30-second commercials. The third stop was unlimited piggyback commercials. In 1971 the basic unit of commercial time became 30 seconds. . . . Now, under the guise of integrated commercials, we face a situation where 15-second messages could become a

fact of life, two within each 30-second unit, four within the minute.

Since Rule's speech the 15-second message had indeed become a fact of TV life. Furthermore, the NAB Code allowing a maximum of 16 minutes of ads to the hour was frequently flouted, as frequently on the news as anywhere. In entertainment programs and the late night movies such staccato interruptions were bad enough. On the news, which even at its most active still was supposed to reflect reality, the commercial's insistent intrusion was intolerable.

In a monitoring project undertaken for the Survey by the American Association of University Women, half-hour news programs at 262 local television stations across the country were found to have an average of fifteen commercials, totaling an average of 8 minutes per half hour. Forty-three percent were reported over the recommendations that one could deduce from the general guidelines of the NAB code, and one station had an astounding 15 minutes and 45 seconds of commercials in its half-hour broadcast. An average of 5½ interruptions per half hour was reported for commercials. Though clustering was reported at 80 percent of the stations monitored, commercials were still found to be more intrusive than in previous years by 25 percent of the monitors. Only 10 percent said commercials were less intrusive.

Weather portions of local news programs averaged 2½ minutes per half hour. Sports averaged 3 minutes. This left an average of only 16½ minutes per half-hour program for news items—which included ever-increasing features, billboards of upcoming items, and happy talk among newscasters.

An average of fourteen and a quarter stories were covered in these 16½ minutes.

A trend to more short items was reported at 32 percent of the local stations. More funny items were reported at 31 percent. And human interest stories were on the rise at 56 percent of the stations monitored.

The most frequent lead item on May 1, 1974, the day of the monitoring project, was a local news item at 62 percent of the stations. Eighteen percent led with a follow-up on the White House transcripts released a day before. Nine percent led with the arrest of seven suspects in the Zebra killings case in San Francisco. Twenty percent led with some other sensational item (sex, violence, minor accident, fire, or other attention grabber).

Just how Machiavellian the climate in the nation's newsrooms could become was demonstrated by the stations that were sending tapes of successful rival anchormen to markets where they knew managements were hunting for replacements. One particularly lurid example was reported in *Variety* in January 1974, when on the basis of a Magid survey KSTP-TV, St. Paul, dumped its anchorman and hired newscaster Ron Magers away from the much put-upon KPIX, San Francisco. Magers had already been set to move to WBBM-TV, the CBS-owned station in Chicago, which, thanks to the long-term success of WLS, was doing some drastic hiring and firing for the third time in as many years. Then "a rival San Francisco outlet" sent a tape of a Magers newscast to KSTP in an effort to further undermine the competition. Magers changed his mind at the last minute, standing WBBM up in favor of KSTP. When the plot was revealed, both KSTP and the competition it was trying to beat out in the twin cities, WCCO, confessed to employing similar tactics, "sending tapes of another's air personalities to other stations seeking replacements." Indeed, an astute news consultant working for stations in two markets could accommodate both clients by engineering such a defection and get paid for good advice by both.

In June 1974 WABC-TV, another of McHugh-Hoffman's satisfied customers, was revealed to have retained Magid as well—just to keep the latter from advising any of the heavy competition in the New York market.

Perhaps the most depressing picture of all, however, came from the Winston-Salem, North Carolina, *Journal and Sentinel*, which, in the spring of 1974, did an extended feature on the TV news in the Winston-Salem region, the nation's forty-eighth TV market.

There was a description of the late night news on WXII, the local NBC affiliate. Without benefit of consultant, WXII had dressed its news-director-anchorman, Dick Jensen, and its reporters "like refugees from the Sunday morning gospel hour in matching lemon yellow blazers. . . . The program opens with three or four news headlines . . . then shifts abruptly to sports, followed by more sports—fifteen minutes in all. A weather forecast and 8 minutes of news bring up the rear."

"This is commercial television and the profit motive is definitely involved," Jensen was quoted as saying to explain his new arrangements. "The name of the game is getting more people to watch you, and everything we can do within reason and ethical bounds to increase the number of people watching our news shows, we will do." Jensen said frankly that investigative reporting was a luxury he could not afford. And since he came to the station, WXII had not broadcast a staff-produced documentary. In six months Jensen's tactics had moved him from a weak second to a strong second in the local news ratings.

There was some hope, however, in the fact that the bottom station in the market had stayed on the bottom even with the services of Frank Magid Associates, and that the station that remained number one, WFMY, had a news director who maintained stoutly:

> We recognize we are in a competitive situation, but we're not going to attempt to dazzle people with a new set or some new promotion. In the long run, I think it's good writing and good journalism that makes the difference. A lot of the stations [that have been overtaken] are rolling over and playing dead when they get some competition. They thought they were communicating and they weren't. . . . We're concerned about the numbers—they're good now but we would like them to be even better. The answer to the challenge of Mickey Mouse formats is improving the journalistic quality of your product.

The really bad news came from an observer a little off the scene, John L. Greene, Jr., the news director of WBTV, Charlotte, proprietor of the only hour-long newscast in North Carolina, a program that outrated any show on the air locally except for "The Waltons." Greene reported:

> The trend now is away from "happy talk," and toward "top 40," a hard and fast approach with the announcer covering a lot of 15- and 20-second stories, instead of several 60- to 90-second stories now. Film clips are also shortened to about 20 seconds.

News consultants and hold-the-line newsmen of the traditional sort, as well as anyone concerned with the future health of the nation, both might take alarm at this bit of news.

6 • Where the Action Wasn't
Government and Commercial Broadcasting

IN THE SPRING OF 1973 RCA board chairman Robert Sarnoff had fighting words for the affiliates of the National Broadcasting Company, gathered full force in the ballroom of Los Angeles' Century Plaza Hotel:

> . . . the growing intensity of government assaults on broadcasting must give us new and genuine concern. Most visibly, we have had the unprecedented spectacle of high federal officials attacking the national news media in general and television network news in particular. It is plainly an effort to impair the credibility of the news and to influence how it is reported. It seems aimed at a state of public information fed by government handout and starved by official secrecy on matters that are the public's business.
> The effort to discredit television news has coincided with another development—the emergence of a new official voice that speaks for the White House on broadcast policy. The Office of Telecommunications Policy has some antecedents as a technical unit in the Executive Branch, but now it has become an activist agency—something new not only for broadcasters but for the FCC and the Congress to contend with.
> Here are some of the policies the OTP has been pushing. The agency seeks to force-feed cablevision beyond its natural growth in order to offset broadcasting. It wants to limit repeat programming with no comprehensible justification in the public interest. It has assaulted network news with colorful generalities that defy definition. It has sought to turn the stations into censors of network news by linking such a role with proposed licensing arrangements we all seek. . . .
> The government's efforts to make the news media docile and accommodating rely heavily on the technique of intimidation. This technique works only against those who are willing

to be timid. But there is another threat that is not sufficiently recognized. That is to strike at national broadcast journalism through actions and proposals attacking the economic capability of networks. I am not suggesting that the government has adopted such a design, but I am concerned that an atmosphere has developed where networks are perceived as fair game.

Whatever may be the motives of this growing pressure on broadcasting, it is important for us—and even more important for the public—to recognize an essential fact: weakening the economic structure of networking could impede the flow of independent information to the people.

And in our society, which depends on an informed electorate and an open market of ideas, that would be a calamity.

Sarnoff's words sounded a note frequently heard in recent months in the speeches of broadcasting's top brass. Whereas in the past the justification for a network's stance usually involved ratings, profit and loss, disgruntled stockholders, or, if really pressed, the survival of the free-enterprise system, now network spokesmen singled out the First Amendment as their rallying point and their news and public affairs departments as their primary reason for being.

There was a significant oversight in Sarnoff's otherwise compelling argument, however. Although there was admittedly a great deal of flack flying in the networks' direction, their economic base had remained remarkably firm. Sarnoff could have reported record-breaking profits at NBC, a story that could be repeated at both of the other networks.

ABC, claiming to be in the black for the first time in a decade, had marked the occasion with a long overdue, top quality, prime-time news and public affairs series, "Close-Up." On the other hand, Sarnoff's own network and CBS, neither of which had had an unprofitable year within memory, and whose income had just made a giant leap forward continued their lowest commitment to regular prime-time journalism in history. Nor were things turning out that badly for them in the nation's Capital.

It was true that Nixon's landslide victory in 1972 promised "interesting" times ahead for the broadcaster. Initiatives had already been taken which broadcasters saw as a concerted effort to contain and diminish what the president's men had labeled "the unwarranted power of the networks" as well as their profits. The votes of the American people seemed to give added authority to the Administration's clearly established bent.

As Watergate unfolded it was sometimes difficult to remember that the battle between network news and Nixon was not the only conflict. There was also the continuing struggle between the broadcasting industry and its would-be regulators. The two conflicts had different battle lines and different objectives.

Among the gestures Sarnoff and other broadcast executives saw as punitive was the president's suggestion that something needed to be done about network reruns. In a letter to John Gavin, president of the Screen Actors Guild, dated September 15, 1972, President Nixon wrote:

> I am convinced that, in cutting the amount of original programming, the television networks are failing to serve their own best interests, as well as those of the public. No one will gain with this network practice, which has the long range effect of drying up the domestic sources of new programming.
>
> Given the potential serious effect of this practice, I have instructed Mr. Whitehead* to thoroughly investigate this problem. I am hopeful Mr. Whitehead, working with the networks, will find a voluntary solution, otherwise we will explore whatever regulatory recommendations are in order.

The networks' answer: rising costs made reruns imperative. Besides, since 86 percent of the potential audience missed any given program when it was first shown, to run it again was in the public interest.

"If the FCC required that at least 50 percent of network programs or syndicated shows be new material," said John Bass, head of the FCC's Office of Network Study, "I do not think that would cause a dramatic economic dislocation."

Even more threatening than limiting reruns were the antitrust proceedings the Justice Department had instituted in April 1972 to sever the networks from the production of entertainment programming. The suit, which had sat around the attorney general's office for a year and a half, used figures from 1967 to show that CBS had ownership interests in 73 percent of its prime-time entertainment programs, NBC had 68 percent, and ABC 86 percent. As an example and justification for their suit, proponents of the action pointed to the successful 1948 antitrust action that separated the motion picture producing industry from its owned and operated exhibition arms.

* Clay T. Whitehead, chief of the Office of Telecommunications Policy.

The networks replied that the figures used by the Justice Department were outdated. Since a 1970 FCC ruling barring networks from acquiring financial or proprietary interests in programs of which they were not sole producers, their part in entertainment programming had dropped considerably. By the last quarter of 1971, CBS said it produced only 8.2 percent of prime-time entertainment shows, and NBC and ABC both said they produced less than 10 percent. When the antitrust suit was completed, with FCC rumblings about prohibiting the leasing of network studio facilities to outside producers, the networks protested that not only would their economic base be destroyed, they would lose their capability to broadcast news and public affairs and cover events of national importance such as political conventions and elections.

There was also the prime-time access rule, which had been introduced to encourage the production of worthwhile local programming and reduce, at least by four and a half hours a week, the networks' dominion over the nation's evenings.

According to a report to the FCC entitled "The Economics of Prime Time Access," the results had been different from those intended.

> Regularly scheduled network produced public affairs and documentary programming almost totally disappeared from the prime-time schedule as a result of the rule. There was approximately a 30 percent reduction in regularly scheduled public affairs programming in prime time as a direct result of the prime-time access rule.

The report found that for the 1973–1974 season the 150 stations subject to the access rule were offering 145 half-hours of local interest programming—less than one half-hour per station. Of those, seven half-hours were in Washington, D.C., and thirteen on the three Boston affiliates. According to another FCC tabulation, the median station among the top fifty VHF affiliates with at least $5 million in revenues was devoting only 1.4 percent of its prime time to local public affairs. Despite the fact that prime-time access had aspects beneficial to them, NBC and CBS still rated it a hostile act.*

* ABC was enthusiastically for the rule, since it was given credit for boosting the network into the black by reducing its overhead. NBC came around to supporting the rule in modified form in the fall of 1974, leaving only CBS holding out against it.

To round out the list of network harassments there was continued pressure from the FCC, FTC, and Congress to reduce TV violence and raise the tone of children's TV programming and advertising.

Not all government actions relating to broadcasting could be interpreted as punitive. There was a reassessment of the Fairness Doctrine by the FCC, which had been under way for three years. It bore some promise of limiting the increasing use of the Doctrine as justification for attacks on the broadcasters' advertising and employment practices as well as their programming.

Also, no less than 125 separate pieces of licensing legislation friendly to broadcasting had been proposed in Congress, most of them incorporating features that would lengthen and strengthen the broadcasters' hold on the public air and protect them from the license challenges that were being threatened with increasing frequency from coast to coast.

The ambivalent attitude of Congress and federal agencies toward broadcasters was probably most clearly demonstrated in the "ideological plugola" speech delivered in Indianapolis by OTP chief Clay T. Whitehead a month after Nixon's reelection (see DuPont-Columbia Survey 1971–1972). Juxtaposing criticism of network news with a tempting proposal to authorize station licenses of five years' duration, Whitehead outraged the networks and many local broadcasters by his obvious appeal to the latter's baser instincts.

Whether it was the growing chill of Watergate or the paralysis of impeachment politics, Whitehead's speech turned out to be the peak of the Nixon administration's *quid pro quo* approach to commercial broadcasting. During Nixon's truncated second term few of these threats or promises, from Whitehead or anyone else, were realized.

After their preelection pitch to workers in the film industry, Nixon and Whitehead never followed up demands for fewer TV reruns. However much it might have benefited the public by opening up the prime-time schedule to more worthwhile programming, neither voluntary action from the networks nor regulative proposals from Whitehead were forthcoming.*

Nor did the antitrust suit to separate the networks from their entertainment production make much headway. The motivation

---

* In October 1974 the FCC reopened the matter of reruns with what *Broadcasting* magazine described as "obvious reluctance."

for the suits was questioned as growing evidence of Administration pressure on the networks, revealed in White House memos and on tapes as well as in depositions from major industry figures, and threatened to turn the Justice Department action into a mini-Watergate. The resulting uproar, and Watergate itself, made an early decision unlikely.

The prime-time access rule was modified to open up time for quality network weekend programming. But after howls of protest from program syndicators, the courts postponed the change for another year and the dispossessed low-budget-profit shows got their time back before they had relinquished it. In this round trip to nowhere, the only weekly network prime-time news and public affairs program scheduled for the 1974–1975 season, NBC's Saturday evening hour, appeared and disappeared like a mirage in a vast wasteland of fun and games.

The agitation against violence and children's programming had led to some network and local station modifications, most notably the voluntary reduction of commercials on Saturday morning network kiddy shows and a commitment by station KTTV, Los Angeles, convinced by a license challenge, to reduce the list of permissible children's features the station would clear for air. But more drastic changes had been delayed by promises of industry self-regulation.

CBS president John Schneider in a speech to the Hollywood Radio and Television Society explained his network's reluctance:

> The most pressing assault on our freedom of operations is currently found in television programming designed for children. The assault is aimed at both its advertising and program content. Simple economics demonstrates that the two issues are inexorably intertwined. Advertising pays for programs—not government funds, not donations from Action for Children's Television—but advertising. Decrease advertising and you risk decreasing program quality. Now obviously, such advertising must be monitored carefully—a job thus far well done I might add, by the broadcaster. . . . We are in danger of being led into a restructuring of television, not in an evolutionary fashion as has been true with most of our social institutions but in vast, sweeping ways. Some of this may come about through government fiat, which too often results in large measure from the pressure of small, well-organized special interest groups seeking to mold television in their own image. It is a dangerous threshold to cross, but we are almost there. It

is time for wise men and women to ponder these questions carefully, to avoid having emotions destroy what careful thought and many years of dedication have built.

Other actions that broadcasters might have interpreted as hostile, but which made few real waves, included Clay T. Whitehead's scheme to drop an additional sixty-seven VHF stations into a national TV grid, which both network and local broadcasters insisted was already saturated. After causing a mild furor and considerable criticism on the part of technical experts, it was taken back for reconsideration and resubmitted to the FCC in May 1974 with a whole new set of figures.

Another action, also Whitehead-generated, was the White House report on cable TV. Although intelligent and sympathetic, the 122-page booklet (despite Sarnoff's fears) contained few recommendations to move the sluggish new technological miracle out of its current becalmed state into a position where it could hope to compete with over-the-air TV, nor did FCC actions promise much help.

As for actions that might have benefited the broadcaster, they too made very little headway.

Broadcasters' agitation against the Fairness Doctrine reached a climax in the frontal attack delivered by CBS board chairman William Paley at the dedication of the Newhouse Communications Center at Syracuse University (New York) in May 1974. Paley called the Doctrine:

> . . . a tempting device for use by any administration in power to influence the content of broadcast journalism. . . . Despite its good intentions the Fairness Doctrine had implicit dangers in that it conferred upon a governmental agency the power to judge a news organization's performance. In recent years, this danger has become real as the FCC began considering complaints on a broadcast-by-broadcast basis, almost line-by-line and minute-by-minute . . . a springboard for efforts to restrict the freedom of broadcasting from operating fully in the public interest, as the press always has, unhampered by judicial commands, bureaucratic reviews, administrative probings and executive reprisals. Attempts have been made to extend the enforced Fairness principle to entertainment and advertising. "The Autobiography of Miss Jane Pittman," the story of a former slave shown on television, was the subject of a complaint, wisely rejected by the FCC alleging that it reflected unfavorably on whites. In commer-

cials, complaints assume the militant guise of "counter advertising" demanding, on the vaguest grounds, free time for
replies to specific advertisements. This could endanger broadcasting economics enough to reduce its ability to carry out its
journalistic responsibilities.

Government's intrusion upon broadcast journalism has led
to open attacks upon the basic principle of the free press which
is that the value of whatever is published—whether printed or
over the air—is best left to the people.

Attacks by the Administration have been directed at
impugning the integrity of able reporters: setting up monitoring systems to determine whether Government agencies
could be used to intimidate offending media; splitting affiliates
from networks by threatening nonrenewal of licenses; and
weakening the economic base of news operations by clumsy
appeals to advertisers to boycott broadcasters failing to report
the news as the White House sees it.

The inescapable impression emerges that there are those in
positions of power and trust who oppose a free press because
they think it will distort some facts and know it will disclose
others.

To strengthen broadcast journalism's freedom, it is time to
repudiate the Fairness Doctrine, specifically immunizing news
and public affairs broadcasting from any form of governmental supervision.

Paley's attack was not without provocation.

There had been 2,406 Fairness complaints in fiscal 1973, almost
three times more than five years earlier. Yet only 94 of the
complaints had been forwarded to broadcasters for comment, and
of those "no more than five" had been decided against the
broadcasters.

Of these five, the single instance that seemed the most threatening to journalistic integrity concerned NBC's Peabody Award-winning documentary "Pensions: The Broken Promise."

The complaint against "Pensions" was one of eleven brought by
Accuracy in Media, Inc., a conservative watchdog organization
based in Washington and headed by Federal Reserve Board
economist Reed J. Irvine. AIM contended that the program, an
examination of faulty and inadequate pension plans, was "gro-
tesquely distorted" and failed to give fair treatment to the vast
majority of pension plans in the country that were honest and
effective. Particularly since there was pertinent legislation pending
in Congress, AIM demanded that the network give air time to
opposing views.

NBC, answering that an admission of error and the implementation of corrective action on its part was not only unnecessary but would be damaging to all investigative reporting on TV, stood its ground even after the FCC ruled against the network.

Reuven Frank, ex-president of NBC News, said in an affidavit filed with the FCC:

> Almost all the great television documentaries dealt with problems. Most of them would have been impossible under this rule. There seems to be agreement that examination of problems of society is a high calling of journalism. Journalists follow many definitions of news, but generally these agree that news is the atypical. Sunshine is a weather report; a flood is news. A fire is reported, but not the houses which didn't burn.

Press critic Ben Bagdikian agreed. Writing in the *Columbia Journalism Review*, he said:

> "Pensions" was not an ideal program, but it was not reckless or manifestly unfair. If the AIM and FCC judgment is upheld, instead of stimulating robust debate on controversial issues (the stated goal of the Fairness Doctrine) the judgment threatens to force broadcast journalism to retreat even further from investigating the most urgent problems of society.

However, ex-CBS News president Fred Friendly saw the confrontation as unnecessary and dangerous. Speaking to the Federal Communications Bar Association in Washington, Friendly said:

> I don't know which alarms me more—prosecutors and jurists flooding the courts with subpoenaed reporters and contempt citations or newsmen and publishers crying "First Amendment" every time they are challenged. I do know that when these excesses are combined with those of an Administration which tampers with the integrity of both courtroom and newsroom, we have enough to cause the nervous breakdown of the First Amendment. . . . One can regret that NBC News in its fair-minded tradition did not choose to use its own air to ventilate the issue once the controversy arose. The vent of more air time is the only escape valve for a pressurized situation. . . . Pursuing it further instead of smothering it might have kept the FCC out of the newsroom and NBC out of the courtroom. Even now they could advance the public's consciousness on the issue of pensions and the controversy

over the Fairness Doctrine by scheduling a comprehensive documentary on the chain of events which have occurred since the original broadcast 18 months ago. A provocative title might be 'Pensions: the Broken Promise, and the Fairness Doctrine, the Broken Record.' "

To Friendly, the Doctrine, properly interpreted, "merely makes the broadcaster the public trustee he is obligated to be." In late September the U.S. Court of Appeals reversed the FCC's ruling, an action that left NBC vindicated and the Fairness Doctrine more inscrutable than ever.

Dean Burch, who shortly after his arrival at the FCC in 1969 had called the Fairness Doctrine a "chaotic mess," left four and a half years later having come to the conclusion that it was "difficult, arcane, but perhaps as good as we can devise."

The report he left behind, after dozens of hearings and a year of final deliberations, was entitled "The Fairness Doctrine and the Public Interest." Ironically, what relief it contained for broadcasters had already been anticipated by the Supreme Court in its decision on the case brought by the Business Executives Move for Peace in Vietnam against WTOP-TV, Washington, D.C.

The ruling—that stations could refuse advertising of a controversial nature—according to Tracy Westen, lawyer for BEM, could lead to "capital punishment," i.e., petitions to deny license renewal. It was, however, accepted as good news by the broadcasters who had been appalled by the growing application of the Fairness Doctrine to advertising.*

The report, however, which broadcasters hoped would limit the Doctrine even further, waffled. If on the one hand it recommended that the FCC be relieved of any responsibility for overseeing advertising, on the other it left the Doctrine wide open for future interpretations.

"The hard truth remains," said *Broadcasting* magazine, "you can't have a First Amendment and a Fairness Doctrine, too."

Confirming *Broadcasting*'s contention, Senators William Proxmire and Alan Cranston had called for legislation that would eliminate the Doctrine altogether, and with it the equal-time ruling and any other form of government regulation that might interfere with the broadcasters' First Amendment rights—including licensing.

* The ruling also seemed to counter the court's decision in the controversial Red Lion Case, which held that the citizen's access to the air took precedence over the station owner's First Amendment rights.

Petitions to deny licenses had reached an all-time peak in 1972, and threats to petition, sometimes equally effective, were even more widespread. How effective such threats could be was indicated by a report from the DuPont correspondent in Austin, Texas:

> Two community groups won significant promises from the three commercial stations in Austin by threatening to file petitions to deny. The groups are the Austin Black Media Coalition, an ad hoc group of about 20 blacks, and the Austin Television Action Council, an even more ad hoc group made up of law students, feminists, Chicanos, and others.
>
> In response to the demands of these groups, KTBC-TV agreed to hire a black news staffer, to produce 10 local documentaries in the remainder of 1974 and 8-12 annually thereafter, and to expand its evening news program from 30 minutes to one hour.
>
> KTVV agreed to hire an additional black staffer, produce at least six local documentaries a year, and enter into an internship program with Huston-Tillotson College, a predominantly black school in Austin.
>
> KVUE-TV agreed to hire a black news staffer, carry a weekly black community affairs program, establish an internship program, and consult with a black advisory board on production of local documentaries.

The local stations, like the networks, found license challenges even more upsetting than the Fairness Doctrine. Among complaints sent to the Survey:

> I feel that this year we have finally reached the stage where we must begin, through our representatives in government and through our professional organizations and societies, to effectively fight the growing movement by government and special interest and self-appointed minority groups to seize control of broadcast journalism. I feel that we have been tolerant to the point that we have in effect encouraged these people to feel that taking over the programming direction of a broadcast station requires little more than an open throat, a reasonably articulate lawyer, and a cursory knowledge of how and when to complain to the FCC. If we do not bring more pressure to bear in our own behalf, the broadcaster is going to become a minor influence in how his own station is programmed. . . . Having just gone through the preparatory processes (of license renewal) and now waiting the suspense of whether this minority group or that will file an application to deny be-

cause we refused to sign a contract with them has me seriously
questioning the haphazard manner in which we are regulated through the big stick of the license renewal. Common sense must enter the picture somewhere . . . and
soon.—*KCBD-TV, Lubbock, Tex.*

Since we do use the public's airwaves, there must be some
form of regulation. The current system, however, has a chilling
effect. The Fairness Doctrine, 3-year-renewal periods and the
cost of FCC litigation can cause newsmen (and/or management) to lose the faith. The danger lies not so much in losing a
license as in the cost of defending the license against challenge.—*WBAL, Baltimore*

Pressure groups with invisible constituencies and unlimited
typewriters have buried us under a Himalaya of paper, and
responding to their senseless charges has become a full-time
occupation. Tragically, the real needs of the poor and the
disadvantaged become buried, as we are, under the phony
mountain, and broadcasters have responded to these demands
in kind with phony programs that make much noise but say
nothing.—*WVUE, New Orleans*

The First Amendment is in jeopardy in Milwaukee as far
as television is concerned. We have encountered repeated attacks on our responsibility to give large blocks of time to
marginal spokesmen for marginal causes under the Fairness
Doctrine. We now tend to "back off" political controversy.
—*WITI, Milwaukee*

While Proxmire would have eliminated all such threats to the
First Amendment by wiping out both the Fairness Doctrine and
licensing, most broadcasters would have been quite happy with the
legislation that passed the House in the spring of 1974 by a vote of
379 to 14. This licensing law, enthusiastically supported by the
National Association of Broadcasters, strongly resembled the one
suggested by Whitehead in his unfortunate speech in Indianapolis.
Among its more attractive features were the extension of the
licensing period from three to five years and the elimination of
cross ownership as a reason for withholding a license.

The cross-ownership issue had been a hot one even before 1972
when the courts finally decided after seventeen years to give the
license of WHDH, Boston, the station of the Boston *Herald-Trav-*

eler, to a challenger. The *Herald-Traveler*, in severe financial trouble, was shortly thereafter sold to the Hearst chain and the specter of cross ownership still haunted the industry. The ghost was vividly aroused in 1973 when the Justice Department instituted suits against several newspapers asking that they divest themselves of their broadcast properties on the grounds of media concentration.

Although the licensing bill had run into trouble in the Senate, and both articles mentioned above were scratched in the Senate Commerce Committee, in October 1974 the full Senate reinstated five-year licensing and voted 61 to 10 in favor of the revised bill. However, it was still stalled in Congress two months later.

To make matters worse, in September 1974 eight stations of the Alabama Educational Television Commission had their licenses removed in a surprise action by the FCC, which reversed the recommendation of its own examiner. The grounds for denial were the stations' long history of discrimination against blacks in both hiring and programming. It was the first time in history a license denial grew out of citizens' complaints. The action was greeted by Dr. Everett C. Parker, director of communication for the United Church of Christ, as "a fantastic thing. This is the first indication we've had that the FCC is really concerned about the public interest requirements of the law."

Dr. Parker, as the nation's leading license challenger with a long record of partial hits and near misses behind him,* may have been overreacting. There was little other evidence that the FCC, with a full complement of Nixon appointees on the panel, was that different from what it always had been.

Chairman Burch talked about his tenure, the second longest in the history of the FCC, before departing for a hectic summer in the White House as Nixon's chief counsel. After listing the major business of the commission, he said: "All these issues remain on the agenda and, if anything, they are getting more difficult instead of less. Whether I am on the Commission or there are seven geniuses—should that be genii?—the issues won't be resolved easily."

Indeed, setting aside one very important segment, broadcasters and broadcast journalism, for all the attacks, the alarms, and the excursions, had not fared too badly in Washington under an actively hostile Nixon regime. If the industry's gains in the agencies and Congress were minimal, so were its losses.

---

* His greatest success had been the lifting of the license of WLBT-TV, Jackson, Mississippi (see DuPont-Columbia Surveys 1968–1969, 1969–1970).

The important segment that had to be excluded from such a generalization was public TV, and particularly public TV journalism. For the reporters and documentarians of nonprofit broadcasting, the Nixon years had been an almost unmitigated disaster.

7 • Where the Action Was
Government
and Public Broadcasting

IN APRIL 1974 Clay T. Whitehead had placed on President Nixon's desk a bill that was intended to insure adequately insulated funding for public television on a graduated annual scale of $70 million to $100 million over the next five years.

In July the bill was finally presented to Congress, according to reports, against the president's will. Considering the enthusiastic congressional response to the public TV funding bill of 1972, which the president had then preemptorily vetoed (see DuPont-Columbia Survey 1971–1972), the new bill, coming from the White House, seemed to stand a good chance of passage.

Whether passage, when and if it occurred, would be occasion for celebration was another question. First, the amount of money recommended in the bill was considered by many (though the most generous proposal to date) to be too little.* More serious than the inadequacy of cash proposed, however, were the tardiness of the legislation's arrival and the changes in public TV's structure that had preceded it.

If the suggested funding was perhaps too little, the bill was almost certainly too late to save much that was best in public TV. This was all the more painful since in their coverage of the Senate Watergate hearings and the House impeachment debates, public television and its national public affairs unit, NPACT, unquestionably had had their finest hour.† Public television had committed itself to complete Watergate coverage four weeks before the commercial networks decided to do so and stayed with the proceedings long after the others had departed.

---

* Estimates of how much it would cost to run an adequate public TV operation in the United States varied. In 1972 Wilbur Schramm and Lyle M. Nelson of Stanford University had suggested a minimum annual budget for public TV of $432 million, or $2 a person. This seemed generous until one compared it to the $11.40 per head public broadcasting cost the Swedish or the $7.00 per head it cost the Canadians.

† See page 166.

Day by day, night after night, public TV broadcast the complete, unedited hearings, accompanying them with the most consistently literate and informed background sessions of any of the four national networks. In such programs as Bill Moyers' "Essay on Watergate" (WNET) and "Behind the Lines' " "Watergate and the Press" (WNET), as well as the regular "Washington Week in Review" (NPACT), * public TV showed its independence, originality, and intelligence in putting unfolding events into perspective. These services were rewarded by the largest audiences and cash contributions in public TV's history.

Some saw in public TV's exemplary performance the salvation of an organization that was within an inch of extermination, a parallel to those defiant actions by victims of political terror who survive simply by keeping their visibility and their volume high. Others felt that as impressive as the coverage was, the Watergate performance was public TV's swan song, and that the leadership of public TV had already given up or negotiated away its most important talent and privilege—the airing of expert, hard-hitting public affairs programming.

As recently as 1971 public television had set the pace for the commercial networks in dealing at length with difficult and controversial subjects, claiming more documentaries in prime time than the three commercial networks combined. Indeed it was to such provocative programming that its present troubles were attributed. Within the past two years virtually every respectable news and public affairs series on public TV had been canceled or threatened with extinction. Political pressure in some cases and special outside support in others brought back a few programs, but many, equally worthy, had disappeared forever.

That public TV had enemies in high places had long been known. How high, and how hostile, presidential communications aide Patrick Buchanan spelled out on the Dick Cavett show in March 1973. It was a performance that CPB chairman James Killian was later to describe as "one of the striking examples, I think, of hubris on the part of a member of the White House staff."

"So they sent down their $165,000,000 package voted 82 to 1 out of the Senate," Buchanan reported with obvious relish, "thinking that Richard Nixon would therefore—he would have to sign—wouldn't have the courage to veto something like that. And Mr. Nixon, I'm delighted to say, hit that ball about 450 feet down the

* See page 166.

right foul line right into the stands—and now you've got a different situation in public television. . . . You've got a new board on CPB. You've got a new awareness that people are concerned about balance." *

Then Buchanan proceeded to name those he found particularly unbalanced. They included Sander Vanocur, "a notorious Kennedy sycophant" who had already left public TV, and Robert MacNeil, who would leave in August. There was Elizabeth Drew, "definitely not pro-Administration," who did her last "Thirty Minutes With . . ." interview in June. Also mentioned by Buchanan were "Washington Week in Review," "Black Journal," "Bill Moyers' Journal," and "then, for a figleaf, they throw in William F. Buckley's program."

All, including Buckley, in the period immediately prior to Buchanan's attack, had been scheduled for oblivion.

There were others in positions of power who were unkindly disposed to public TV and its journalism. As early as Clay Whitehead's Miami speech to the National Association of Educational Broadcasters in 1971 (DuPont-Columbia Survey 1971–1972), the threat of Administration punishment had been quite clear. Since then many of those men in public television who felt it had an important national mission to fulfill beyond its obvious local responsibilities had been demoted or had disappeared entirely. Among them were the first CPB president, John Macy, chairman Frank Pace, the former head of NET, James Day, and a long list of talented producers and reporters.

As they departed, ragged battle lines were drawn. On one side was the government-chartered Corporation for Public Broadcasting—with all the money and power. It was dominated by Administration men, notably Macy's replacement, Henry Loomis, a loyal Nixon bureaucrat who made no bones about his lack of enthusiasm for public TV journalism, backed up by a board of fifteen presidential appointees. Opposite was the Public Broadcasting Service, which for the moment chose most of what public TV put on the air coast to coast but with no money or status before the law. It was led by Hartford Gunn, Jr., not noted for his dedication to outspoken journalism in the past.

In November 1973 CPB president Loomis proposed directly to public TV station managers that they carry twenty-one hours of

---

* Off the air, Buchanan was less restrained, telling one public TV executive at a Washington party, "If you don't do the kind of programming we want, you won't get a f——ing dime."

live coverage of the Apollo 17 moon mission. An indignant outcry from PBS at being bypassed and a negative vote from the station managers seemed to give Loomis a temporary setback.

However, in January 1973 the Corporation for Public Broadcasting, heretofore inactive in the field of programming, announced its intention to take over. A CPB board resolution, passed unanimously, stated that CPB would call back from PBS "the decision-making process, and ultimate responsibility for decisions, on program production support or acquisition" and "the pre-broadcast acceptance and post-broadcast review of programs to determine strict adherence to objectivity and balance in all programs or series of programs of a controversial nature."

The board had already voted to withhold approval of PBS' proposed public affairs offerings and to retain the right to prohibit the use of the PBS interconnection for any outside programs of which it disapproved.

What Loomis and his board intended was made clear when he added that he felt "that we ought to be spending our money on the kinds of programs that would stand up timewise for six months or a year," or as one PBS official said, public broadcasting had "no business getting into controversy, and we ought to stick directly to education things, pretty ballets and plays."

PBS president Hartford Gunn had said: "When you have all the power in the CPB's hands, all the necessary conditions are present for the corporation to become a propaganda agency."

It was just such an agency that Buchanan envisioned in his Cavett appearance. Much of the PBS news and public affairs schedule had been canceled. Two months short of its spectacular coverage of Watergate, public TV was totally demoralized. And the sentence of doom that seemed to be hanging over it was all the more depressing since it was pronounced not only by PTV's enemies, but also by those who considered themselves its friends.

The excuses used by both friend and foe to justify turning off public TV journalism were "the bedrock of localism" and "objectivity and balance." Both concepts were already familiar from the struggle between the Administration and the commercial networks.

If the Administration had failed in its attempt to drive a wedge between the networks and their local affiliates and thereby deflect the impact of network news and public affairs, it had been more than successful in promoting the concept of "localism" in public TV. In this it was helped by the wording of the Public Broadcasting Act of 1967 and the Carnegie Commission Report, on which it was based, both of which had affirmed localism as one of their basic tenets.

"Turning public TV into a village handicraft industry," protested Douglass Cater, who was one of the principal draftsmen of the 1967 legislation, "would be prohibitively expensive or deadeningly dull." Still, localism remained attractive to the ideologues of public TV, and in its name much damage had already been done to PTV journalism.

The second and even more dangerous assumption was that "objectivity and balance" were more important to public TV journalism than they were to its commercial counterpart. The phrase also was found in the Public Broadcasting Act of 1967 where it had been put by nervous legislators in a last-minute compromise to get the bill passed.

If the Fairness Doctrine, itself a highly controversial measure among commercial journalists and management (see Chapter 6), permitted a commercial TV station or network to demonstrate its broad-mindedness over its entire schedule and during an extended period of time, public TV, according to CPB's argument, had no such latitude. It must demonstrate balance and objectivity in any individual program that might be considered controversial.

To put the CPB position in its most depressing terms, in the words of Neal B. Freeman, president of King Features and a board member of the Corporation for Public Broadcasting, "it is a bit late in the game for those of us in public broadcasting to pretend that we are part of the free press."

Dr. James R. Killian, who as head of the 1967 Carnegie Commission had had nothing to do with the "balance and objectivity" afterthoughts of Congress, was not quite so sure. "Congress sought to give public television the attributes of freedom of the press—I think that is clear in the bill. It speaks of the board [CPB] affording 'maximum protection to public broadcasting from extraneous interference and control.' This subtle and almost metaphysical question of what constitutes objectivity and balance is terribly difficult to handle." Killian hoped that trying to achieve these elusive qualities "wouldn't result in timidity in programming."

Again, as with "localism," there was little or no discussion of whether "objectivity and balance," despite their presence in the Public Broadcasting Act, were desirable attributes for broadcast journalism or whether they actually precluded the presence on public TV of strong-minded public affairs of national and international consequence. It was easy enough to see why the politicians who insisted upon adding the phrase to the Public Broadcasting Act wanted it there. What most politicians meant by preserving balance was in reality clearing space for their own opinions, no matter how unfriendly the facts. The importance of balance rested on the assumption that TV news and public affairs was essentially an instrument of propaganda and not of truth.

And yet the desirability of balance was conceded by more and more of the hierarchy of public TV, including Hartford Gunn, Jr., who, as president of PBS, found himself at the head of the forces fighting against the CPB take-over.

Anyone who wished to see public TV out of journalism had other reasons to rejoice. Following CPB's January 10 putsch, PBS had done a hasty reorganization, taking power away from the station managers and sharing it with the chairmen of the boards of local public TV stations. The boards, usually made up of bank presidents, educators, successful businessmen, or other "civic leaders," were supposed to promote localism and give the people more of a voice than ever before in public TV. Although the action brought in some dedicated and powerful friends of public TV, it could ultimately take decision making away from professionals and deliver it up to amateurs.

A plan had already been proposed to distribute most of the money at CPB's disposal to local stations and to cut back the allotments to the New York and Washington production centers heretofore responsible for the lion's share of documentaries and public affairs.

In April Thomas Curtis, chairman of CPB, presented to his board a "compromise" agreement with PBS, which established a review board to screen all possibly controversial programs before airing and permitted "approved" outside material onto the interconnection. But even such meager concessions appeared to be unacceptable to the White House, which was reported maneuvering behind scenes to remove all power from PBS and insure that public TV would never attend the Watergate hearings. The compromise was tabled and its chief sponsor, Nixon appointee Curtis, handed in his resignation in disgust. One station president, David O. Ives of WGBH, Boston, immediately demanded an explanation. "We want the absolute assurance that the corporation will never permit their discussions with the White House or the Congress to include any bargaining for or against particular programs, be they in the area of public affairs or in any other area."

If his station thought such bargains were going on, Ives said, "we will not hesitate to refuse corporation grants to WGBH, even if that means dismantling a large part of our activities."

By late April indignation had built up among public TV personnel, fed by Curtis' reports of extreme White House pressure on CPB members to defeat his compromise. In May Dr. Killian, whose credentials were impeccable, was elevated to the chairmanship of the corporation to replace Curtis. The CPB board reconsidered the compromise, this time agreeing to almost exactly the same terms it had hesitated to accept less than two months before.

Although it was greeted as a victory for the pro-PBS contingent by some, the review board and the redistribution of funds remained and most of the damage to broadcast journalism was left unrepaired. What repairing was done was accomplished by the application of Ford Foundation money to the injured areas. That this could not be a permanent cure was dramatized by the fact that even as Ford millions came to the rescue of some areas of public TV news and public affairs, the foundation made the announcement that four seasons and $40 million in the future it would depart from public TV forever.

One of Ford's final legacies was the Station Program Cooperative plan, a scheme that was intended to give the local stations some responsibility in the selection and production of the national fare that would go over the interconnection and at the same time give respectable national fare a chance for survival.*

Well-meaning as this scheme was, it sounded the death knell, immediate or in the near future, for most of the programs Buchanan and his associates had been so anxious to get off the air.

The 152 licensees in the Public Broadcasting Service were offered ninety-three possible programs by thirty different programming sources at prices that depended on the size of the individual station's operating budget and potential audience. The survival point for a given show was approval by at least sixteen licensees. Theoretically, one station could have bought a program by itself. But a 75 percent discount, provided in the form of $10 million worth of matching funds by the Ford Foundation and CPB, was

---

* Loomis described the plan in testimony before the Labor-HEW Subcommittee of the House Appropriations Committee in March 1974 as follows: "This system would permit the purchase of national programs by local public television stations in keeping with the policy of further station independence and less centralized staff decision-making. This would provide local stations with an opportunity for a greater determination of what programming to select for their communities."

given only to programs that could muster firm purchase commitments from at least 10 percent of the licensees. And the more stations purchasing a particular show, the cheaper it was for all involved.

By July, after a dozen rounds of bidding, eliminating, and finally purchasing, only twenty-five shows had survived. Of these, seven were in the news and public affairs area. Some of the more respected fatalities were "Behind the Lines," "Washington Connection," and "The Advocates." All proposed documentaries were voted down, including "Primate," an already completed show by DuPont prizewinner Frederick Wiseman, and a package of six NPACT documentaries on subjects ranging from mental institutions to new immigrants to retirement communities.*

The most popular bit of journalism to survive without an outside transfusion was "Washington Week in Review," which rated fourth in popularity, just below the "Japanese Film Festival," "At the Top" (jazz), and "Sesame Street." Among the other winners were "Evening at the Symphony" (the Boston Symphony), "Soundstage" (contemporary music), "Electric Company," "Book Beat," "Solar Energy," "Woman," "Black Perspective on the News," "Romagnoli's Table" (cooking), "Consumer Survival Kit," and "Lilias, Yoga and You."

One encouraging sign was the purchase by 129 of the 152 public TV licensees of NPACT's special events coverage and the $1.3 million voted to finance it. This money insured the presence of the impeachment debates on public TV but left comparatively little for future events, and the funding was guaranteed for just one year.

Another optimistic sign was the survival of shows like "Washington Straight Talk," "World Press," "Black Journal," and the replacement for "Bill Moyers' Journal," "Assignment America," which was approved only after Ford agreed to absorb half the production costs, thereby lowering the price. But according to the rules of the Station Program Cooperative, which was to provide a full one-third of the programming sent out over the PBS interconnection in 1974–1975, only those stations which had purchased a show could broadcast it. This meant that a show like "Black

---

* Several shows voted down by the cooperative were later scheduled to go on the air anyway—saved by funding from different sources. Among them: "Behind the Lines" (Martin Weiner Foundation and Ford Foundation), "Primate" (WNET), U.N. Day Concert (CPB), "The Weather Machine" (Champion International Corporation), "Walsh's Animals" (WGBH and the Latham Foundation), and "Zee Cooking School" (South Carolina Educational Television Network).

Journal," approved by only thirty-nine licensees, would have its
potential audiences cut back as much as 70 percent.

Some of the shows were produced by stations that had never
before fed regular programming over the interconnection, among
them "Solar Energy" from KNME, Albuquerque, New Mexico,
and "At the Top" from WXXI, Rochester, New York.

However praiseworthy such democratization of the system was,
the unpleasant suspicion remained that cheapness and popular
appeal rather than quality and importance motivated most of the
station selections.

"The schedule we were able to accomplish was basically a
bread-and-butter schedule," said Warren Park, director of programming and operations at the Maryland Center for Public
Broadcasting, whose "Consumer Survival Kit" (at $301,852 for
twenty-six half-hours) won out over the livelier and more hard-hitting WTTW "Consumer Game" (at $336,000 for eighteen half-
hours). "We weren't able to buy those little gems you need to give
luster to your schedule. Had we had a little more money, we could
have picked and chosen as we wished."

Gunn, who had originated the scheme two years before, said,
"the cooperative was born out of desperation. We had to get the
stations to part with some of their money. We have redesigned the
system so that it is more viable. The board is no longer one board,
whether CPB or PBS, the staff is no longer one staff, whether CPB
or PBS. . . . Here you have the stations making hard and critical
choices, and it is their money involved. They can't back away from
decisions. And I have to think that will help national programming."

Nevertheless, the figures were not promising. Program repeats on
public TV had jumped from fifty hours in the 1971 season to three
hundred in 1973. In 1974 public TV would spend a total of $40
million for programming as against $1 billion for the three
commercial networks. Since 1971, funds for national evening
programming on public TV had declined from $22 million to $13
million, and the percentage of time allotted to news and public
affairs had been cut in half. NPACT had had its budget cut by a
third.

Nor did the situation seem any more encouraging when one
compared it to the vision contained in the final paragraphs of the
Carnegie Commission Report of 1967, which was so frequently
alluded to as the firm foundation on which current public TV
policy was built:

If we were to sum up our proposal with all the brevity at our command, we would say that what we recommend is freedom. We seek freedom from the constraints, however necessary in their context, of commercial television. We seek for educational television freedom from pressures of inadequate funds. We seek for the artist, the technician, the journalist, the scholar, and the public servant, freedom to create, freedom to innovate, freedom to be heard in this most far-reaching medium. We seek for the citizen freedom to view, to see programs that the present system, by its incompleteness, denies him.

Because this freedom is its principal burden, we submit our report with confidence: to rally the American people in the name of freedom is to ask no more of them than they have always been willing to provide.

The painful fact was that although commercial broadcasting's newsmen, thanks to Watergate, had declared and demonstrated their independence, many of public TV's equally talented journalists were being effectively silenced.

As long as the networks and courageous individual commercial stations continued to support and take pride in their news and public affairs departments as they had in the months under consideration, the situation, though depressing, was not desperate. But, should their enthusiasm flag, as it had in the past, there was a possibility that no poor but proud competitors in electronic journalism would be left to shame them by their example.

8 • Out of the Shadow

The Broadcasting
That Made a Difference

FROM HIS SECOND INAUGURAL in January 1973 until he left the White House in August 1974, the thirty-seventh president of the United States and his tangled affairs were the lead story for all American journalism. In Watergate's deep shadow other news was shunted sideways and grew dim. It was not unusual for half the national evening newscasts to be devoted to items having something to do with the scandal. Rumors proliferated that the Watergate glut was having a negative effect on network news ratings, particularly those of CBS and the dean of TV newsmen, Walter Cronkite.

Actually, the opposite was the case. Although network newscast audiences grew slowly, the growth was steady, rising early in 1974 to two million more viewers than in the months immediately preceding the Watergate hearings. In the summer of 1974 Cronkite still was holding his narrow lead over the competition.

Nor was there any indication that TV's prestige had slipped. In April 1974 *U.S. News & World Report* asked five hundred U.S. "leaders" to rate organizations and institutions "according to the amount of influence . . . for decisions or actions affecting the nation as a whole." TV came in first with a score of 7.2 on a scale of 1 to 10. The White House tied the Supreme Court for second place, and newspapers came next. In Burns Roper's 1973 report on the information preferences of the nation, TV was still at the top, with 64 percent of the population.

In a special study of public institutions done by Louis Harris for the Senate Subcommittee on Intergovernmental Relations, TV news was found to have made by far the greatest gains in public confidence since 1965—overtaking the military, organized religion, the Supreme Court, the U.S. Senate, the House of Representatives, and the executive branch of the federal government.

Television's first call on the attention of Americans made it all the more important that stories of primary importance get decent visibility. Elmer Lower, who was promoted from president of ABC News to vice-president of corporate affairs in the summer of 1974, addressed the Radio Television News Directors Association convention in Montreal in September 1974:

> Are we giving people enough news? Back when I started in television, we wondered if fifteen minutes of John Cameron Swayze on NBC and Doug Edwards on CBS wasn't overdoing it a little. Today we wonder if the half hour of news we give the nation via the network is enough to help viewers understand what's really going on. We've already taken some surveys and studies regarding the practicality and potential of a full hour of news on the network. Personally, I know it's possible and I think it's not only desirable, but practical. My own prediction is that an hour news program on some network in the evening will be a fact of viewing life in the not too distant future. Five years at the most; more likely earlier.

Variety was already speaking of all-news TV. Still there was no indication that any of the three networks would increase their news coverage in the immediate future. Robert Wood, president of CBS, at the annual affiliates' meeting in May made a point of scotching persistent rumors that "The CBS Evening News" with Walter Cronkite would be lengthened, although CBS would "reserve the right to reopen the subject" should another network announce expansion plans.

The average length of local newscasts on network affiliates in the top twenty markets had risen steadily from an average of 43.5 minutes in 1969 to 54 minutes in 1974. A 90-minute block of local evening news was now increasingly common, and early in 1974 WNBC, New York, joined its fellow network-owned station KNBC in Los Angeles in a straight two hours of local news nightly, preceding the half-hour network newscast.

Although network coverage of news out of prime time went up, there was not a single regularly scheduled weekly prime-time news and public affairs program on any network. Nor, except in the case of Watergate, did public interest in extended news coverage when it had an entertainment alternative noticeably increase. In the Nielsen ratings of prime-time series, "NBC Reports," the only news and public affairs show qualifying for the list, was consistently within five places of bottom, just above "The Partridge Family" and below sixty to seventy entertainment shows.

On *Variety*'s annual list of prime-time specials the only news programs to get in the top 150 were CBS' program on Gerald Ford's nomination to the vice-presidency and its follow-up of the Nixon resignation—numbers 129 and 138, respectively. Most of the others were clustered at the bottom of a list numbering 363.

Again local newscasting had become completely competitive with entertainment programming, ranking first or second in many markets and in the top ten in a total of twenty-two out of the fifty largest. However, audience for local documentaries and public affairs lagged far behind.

Although at least one non-network news source, Television News, Inc., had made significant strides in building its staff and clientele, feeding thirty minutes of national and international news to a total of thirty-seven American and thirty-five Canadian stations daily, and the Capitol Hill News Service, catering to local TV stations, had been established in Washington, D.C., the principal source for out-of-town stories for local TV newscasts remained the network feeds and the wire services.

Of the major stories breaking during Nixon's second term, the Yom Kippur War and its formidable companion, the energy crisis, rose most conspicuously above the Watergate flood.

CBS News was particularly attentive to events in the Middle East. In addition to regular reports by ten of its top correspondents and fourteen camera crews deployed from Cairo to Damascus, two outstanding prime-time documentaries were aired. "The Israelis," narrated by author Amos Elon, was free from the condescension and special pleading that so often has marred coverage of the embattled Jews. Made half before, half during the war, it ended on a surprising note of reconciliation and wry reason: "Palestinian Arabs," said Elon, "should not become the Jews of the Jews."

The Palestinian guerrillas, the adversaries of the world, were handled with comparable detachment, perhaps a much harder job. "The Palestinians" showed them at home, at work, and in guerrilla training camps. Neither their tragedy nor their intransigence was played down. Correspondent Bill McLaughlin accurately nailed down two harsh truths about the refugees' painful situation: "The promised land has been promised to two different people at the same time," and "Killing civilians makes headlines; killing soldiers doesn't!"

In a growing trend, several local stations sent crews overseas to cover events in the Middle East. Of a half dozen, the best was WTVJ, Miami's "Israel: After the War—Before the Peace," which presented a sensitive subject to the large Jewish population of its community, respectfully and without clichés.

Coverage of the energy crisis was led by Fred Freed's monumental three-hour evening on "The Energy Crisis," * which opened the 1973–1974 documentary season and stood as a capstone to the career of one of America's most talented TV journalists. For 180 minutes Freed ranged his vast subject, from strip mining in Montana to deep-water porting in Maine. The Freed rhythm and pace carried it off, sometimes leisurely, sometimes staccato, juxtaposing pictures and words in unexpected and exactly appropriate ways. Nothing was simple, nothing was dull. "Profit for profit's sake is not sufficient," said a middle American in his shirt sleeves.† If Americans want fuel for their cars they have to change their policies, said King Faisal of Saudi Arabia, interviewed for the first time on American TV since 1957.

The energy evening was just one part of Freed's formidable output in what was to be his final year on TV. Two other hour-long programs on energy later in the season tried to help Americans sort out their priorities and find solutions. More typical perhaps were two gentler essays filled with the familiar Freed irony and questioning. "In White Collar America," the story of the second-string executives in an Atlanta insurance office, seemed an answer to the nostrum "Sunny days and salesmen aren't news; hurricanes and hijackers are." The go-getters and plodders in this large, bright, glassy tower had something quite new and sharp to say to their fellow Americans, thanks to Freed's unerring eye and ear.

"But Is This Progress?" filmed in San Jose, "the fastest growing city in California," was filled with those unexpectedly articulate and complex people Freed had such a talent for spotting and getting on film, including this time a beautiful twenty-five-year-old blonde, ex-runaway, ex-drug addict and Jesus freak, ex-housewife who now programs computers and says softly, "Purpose is something my generation is totally lacking in."

One of the program's messages, which might have been Freed's

---

* See page 166.

† Equal time on another network was given to the president of Phillips Petroleum on Jay McMullen's first-rate CBS investigation of "The Corporation." "Our fundamental purpose has to be to make a reasonable profit," said W. F. Martin on the program, which went on the air two days after the Bartlesville, Oklahoma, conglomerate had been fined $5,000 for making an illegal contribution of $100,000 to President Nixon's campaign for reelection.

own final, tolerant comment on his fellow countrymen, was "Technology allows them to have what they used to have before they had technology." The show went on the air in July 1973. By the next July both Freed and the man who read the words, top NBC newsman Frank McGee, were dead.

Two stories that got repeated attention were inflation, which spread everywhere and affected everyone, and the Patricia Hearst–Symbionese Liberation Army tragedy, which for different reasons also touched most Americans.

Inflation seemed particularly hard for TV to grasp and communicate. Food was the most immediately accessible handle by which to move the huge unmanageable story, and after an endless procession of supermarket carts pushed by poker-faced women reporters reading off rising price tags, "The Food Crisis—Feast and Famine" ("CBS Reports") made a notable impact. It asked the necessary embarrassing questions: Is the food industry taking excessive profits? Is it working at full capacity? Is it engaged in a romance with government with the public paying the tab? The answers provided in sixty minutes, if not definitive, were at least illuminating and disturbing.

Inflation was very much on the minds of local newsmen too, with WMAQ, Chicago's "How High Is Up?" a prime example of a station going into its own community, visiting the real victims—the poor, the old, the hard-pressed middle class—and giving flesh and blood to a story too often reduced to a ringing cash register.

Focusing even tighter was KGTV, San Diego's series on Buck and Dee Buckland, their low-income ($92 a week), non-welfare family of four, and the difference inflation was making in their lives. "What we lack in worldly goods we make up in love," said Dee wistfully. But spunk and heroic measures were obviously running out for the Bucklands, as for many other Americans.

In February 1974, "Today" gave its breakfast viewers two hours tagged jauntily "Up, Up and Away." The information on America's cost of living was unusually complete and relevant, but anything but cheerful. Indeed "Today's" obligation to cheer America up each morning seemed to have gone the way of J. Fred Muggs. One of Washington's favorite programs, "Today" started day after day with interviews of government bigwigs who were more likely to make disturbing news than soothe. The season's record for news-making was undoubtedly the program of January 18, 1974, when two segments back-to-back commanded front-page headlines the morning after. Admiral Thomas H. Moorer, chair-

man of the Joint Chiefs of Staff, confirmed the story, in a "Today"
exclusive, that Yeoman Charles Radford had indeed been snitching
secret documents from Henry Kissinger's office and delivering
them to high-ranking navy friends. In addition Special Watergate
Prosecutor Leon Jaworski told "Today" viewers that he was at the
moment plea-bargaining with more than one Watergate defendant.
Given Counselor Jaworski's astuteness, this bit of fascinating
information was not easy to come by or easy to interpret. Flanking
Jaworski were Bill Monroe, "Today's" Washington editor, and
correspondent Carl Stern, NBC's legal expert. The talk with
Jaworski was a textbook study of how one lawyer can quiz another
and still make it almost comprehensible to an uninitiated outsider.
Stern, along with CBS' Fred Graham, represented a new breed of
newsmen brought to prominence by Watergate. His encounter with
Jaworski may have been indigestible for the moderately well
informed, moderately wide awake American who makes up
"Today's" audience, but it was certainly worth his time and
attention. The new "Today" was a credit not only to NBC and to
Stuart Schulberg, the show's resourceful producer, but also to the
American people who were willing to put up with such rich fare so
early in the morning.

A little harder to swallow was the fact that though the hard news
content of "Today" climbed, the people who put it on the air were
still required to double as pitchmen and pitchwomen for the
formidable list of advertisers the program accommodated, a
hangover from "Today's" earlier happy-go-lucky days and from
the rip-and-read operations of boondocks broadcasters.

Unlike the diffuse story of rising costs, the story of Patricia
Hearst and the SLA seemed at first the classic tabloid thriller, easy
to grasp, compact, fast moving, with a beginning, middle, and
foreseeable end. But over a period of weeks the beautiful young
heiress, kidnapped and waiting to be rescued, changed character. A
family tragedy became a social parable with ramifications far
beyond the original dimensions of the story.

No one was quicker to see this than San Francisco's public TV
station KQED * and its star reporter, Marilyn Baker, who had
been far ahead of the authorities in tracking the SLA. When the
terrorists' story joined that of Miss Hearst, Baker still managed to
keep several steps in front of the field. Thanks to Baker, KQED
was ahead of the police in identifying Nancy Ling Perry as a

* See page 167.

member of the Symbionese Liberation Army, the first after the kidnapping to identify Field Marshal Cinque as escaped convict Donald DeFreeze. The station not only was first with item after item, it also explored the human dimensions of the tragedy, most notably in the program produced by news director Joe Russin that recapitulated Miss Hearst's gradual and painful alienation in an expertly spliced sequence of film, audio tape, stills, and spare comment.

The shoot-out in Watts, which brought the SLA-Hearst story to its violent climax, was heroically covered on TV by the news team from KNXT, Los Angeles, which braved tear gas and gunfire to keep its picture on the air. Live coverage was shared with several other TV stations in Los Angeles and across the country. Although new lightweight equipment permitted KNXT's TV crew to get in close and stay long, it was still Los Angeles' all-news radio station, KFWB,* whose team of four reporters got in the closest and stayed longest. Their coverage gave the sense of danger, violence, and tragedy, detail by detail. Appropriate comment, rare under such pressure, made five consecutive hours on the air into a single chilling and coherent whole.

However admirable the newsmen's courage under fire, some critics saw in the media's relationship to the Hearst-SLA story, with its mutual exploitation and manipulation, a prime example of the "media coup d'état" that put access to the press and the public directly in the hands of small groups of violent and single-minded people. However futile the result, for a few weeks the SLA, the world's smallest army (maximum complement estimated at twelve souls), commandeered the world's largest information machine at will.

The SLA's tactics—placed beside those of the Indians at Wounded Knee, the convicts at Huntsville, Texas, state prison, the Black September operatives, and the Japanese Red Army terrorists, to name only a few of the groups that made successful media take-overs in recent months—were unmistakable indications of a growing trend. Whatever the justice of the ends, the means, coming as much from media naïveté and overeagerness as from cleverness on the part of the preempters, were impermissible. Former CBS newsman Desmond Smith, writing a harsh evaluation of Wounded Knee in *The Nation*, invented the term "media coup d'état" and elaborated:

* See page 166.

The techniques of TV and press take-over are in their infancy, but we may be sure that wherever the obsessed are gathered there are such thoughts. To put an end to the collective penalization of innocent people is a priority for government and electorate alike. At the present time newsmen are helpless victims in the adventurist game of media blackmail.

Or as *TV Guide* news watcher Edith Efron described the press's sometimes confused and ambivalent coverage of the Hearst-SLA story:

> Probably every reporter involved was personally horrified by the crimes. So how *did* it happen? The answer, apparently, is this: as liberal leaners, mostly, the reporters have no natural antibodies against the left—which often voices, in more extreme form, their own values and goals. The reporters can be easily had—and "we wuz had" has been a common confession since leftist violence broke out in 1968. In the Patty Hearst case, many Los Angeles and San Francisco reporters were gradually kidnapped—*philosophically* kidnapped by the left and, in the crunch, unconsciously joined their kidnappers.
> Like Patty Hearst herself.

Mini variations of the media coup d'état also proliferated. The kidnappers of Reg Murphy, editor of the Atlanta *Constitution*, had the commandeering and reforming of the press as one motive for their foolhardy act.

Even more pathetic, two teen-age bank robbers in Rancho Cordova, California, surrendered seventeen hostages and $1 million in ransom in exchange for a promise that a TV interview with them would appear on the Sacramento TV station (KCRA)—a strange inversion of the SLA's demands that Joseph Remiro and Russell Little be permitted to tell their story to the nation via network TV.

No media coup d'état accompanied other stories that promised more serious consequences for the American people and got only fitful attention on the air: the famine in Africa, the continuing war in Southeast Asia, events in Portugal and Ethiopia. The junta take-over in Chile, which involved the overthrow of an elected government in a nation of 11 million, was largely ignored or misreported.

Over a year later the facts were still emerging. One of the more distressing examples of media manipulation and the other side of the coin from a media coup d'état accompanied the U.N. appearance of the widow of the murdered president of Chile, Señora Hortensia Allende. In an accommodation arranged by the Netherlands and the U.S.S.R. with the United States' tacit agreement, it was decided not to permit her speech to be broadcast, ostensibly because she might put the medium to propagandistic use. Preventing propaganda was a strange excuse to apply to U.N. pronouncements. Turning off Señora Allende also amounted to prior censorship. Requests for the speech by CBS, UPI-TV, East German TV, and Vis News were ignored.

Overt intrusion in news programming was comparatively rare. In July 1974, the Soviet censors twice interrupted scheduled newscasts on the actions of dissidents, causing some inconvenience and indignation at the networks. Earlier Dick Cavett had been prevented from putting on the air an innocuous program featuring four 1960's U.S. radicals, Jerry Rubin, Abbie Hoffman, Tom Hayden, and Rennie Davis. The program was rescheduled a month and a half later, with a 30-minute rebuttal from the political right by conservative Fran Griffin and news commentator Jeffrey St. John tacked on for "balance."

In the hinterlands, one of the most striking examples of management intervention was KENS-TV, San Antonio's abrupt cancelation of a televised vasectomy at the local Planned Parenthood Center, which had been scheduled for prime-time viewing.

If Watergate distracted networks from some worthwhile stories at home, or gave them an excuse to neglect their overseas beats,* it had other, beneficial repercussions in network and local newsrooms.

Elton Rule, president of ABC, the network least attentive in the past to the demands of broadcast journalism, told his affiliates in the ballroom of the Century Plaza Hotel in Los Angeles on May 23, 1973:

> If there is anything to be learned from the exposure of Watergate and its widespread ramifications, it is that what is needed is more investigative reporting and a more resounding affirmation of the principle of separation of government and a free press. For our part, we intend to expand our activities in the investigative area. . . . On a national scale, there is ample

---

* Rising expenses and growing public indifference to foreign news were given as others.

evidence in Watergate of what investigative reporting can accomplish; if the journalistic function was only to reflect official positions and public opinion, would the incredible dimensions of the Watergate scandal ever have become known? . . . While the public may have believed there were higher officials involved than those actually captured at the Watergate, the public at first appeared not to care about the matter.

If the press had chosen to remain silent along with the majority, it would have been an abdication of the truth. Instead, we have seen the power of the truth arouse that public, and, as the latest polls indicate, make it vocal once again in asking that justice be done. . . .

If we should ever fail in our responsibility, to whom could the people turn for the truth?

As earnest of the network's good faith, Rule pointed to the announcement of twelve one-hour investigative reports that the network intended to broadcast in prime time once a month during the coming year.

The news of the documentary series had been greeted the day before with polite applause by the affiliates, who would, no doubt, have preferred to be informed of a surefire new entertainment series like "The Streets of San Francisco" or "Marcus Welby M.D."

The industry, which had heard such promises before, also received Rule's words with some skepticism. However, what Rule promised turned out to be the admirable "Close-Up" series,* the single most impressive journalistic fallout from Watergate.

"Close-Up's" executive producer, Av Westin, a veteran of the Public Broadcast Laboratory as well as "The ABC Evening News," put together a stable of top TV documentary talents, including Paul Altmeyer from Group W, Martin Carr from CBS via NBC, Pamela Hill from NBC and Marlene Sanders and Stephen Fleischman from his own shop. With sufficient time (five to six months) and adequate budgets ($150,000 per show), these talented producers gave the TV audience the most consistently gripping and outspoken series of TV reports since "See It Now."

In a list that included superior inquiries into death and what was really going on in the coal business, the oil business, the food business, and the art business, the standout was an essay on "Fire,"

* See page 166.

a subject that for years past had been the main staple of every local TV newscast.

The sixty minutes produced and written by Pamela Hill was a demonstration of the uses of network TV, replacing the morbid fascination with the misfortunes of others that has characterized most treatments of the subject by a shattering human story exposing a national scandal of major proportions. "Fire," as seen by "Close-Up," was not the product of an arbitrary and malevolent fate, but the result of the deliberate oversights and misrepresentations of men who claimed once more to want no more than to turn a decent profit. Seldom had the cutting of a corner to make a buck been shown to have such excruciating and unforgivable results in the maiming and death of the innocent and unwarned. Nor were the culprits two-bit shysters. In the course of the program, a long list of the nation's top corporations, seventeen of them ABC advertisers, were accused by name.*

This unique willingness to dig out evil, show it unvarnished on the screen, and then give it a name and address ran like a patrol-car light and siren through "Close-Up" after "Close-Up" until the only skepticism remaining was, Could they keep it up for another season?

The best weekly display of TV journalistic resourcefulness continued to be CBS' high-quality magazine show "60 Minutes." † In its sixth year it was still delivering both hard news and stylish features with an expertise that no one else on the air managed or indeed any longer attempted. In one of its brightest seasons to date "60 Minutes" offered "End of a Salesman," in which a sixty-year-old minor executive was given equal fire power with one of the world's largest corporations, Standard Oil of California. Arbitrarily retired before his time and against his will after thirty-three years of service, Clyde Shearer joined with three fellow victims to tell his story for the CBS cameras. Following the program, corrective action was taken by Standard Oil to rehire 120 of its former employees and make cash settlements with 40 others. Ironically, Mr. Shearer was not one of that number.

Another striking segment was "I Was Only Following Orders," showing scientific experiments which gave a chilling explanation

---

* One 43-second segment showing a burning crib was deleted before broadcast because of a court injunction brought by the crib manufacturer, a rare instance of prior restraint in broadcasting history, which ABC contested and eventually won. None of the other culprits were heard from.

† See page 166.

for the psychic origins of the Nazis, My Lai, and perhaps Watergate.

As always, the interviewing was first class, particularly in revealing segments devoted to the Reverend John McLaughlin and Charles Colson, two men who had found religion in Watergate, and John Ehrlichman, who was about to meet his nemesis there.

Of the year's interviews the most amazing, however, was once more the work of Mike Wallace, who on camera fought the Shah of Iran to a stunning draw. Although neither gave an inch he didn't choose to, a rare occurrence in a Wallace interview, there was both intimacy and generosity in the session. A typical interchange:

WALLACE: Why did you survive?
THE SHAH: I believe in God, ask him.

That such a dialogue did not sound pompous, pious, or pretentious was a tribute to both men's stubborn honesty.

Other important segments on "60 Minutes" included two examples of hard-nosed journalistic soul-searching, "Local News and the Rating War" and "Press Junkets." Following the latter segment the Radio Television News Directors Association, fingered for having been lavishly entertained by Chrysler Motors Corporation at its 1973 convention, announced a policy of no longer accepting or soliciting "any commercial sponsorship or underwriting of any conference-related function."

Elsewhere the most thorough job done by the TV medium on the media was WNET/13's "Behind the Lines," which for the season had an hour at its disposal once a month. Particularly fine were its investigations of the press and Watergate, and the press coverage of the energy crisis. The program also called attention to a disturbing phenomenon, the growing bombardment of TV news directors with filmed press releases, and the growing willingness of the newsmen, harassed, understaffed, or just plain lazy, to use the releases without editing or identifying the source.

The investigative fever, spread by Watergate, hit an impressive number of the nation's local broadcasters.

In a special survey conducted in conjunction with the American Association of University Women, over 500 monitors covering 425 different stations coast to coast found that more than half had added full-time investigative reporters to their staffs or in some way increased their investigative activities.

Of the more than 200 news directors reporting directly to the

Survey in 1974, a third said they had increased their investigative assignments. One commented on the results:

> We are attempting to concentrate our reporting efforts on investigative and enterprise journalism. However, the scheduled event syndrome is hard to break for a TV newsroom. I hope we win the battle and put something of significance on the air regularly. Otherwise, I suspect that the truck driver who has been getting 90 percent of his news from the tube is going to wake up some morning saying—damn it . . . I'm completely uninformed. I don't know what's going on, and I don't know who's doing what to whom in my town. That box has deceived me. While they were showing me ribbon cuttings, my taxes were going up, and the politicians were stealing the Court House. I'll never believe that boob tube again—Click.
> —*WITI, Milwaukee*

Another:

> What an opportunity. And we are accepting the challenge. It is seen daily in editorial commentaries; in-depth news reports and mini documentaries. What's more, we are competing with the daily papers for our share of exclusives, the investigative pieces, the analytical reports. It has made for a healthy competitive market. And the beneficiaries are the people who have been made not only more knowledgeable but who have found that they have strong ombudsmen serving their interests.—*WCKT-TV, Miami*

WCKT's investigative energy was indeed phenomenal. A half-dozen series aired on its evening news in as many as fifteen segments dealt with, among other subjects, police honesty, hitchhiking, and with particular tenacity and effect, local governmental corruption.

In the WCKT coverage a character who was growing more and more commonplace in TV news appeared, the reporter provocateur, impersonating doctors, women in search of silicone treatments for their breasts, auto owners with problem carburetors. Whatever the ethical considerations, this new breed of reporter took unaccustomed risks and frequently came back with a fascinating story.

Among the most distinguished pieces of local investigative reporting was WPVI-TV, Philadelphia's "Public Bridges and

Private Riches." * Taking a Delaware Valley scandal, WPVI's reporters ranged wide and then in a carefully built 30-minute program circled in ever-tightening spirals and finally swooped down on the venal public servants who were benefiting themselves and their relatives at the public's expense.

For radio, WNEW, New York, did an equally impressive job on the failure of airports to adequately screen the cargoes of passenger planes. In "The Hidden Passenger," † the frightening tale of explosives, acids, radioactive materials, and disease viruses traveling under unwitting travelers' feet was pieced together over a year's time by John and Christine Lyons. Aired in a series of twenty-one reports and two weekend documentaries, it resulted in legislative proposals and in John Lyons' being assigned duties as consultant on hazardous cargo to the New York Port Authority.

Among the dozens of first-rate investigations that got on the air as newscast series or documentaries:

• "Scandal Rides the Ambulance" (WFSB-TV, Hartford), which led to the arrest of three ambulance proprietors who in the interest of profits were not referring emergency cases to competitors, sometimes with fatal results.

• "Democracy C.O.D.," one thoroughly researched segment among many done by "LA Collective," KCET's savvy local TV magazine. The prickly subject: campaign financing.

• "Art Museum Controversy" (KAKE-TV, Wichita), pulling the chain on local businessmen hoping to profit from the building of a new cultural institution.

• "How Safe Is Logan?" (WCVB-TV, Boston), an exposé of the frightening chances being taken at the world's eighth busiest airport.

• "Migrant Workers" (WHEC, Rochester, New York), a local problem pursued out of state.

• "Big Thicket" (KERA-TV, Dallas) and "Okefenokee" (WTVT, Tampa), two sensitive and upsetting investigations of what was happening to wilderness areas rich in tradition, character, and natural beauty, clearly held up to the viewer to see who was responsible and what was worth preserving.

• "Moore on Sunday" (WCCO-TV, Minneapolis), a weekly magazine show, which regularly stirred its community up whether it was investigating mass transit, or homosexual marriage.

* See page 166.
† See page 167.

• "CIA Reports," * a monthly documentary series on WCIA-TV, Champaign-Urbana, Illinois, which demonstrated how a modest station in a comparatively small market could consistently examine the local ramifications of major human problems and present them thoroughly and fairly to its community. Among those subjects considered were welfare, energy, old people, economic discrimination, and ecology, in each instance approached through sharply and sympathetically observed manifestations close to home.

Service to the community of another sort was rendered by WHAS, Louisville,† through both its radio and TV outlets when twenty-one separate tornadoes scythed through its coverage area on the afternoon of April 3, 1974. WHAS helicopter traffic reporter Dick Gilbert risked his life to keep WHAS listeners and viewers informed and was credited with saving dozens of others during the stations' 9 hours and 58 minutes of continuous coverage.

One of the few network or local programs during the period that attempted a global view of mankind's problems was KNBC, Los Angeles, in its 90-minute tour de force "The European Connection." ‡ The station sent reporters and cameramen to England, France, Holland, and Germany to see how the natives were coping with the same problems—inflation, pollution, crime, mass transit, racial intolerance—that afflicted the local Angeleno. The resulting ninety minutes not only illuminated the southern California way of life but gave a coherent and overarching sense of spaceship earth, which TV only rarely and fragmentarily conveys.

"The European Connection" illustrated another trend, the maxi documentary and public affairs program. Along with hours of Watergate and Fred Freed's three solid prime-time hours on energy, there were dozens of public affairs offerings cross country that exceeded the statutory 30- to 60-minute time span. Surprisingly, they often deserved all the time they were allowed.

KQED did a 2-hour and 20-minute profile of a POW, U.S. Navy Commander Richard Stratton. "2,251 Days" § was the most exhaustive and revealing inquiry into one man and woman's family since public TV introduced the Louds to America. It was also head and shoulders above any of the dozens of other treatments of returning POW's, which tended to facile pity and patriotism. "The Beak" was obviously no plaster and braid hero nor was there much

* See page 167.
† See page 167.
‡ See page 166.
§ See page 167.

question about the authenticity of the horrors he had experienced at the hands of the North Vietnamese, "petty, vindictive, mean little people" as he called them on camera.

Other victims of Vietnam, the anti-war exiles in Canada, were also given the blockbuster treatment by WMAL, Washington, in a series of ten mini-docs, which culminated in a fascinating 90-minute live free-for-all in which advocates and opponents of amnesty in Washington spoke with Toronto exiles on camera.

WRTV, Indianapolis, did the most ambitious takeout to date on the motor car and the problems of urban mass transit in its 2-hour and 30-minute investigation of "The Auto and the Alternatives," which traveled far and wide (Kokomo, Indiana; Reston, Virginia; Chicago; Washington, D.C.; Minneapolis; San Francisco) to cover a very big problem thoroughly and well.

KDKA, Pittsburgh, turned over its studio and cameras for a 4½-hour session on the subject of energy. Its sister station, WBZ in Boston, devoted sixteen hours to the controversial matter of women.

The country's largest minority received a little more of the attention and respect it deserves than in previous years. CBS gave a trial run to a daytime "Magazine" on May 2, 1974, using top talent: Perry Wolff, Charles Kuralt, and Sylvia Chase. The result was pleasing enough to confirm five more for the coming season. Women fared less well in the morning on CBS, where Washington *Post* reporter Sally Quinn's short stint as co-anchor with Hughes Rudd was one of the year's causes célèbres.

Out of New York, the AAUW members canvassing their communities found more coverage of their sex in half the stations reported on, and a change in the attitude toward women for the better was reported in almost two-thirds.

In the approximately 350 stations responding to the AAUW's questions, the score on women employed in news departments was: newscasters 233, newswriters 199, technicians 121, reporters 315, producers 184, all other jobs 610.

Two-thirds reported an increase in women employed in news operations, only 17 reported a decrease, the rest remained stable. As for the kinds of assignments given the women reporters, 59 reported definite discrimination, 161 said there was none.

Sex stereotyping also was on the wane, with 138 seeing a decrease, 7 an increase, and 187 no difference from the previous year. Coverage of the women's movement was reported as fair and objective by a surprising 275; 48 found it condescending, 61 humorous, 3 hostile, 15 not covered at all. Among specific comments:

> The attitude toward women in the news stories and programs has progressed from self-conscious and a little silly to matter-of-fact, straight reportage in the past year or two.— *Grand Forks, N.D.*

> Perhaps more effort at consciousness of women's "liberation" with result of some condescension, but also more honest effort at recognizing women's interests.—*Las Vegas, Nev.*

> Feminine movement has had its impact; greater sensitivity. Women and their community efforts and involvements are taken more seriously. We seem to be approaching a more realistic period.—*Buffalo, N.Y.*

> An attitude of "Look what the womenfolk are doing now" seems to prevail.—*Daytona Beach/Orlando, Fla.*

> It appears that there is more effort to present women as professionals as well as mother-housewife-consumers. Yet, I feel that the television medium as a whole, this station included, has a long way to go before it will have accomplished treating women as humans rather than buyers, etc.— *Madison, Wis.*

Of many worthy programs on subjects of particular interest to women, the most remarkable was unquestionably KNXT, Los Angeles' "Why Me?" * a gripping hour on breast cancer. Ten women, picked from seventy local victims of the disease, were persuaded to tell their stories, harrowing but hopeful, with few comments, straight to the camera. Step by step, diagnosis, exploration, surgery, readjustment, their recollections were paralleled by a young woman who was facing the same experiences. The suspense built to an almost unbearable pitch as she entered the operating room and went under the anesthetic, while the other women went on with their stories. The device took the program's producer on a narrow path between bathos and tragedy, which he survived with signal success, thanks to his own and the participants' impeccable taste and sincerity.

Rape and abortion were two of the most fashionable subjects for

* See page 166.

local TV documentaries during the year, many of them doing an important job of informing the public well. Unusual in its treatment was WTVJ, Miami's "The Sex Offenders," * which saw the story as it was rarely presented, from the man's point of view, and placed it firmly in a context of sickness and sexual deviation where it belonged. In the clinic at South Florida Hospital in Fort Lauderdale, eighteen deviants, including exhibitionists, child molesters, and Peeping Toms, as well as rapists, explored their problems with an attractive woman doctor. Wives and victims were interviewed as well. The program was another startling example of TV's unique ability to explain the heretofore unmentionable and unspeakable to the American public. In both "Why Me?" and "The Sex Offenders," the fact that participants were white, middle class, and physically attractive added an element of shock and surprise as well as paradox to the subjects considered.

Racial minorities did somewhat less well than women according to the AAUW. Out of 344 stations reported on, 142 devoted more time to minority coverage, 24 less, and 178 the same.

Specific biases seemed rare. AAUW monitors spotted 37 pro-black stations to 7 anti, 17 obviously left leaning to 26 right leaners, 15 pro-Chicano to 4 anti-Chicano, and 23 pro-youth to 8 anti-youth. By far the greatest number of stations, 246, were reported to have no discernible bias for or against anyone.

Of the steadily increasing number of quality programs directed toward minorities, unquestionably one of the best in recent seasons was WKY-TV, Oklahoma City's remarkable 90-minute "Through the Looking Glass Darkly," † a self-examination and recollection of all that was best and most interesting in the fascinating history of the blacks of the Great Plains. Solidly rooted in local figures living and dead and a rich tradition, it simply and with great dignity evoked the past of a fascinating community. It also served as an example and bench mark for other stations that could tell equally moving stories of ethnic groups in their communities.

A story of a black community that urgently needed telling was contained in WMC-TV, Memphis' simple and compelling documentary "Trouble in Mound Bayou." ‡ The trouble with the small Mississippi community was that its 34-bed local hospital, the only one in four counties serving the poor and the black, was due to shut

* See page 167.
† See page 166.
‡ See page 167.

its doors. A reporter and a cameraman made the 100-mile trip from Memphis and on their own time talked to the people of Mound Bayou and the staff of the hospital in a series of vignettes that proved vividly in terms of life and death the importance of the institution's survival. In nine days the show went on the air and won the station admiring reviews in the local press.

When no other newspaper, wire service, or radio or TV station picked up the story of the hospital's plight, the station's general manager went farther afield, calling WLBT-TV in Jackson and WABG-TV in Greenwood-Greenville to offer an updated version of the program free. David Brinkley, the Washington *Post*, an FCC commissioner, the Congressional Black Caucus, and a vice-president of NBC News were all called to no avail.

In desperation WMC recommended that enough money to keep the hospital open for six months be attached to a Senate bill to appropriate $10 million to reimburse five Mississippi chicken companies which had used contaminated feed. The idea worked. The hospital was allotted $800,000, enough to keep it open for a year—a rare example of virtue persisted in and rewarded.

WNET/13 in New York continued its admirable policy of paying close and sympathetic attention to the hard-pressed ethnic neighborhoods in its area of coverage, adding understanding and evocative reports on the Italians of Coney Island and the Jews of Brighton Beach to their list.

The problems of distant minorities, beset by the wonders of modern civilization, were sensitively and disturbingly conveyed to Americans by NBC's beautifully filmed essay on Sinai, where 60,000 Bedouins stood helplessly by while a centuries-old life-style crumbled away.

Even more upsetting, since America was unmistakably responsible, was WGTV, Athens' and the Georgia Center for Continuing Education's "The Bikinians." It told the grim and pathetic story of what had happened to the 167 natives whose idyllic atoll was ground zero for U.S. hydrogen bomb tests. The tale was biblical in content and message—a people dispossessed and wandering, "for the benefit of all mankind," coming to the bitter knowledge that what they had really accommodated was a search for power, not goodness.

Indeed, if there was any stereotype of a villain on this year's TV, it wasn't the Mafia boss, cattle rustler, or criminal psychopath of prime-time drama, but the slick, confident, unflappable bureaucrat who was "doing his best" and his frequent companion, the captain of industry with his hard chin, clear eye, and fuzzy explanations.

A minority in many ways as remote from today's America as the natives of Micronesia and Asia Minor was evoked in KMOX-TV, St. Louis' hour-long "Sixteen in Webster Grove: Eight Years Later." * Taking "Sixteen in Webster Grove," the controversial CBS documentary of 1966, as their point of departure, the station contacted 421 of the subjects—the Webster Grove High School class of 1967—to find out what had happened to them. What had happened was drugs, student riots, war, racial protest, the sexual revolution, women's lib, Eastern religions, the pill, and finally Watergate. The privileged young of Webster Grove had been on a pilgrimage as hazardous and heartbreaking as the natives of Bikini, and the program gave encouraging proof of their ability to survive.

Youths even more buffeted by fate were the subjects of the season's most masterful and painful documentary, Frederick Wiseman's "Juvenile Court" (WNET),† the result of a month's wandering the corridors, offices, and chambers of the Memphis children's court. Parents and children, officers, social workers, and a singularly understanding young judge acted out their difficult roles like characters in Dickens, battered, herded, isolated, and occasionally rescued by the institutions intended to serve them. Although Wiseman has dozens of imitators, he remains the virtuoso of the nerve-wracking, heartbreaking, naturalistic documentary where neither cameraman nor reporter casts a shadow.

An even grimmer story was told by radio station KAUM,‡ Houston, which set a crew of four reporters and five part-time assistants to dig out the true facts behind the nightmarish sex crimes that took the lives of twenty-seven young men in and around the lower-middle-class section of Houston known as the Heights. Five hundred interviews later, a 43-minute documentary presented a sensational story without sensationalism or likelihood of offense, re-creating an entire social substructure in an unprecedented and totally convincing way.

Unfortunately this remarkable display of news energy and imagination was not likely to be repeated. The station's former news director, Randy D. Covington, explained:

> KAUM is one of seven FM radio stations owned by the American Broadcasting Company. We were the only station

* See page 166.
† See page 166.
‡ See page 166.

that really had a news operation. Now KAUM is pretty much in line with its sisters (which concentrate on rock music). To replace our department, the station receptionist was promoted to rip 'n read three morning newscasts. She reports to the program director, a former disc jockey. She tells me that about the only instruction she has received so far from the program director is to avoid "depressing" stories.

Nor was KAUM alone in radio's losing battle to maintain its standards. WRVR in Manhattan, one of the quality news operations in the city, had been cut back drastically. WBAI, another off-beat New York station, was wavering financially, as were its sister Pacifica stations in Berkeley and Los Angeles. The sad stories of WNCN, New York, and WEFM, Chicago, which, despite devoted and stubborn listeners and a glut of pop music stations were about to be converted from classical music to rock, contributed to the trend. Another blow to radio diversity was proposed legislation to require all car radios to have FM receivers. According to Congressman Lionel Van Deerlin, an ex-broadcaster, it was a rip-off designed to enrich auto manufacturers. Others felt such legislation could make the younger medium, once dedicated to the high-brow and off-beat, no better than its increasingly raffish older sister, AM radio.

Experiments were in short supply in both radio and TV during the season, but a particularly successful one was brought off by a crew of talented youngsters who called themselves TVTV (Top Value Television) and already had to their credit an impressive inside report on the 1972 Democratic convention in Miami (see DuPont-Columbia Survey 1971–1972). Using porta-pak cameras and one-half inch and one-inch videotape, seven two-person teams set out to cover "the most significant event in human history," the international gathering called at the Houston Astrodome by the baby swami, Guru Maharaj Ji. The resulting report, the 60-minute "Lord of the Universe," * was hectic, hilarious, and not a little disquieting. With a heavier and less sure hand, the subject would have been squashed beneath the reporters' irony or contempt. As it was, one more by-product of the Pepsi and Vietnam generation, cult religion, was handed to us, live and quivering, to make of it what we would.

Was the overall broadcasting picture as bright as its many islands of excellence, or sicklied over by its frequent failures of

* See page 166.

nerve? According to the AAUW, the length of newscasts was up at
56 percent of the stations reported on; the size of news staffs had
increased at 63 percent and news budgets had risen at 75 percent.
The audiences for local news and public affairs were also up at four
out of five stations, with the average increase 25 percent. Quality
was reported improved at more than half the stations observed. On
the whole, the monitors found local news less biased than network,
but also less interesting, less serious, and less thorough.

As for those responsible for getting the news on the air, of the
250 news departments communicating with the Survey this year,
many spoke out strongly. Among the voices of those responsible
for what the nation heard and saw—good or bad:

> During the past year we have reported to our audiences on
> a succession of events that were hard to believe, hard to ab-
> sorb. But I think we are trusted more now than in the past;
> whether this is real or illusory, we must not let it go
> to our heads—we're only as trustworthy as our last newscast.
> —*KSD-TV, St. Louis*

> We are the most powerful men in the history of the world,
> and I'm happy to say that, on the whole, I think that power is
> being used in the best interest of everyone.
> —*WDIO-TV, Duluth*

> I am more optimistic than ever. There is little doubt that
> broadcast news has made some giant steps in the past few
> years, and despite carping and criticism from outside the
> media, broadcasting has managed to maintain the respect and
> popular appeal with the public. I think television news is
> getting more gutsy, more inventive, more responsible with
> every passing day, and that there are an increasing number of
> *good* television news stations—even in the smaller markets.
> The danger, I think, is for broadcasters to become too
> cocksure of themselves, too confident of the impact of their
> product, and too little concerned with their continuing respon-
> sibility to be fair and even-handed.
> —*WCCO-TV, Minneapolis*

> I am seriously concerned that a ratings battle will result not
> in the communication of untruths, but in the communication
> of truth about subjects which have little real journalistic value.
> Specifically, the choice of mini-doc subjects designed to

titillate rather than enlighten—all in the interest of higher ratings.   *—WTTW, Chicago*

Print certainly is not dead—and can do so much that we can't, but we can do what print can't, and in this area we can reach people who have TV sets but can't afford or don't want a daily paper. Moreover, we have no national newspaper, so for the national truth, at this time at least, if broadcast journalism doesn't dig it out and show it, who will?   *—KRWG-TV, Las Cruces, N. M.*

Overall broadcast journalism is in trouble. There is too much dependence on news judgments from New York and Washington, too much of a tendency to become obsessed with corruption resulting in almost total ignorance of Sam Jones and family in Omaha and his needs and feelings or even on the economic war waged by Japan. Too many journalism "trainees" are being taught there's no story unless the dirt is found. This is leading to fewer fact-finding and reporting efforts and more "I already know, you prove me wrong" efforts. It's a prevailing attitude I find a real threat. If Sam Jones in Omaha loses faith in the credibility of the media he sees, hears and reads, the purpose of true journalism at its most basic level is lost. That middle-ground must be found and soon. "Communication of the truth" is really becoming a lost art. Perhaps much of the "yellow journalism" newspapers were forced into to sell papers is being practiced to "buy" viewers.   *—KGVO-KTVM-TV, Missoula, Mont.*

I'm more than a bit worried by what I see as a growing public apathy toward the various scandals called Watergate. I'm worried because of the pre-Watergate trend toward official "disregard" for the free press. It could happen again—and with no Watergate to derail the trend, the very concept of a free press could be in trouble. Perhaps we have communicated too much truth to a weary public incapable of absorbing any more.   *—Iowa Educational Broadcasting Network*

We're doing a good job of covering a lot of news and doing it well. But most of us don't have the staff or time to do the real probing pieces needed. It's the same with networks. The quality of production was never better. But there's a lot of "soft" material and too little of a really important nature. Too often I notice a story in the *Wall Street Journal, New York Times* or *Time* magazine and a few days later the same piece—dressed up in film—on a network news show. We're covering too much by trend and news conference. Consumer reporting—someone says—is going big in one area. It's started in another, but with no real substance. News flow is determined too much by the "called" news conference. Too often, an editor knows the story won't be much but figures the competitors will be there, so we better, too.

—*WRTV, Indianapolis*

If we can remain generalists in an age of specialization; if we can find perspective in a time that tends to neurotic myopia; if we can remain disinterested in all the special interests that surround us; and if we can develop a passionate commitment to the average guy trying to survive in a complicated world; then our opportunity for service in this generation is almost without limits.

—*WSVA-TV-AM, Harrisonburg, Va.*

I assumed duties at WTWV-TV August 27, 1973. At that time, the station did not have a newsroom, a weather wire, police scanner, or visual equipment except one Polaroid camera and a defunct 16-mm. camera. In the months that followed my arrival here, a three-man news department has been added, with management approval for three more. A small newsroom is being utilized as a larger, more versatile news central is constructed. Portable videotape visual news gathering equipment is a part of the operation and cities and towns in a predominantly rural area are seeing a television camera and news team for the first time. It's hard to believe that there are still areas of the nation like this . . . but, it is so.

—*WTWV-TV, Tupelo, Miss.*

And from the DuPont correspondent in Akron, Ohio:

Broadcast journalism is riding on a crest of strength and influence. I fear that by some it is being used as a step to selfish power, affluence, and personal or corporate gain, prestige and aggrandizement instead of reflecting the reality of poverty, hunger, uninhabitable shelter, unemployment, poor health care, and continuing racial tensions that are all around us. Broadcast journalists must learn that news is not only what happens, but what *is;* how people and ideals and things exist, and how they cease to exist when the public is unaware of them, or indifferent to them. So many demands are being placed upon the attention of the public, the news cannot be trivial or less than deadly serious without risking being tuned out with the rest of the barrage of picayune, bantered, superfluous information.

Observations

THE LENGTHENING LISTS of awards and citations that this jury is commending say much about the quality of broadcast journalism. When networks and stations set their minds to news coverage and documentary and are willing to expend talent and money, they frequently achieve distinguished results. The jury finds its task of screening prizewinners increasingly rewarding and difficult with every passing year. Whether this means that more of the television day is being given to news and public affairs or simply that more of it is coming to our attention, we hesitate to say, although our watchers tell us that quantity as well as quality is up. We are struck with the high quality of what we have seen. We are convinced that the industry should find deeply satisfying its accomplishment in this area.

Early in the year we heard with some expectancy that ABC intended a series of documentaries to be called "Close-Up." We followed the series and were not disappointed. "Close-Up" was surely one of television's superior achievements of 1973–1974. Conversely, we received with profound regret the news from Group W that it was disbanding its Urban America team. This is a particularly poignant regret, since much that Group W had previously done had won wide recognition, including three DuPont Awards.

We noted much improvement in locally produced documentaries. In some cases more inventive things were being done by small local crews than by the networks. We call to mind a film by the university-related station in Athens, Georgia, that told a moving story of the return of the Bikinians to their bomb-blasted atoll. For technical quality, originality, persuasiveness, and public service we commend the year's output of local documentaries.

The reader will see that we have been more cognizant this year of good works by radio. We do not claim that this signals a general upgrading of the use of this medium, but it is clear that many excellent things are being done. We cite the five hours of coverage by radio station KFWB in Los Angeles of the shoot-out at the headquarters of the Symbionese Liberation Army, an extraordinary demonstration of performance under fire—articulate, immediate, and accurate. Also, an incredibly complex documentary on station KAUM, Houston, detailing with interviews and unsensationalized reports the series of homosexual murders in that city. We are also commending WNEW in New York for its series on the hazardous cargo that rides beneath the unknowing passengers on commercial airlines. We were impressed with the usefulness of radio in disaster situations, as demonstrated by a number of stations' coverage of the tornadoes of 1974, and we single out WHAS in Louisville for its accuracy, thoroughness, courage, and high sense of public service.

Turning to news, we find much that is excellent and altogether too much that is being debased as a result of the ratings wars. Despite claims to the contrary, we find the general level of balance and fairness in network news commendable, and we rise to its defense. The programs deal with matters of daily import and are never trivialized or cosmetized. The trend toward folksiness, chumminess, and triviality in much local television news handling continues to give us cause for worry. We fear that important, though perhaps dull, happenings are being passed over in favor of unimportant, though sometimes interesting, featurettes. Much of this trend is traceable to consultants who are brought in by local stations and who proceed to package a "show" for audience appeal rather than for news content. Many news directors are firmly resisting this usurpation of their professional responsibility, and we salute them. These issues are discussed elsewhere in this Survey and in other journals.*

Public broadcasting surfaced repeatedly in our screening. NPACT's coverage of the Watergate hearings was outstanding, and the "Bill Moyers' Journal" segment on Watergate was equally so. "Washington Week in Review," by any count, is one of the most articulate, intelligent presentations on the air. The probing beneath the surface of the news on "Behind the Lines" seemed to us to be a singularly effective use of television. We saw distinguished journalistic accomplishment from public stations in San Francisco, Los Angeles, and Boston. All of this we commend.

* See Edward W. Barrett, "Folksy TV News," *Columbia Journalism Review*, November/December 1973.

There are still too many areas of the country where public broadcasting is not seen or heard. Too many of its station outlets on ultra-high frequency are limited in range and reception. The system deserves better, more accessible channels.

We honor the public broadcasting output for the year with some anxiety. For details of what the future holds and what our fears about it are, please read carefully Chapter 7 of this Survey.

Coming away from our viewing and listening, we had some general impression of topics that seemed to be high on the list of broadcasters' concerns this year. Disease and health seemed to be one, as indicated by our award to the documentary on breast cancer, "Why Me?" There were dozens of films and tapes on children's afflictions, some of them moving, some shocking. On radio the repeated topics were rape and abortion, and television was not far behind. Indeed, television was a little ahead, as indicated by our award of a year ago. Sensitive, sober handling of homosexuality appeared in numerous programs. Watergate and the energy crisis were, of course, the topical leaders.

The jurors noted in 1973–1974 a fresh discovery of neighborhoods in television journalism. Bill Moyers' show on Gail Cincotta and her neighbors in Chicago provided one example. The series pioneered by Rosanne Alessandro and Gary Gilson on WNET-TV's "The 51st State" introduced a new concept: a leisurely, attentive projection of how a self-contained, vital part of a city lives, feels, looks at things. On "The 51st State," the old-timers of Brighton Beach and the truck drivers and homeowners of Coney Island saw their own lives, living patterns, and values reflected. "Archie Bunker" is a fantasy of the workingman which more highly educated and highly paid persons have produced. Under Gilson's direction and with Alessandro's intuitive approaches, real people who live in neighborhoods like Archie Bunker's spoke for themselves—with a complexity, irony, and humor that did the nation honor.

The jurors also took note in 1974 of a new threat to the integrity of the media—a kind of hijacking of air time by criminals so bold and imaginative that their deeds, as "news," had become well-nigh irresistible. From the first, the Symbionese Liberation Army staged a grand "media event" as calculated as a political compaign. It may even be said that the SLA lived by the media and died by them; for their grand campaign led to fiery death in the midst of exploding ammunition, Molotov cocktails, tear-gas canisters, and flame-wrapped walls. As we said before, the five-hour inferno was brilliantly reported live by KFWB in Los Angeles and—as close as cameras could get—by television, as well. Throughout the long dramatic months, manifesting great poise, good judgment, and investigative legwork, the broadcasting team of San Francisco's KQED-TV often jumped ahead of the police and the FBI in their discoveries and their interpretive skills.

In this case, the performance of the broadcasters was exemplary. But the SLA event showed that the media are more and more a two-edged sword, used not only for reporting news but for staging it, drawn into complicity in the very texture of "events." They have become far more than the mirror of events. They have become a vital component of such events, essential as oxygen is to fire.

Consistent with our observations of other years, we say again that there ought to be more repeated showings of fine documentaries. Actually, we think we see a swing toward replays, a desire to make use of expensive, quality material more than once on the air. We applaud the swing.

> Elie Abel
> Richard T. Baker
> Edward W. Barrett
> Dorothy Height
> John Houseman
> Sig Mickelson
> Michael Novak

The Alfred I. duPont-Columbia University Awards, 1973–1974

Av Westin and ABC News, for **"Close-Up"**

Don Hewitt and CBS News, for **"60 Minutes"**

Fred Freed and NBC News, for **"The Energy Crisis"**

National Public Affairs Center for Television, for **Watergate coverage**

National Public Affairs Center for Television, for **"Washington Week in Review"**

KFWB Radio, Los Angeles, for **"SLA 54th Street Shootout"**

KNXT-TV, Los Angeles, for **"Why Me?"**

WKY-TV, Oklahoma City, for **"Through the Looking Glass Darkly"**

TVTV and WNET/13, for **"The Lord of the Universe"**

Frederick Wiseman and WNET/13, for **"Juvenile Court"**

WPVI-TV, Philadelphia, for **"Public Bridges and Private Riches"**

DuPont-Columbia Citations, 1973–1974

KAUM Radio, Houston, for **"Mass Murders"**

KMOX-TV, St. Louis, for **"Sixteen in Webster Grove, Eight Years Later"**

KNBC-TV, Los Angeles, for **"The European Connection"**

MARILYN BAKER AND KQED-TV, SAN FRANCISCO, for **SLA and Hearst kidnapping coverage**

KQED-TV, SAN FRANCISCO, for **"2,251 Days"**

WCIA-TV, CHAMPAIGN-URBANA, for **"CIA Reports"**

WHAS RADIO AND WHAS-TV, LOUISVILLE, for **tornado coverage**, April 3, 1974

WMC-TV, MEMPHIS, for **"Trouble in Mound Bayou"**

WNEW RADIO, NEW YORK, for **"The Hidden Passenger"**

WTVJ-TV, MIAMI, for **"The Sex Offenders"**

The Alfred I. duPont-Columbia University Survey Awards in Broadcast Journalism

A Report From The Director for the Year 1972–1973

The following report was issued in the fall of 1973 to accompany the announcement of the Alfred I. duPont–Columbia University Awards in Broadcast Journalism for the season of 1972–1973. Awards and Citations for that year are listed at the end of the report.

THE ALFRED I. DUPONT AWARDS, established by the late Jessie Ball duPont in memory of her husband to honor public service and outstanding news commentary by the nation's broadcasters, have existed now for thirty years.

In 1968 the Columbia University Graduate School of Journalism was invited to administer the awards. At that time it was decided to expand the program by making regular surveys upon which five to ten awards—for excellence in broadcast journalism—would be based. Periodic reports growing from the surveys would appraise the state of news and public affairs broadcasting. By naming the sluggards and villains as well as the heroes, we hoped to put the achievement of the nation's best broadcast journalists in proper perspective.

In March 1968 we had little idea of the importance and magnitude of the task we had undertaken. Then came the murders of Martin Luther King, Jr., and Robert Kennedy, the race and student upheavals, the Democratic convention of 1968, and, eventually, on the eve of our first Awards Ceremony and the publication of our first Survey, Vice-President Agnew's Des Moines speech attacking the network newsmen as "a tiny, enclosed fraternity of privileged men elected by no one and enjoying a monopoly sanctioned and licensed by government."

The issue was joined and the full importance of broadcast journalism to all Americans was dramatically acknowledged. In the years that followed, the courage, skill, and forbearance of all journalists, but particularly those in the broadcast media, were tested as never before.

However, the DuPont Survey and Awards are not concerned only with the large national picture. Since 1968, the staff and jurors have spent a minimum of a month each summer screening the best journalism from local stations as well. The material considered represents the tip of an enormous pyramid, which includes, in addition to the day-to-day monitoring of network news and public affairs, the local observations of sixty-five DuPont correspondents and the recommendations of such attentive and concerned national service organizations as the League of Women Voters, the YWCA, and the American Association of University Women. Finally, the news directors of the principal radio and TV stations in all fifty states have been invited to submit their best work and to comment on their own operations and on broadcast journalism in general. More than a thousand have taken part since the Surveys began.

Five years ago the quality of the exhibits, particularly those from local TV stations, however worthy and well-meant, was unprepossessing. The subject matter tended to be parochial; the technical competence frequently was low.

By this past summer, the jurors found the situation greatly changed. Five years ago only one local documentary was found by the DuPont jurors to be comparable in scope and technique to the best network product. This year there were dozens. The same improvement was noted in other areas of news and public affairs.

The problem of giving credit where credit was due was only partly solved by voting eleven citations for distinction in addition to nine DuPont-Columbia Awards for excellence in broadcast journalism. The awards and citations still left unhonored a large number of journalists who rivaled former prizewinners in seriousness and skill.

Local broadcasters were deep into subjects that they had seldom had the will, skill, or money to explore in years past except at the most superficial level—the energy crisis, pollution, land use, law and order, urban decay, minorities, TV journalism itself. Beginning with their local expression, broadcasters opened the problems out to include their national and international aspects. The results, firmly grounded in familiar detail, were frequently more meaningful than their necessarily wide-angled network equivalents. This year only four out of twenty award and citation winners were the work of network news departments, and it was not necessarily because the networks had had an off-year.

Chances had been taken; investigations and experiments launched by local stations that networks with their vast budgets and unwillingness to fail could not frequently risk. The off-network product often had a human dimension, an originality and freshness, a broad-mindedness along with a specificity that the central operations missed.

It would be dishonest, however, not to point out that there were still a great many stations not heard from or reported on negatively by our informants as offering little or nothing in news and public affairs worth a juror's time and attention. The do-nothings outnumbered their betters five to one, and among them were some of the nation's most profitable broadcast operations.

Further, there was the ungrateful consideration that however splendid the examples the DuPont jurors were privileged to see, these hours of splendor, even on stations (and networks) most dedicated to news and public affairs, were few and far between. And, in a few conspicuous and painful instances, the hours were declining in frequency. Some of yesterday's heroes had apparently lost the will to fight.

For however glossy their final appearance on the air, the DuPont prizewinners still represented the end of a long struggle against unfavorable odds. The achievement of the broadcast journalist was all the more impressive when you acknowledged that to dig up a difficult story or pin down a slippery one remained only a small part of his ordeal, an ordeal that in the past five years had in many ways increased rather than diminished.

Ironically, those responsible for the discomfort of broadcast journalists were often responsible—willingly or not—for their triumphs. At various times these friendly enemies assumed the guise of government official, management, sponsor, public, and of the broadcast journalist himself.

According to DuPont correspondents and station news directors reporting to the Survey on the period July 1, 1972, to June 30, 1973, from which this year's winners were selected, the enemies of excellence were still there. Attempts at government interference peaked, dramatically declined, and then rose again. Management became both more enthusiastic and more intrusive. Sponsors, with a few significant exceptions, continued to withhold their support (except for the sure thing). However, the public seemed to lose some of its apathy. And the newsmen themselves, after beginning the year in desperation, ended it with a surge of hope.

Government threats, carefully orchestrated, reached a climax mid-season when, in December, President Nixon's principal broadcast adviser, Clay T. Whitehead, told a meeting of Sigma Delta Chi in Indianapolis: "Station managers and network officials who fail to act to correct imbalance or consistent bias from the networks or who acquiesce by silence can only be considered willing participants, to be held fully accountable by the broadcaster's community at license renewal time."

If he expected local stations, traditionally more conservative than networks, to rush to his support in an obvious attempt to inhibit network news operations, he was disappointed. Of more than two hundred stations reporting their reactions to the Survey, only fifteen saw any merit in Whitehead's pointed suggestions. Many more perceived them as a threat to their own integrity no less than to the integrity of the networks.

Said one Virginia news director in favor:

> Personally, I agreed. The network bias, when it is obvious, is not shared by this part of the country. We broadcasters who accept the network news service should "talk back" to it, and when we remain silent we default on a responsibility that any journalist should take seriously.

On the unfavorable side, which outnumbered those in favor ten to one, a midwestern newsman commented:

> I am not in the position to second-guess the network newsmen, who have a great deal more information of the stories they cover at their disposal. I believe it is poor journalism to second-guess reporters who have covered the story in the field. It's reporting from a point of ignorance rather than a point of informed intelligence. We have no intention of setting ourselves up as censors of the network newscasts.

From South Carolina:

> Either naïve or peculiarly vicious. Could mean almost complete atrophy of meaningful national news coverage. I do not accept that there is "consistent bias" nor that, if there is, it's practical to correct it at the local level. Function of local news departments is primarily local and area news.

From Kentucky:

> An obvious intimidation and threat directly from the White
> House—an attempt to censor all unfavorable news and very,
> very frightening—might have worked if the Administration
> had not gotten into trouble.

The Indianapolis speech was the culmination of a series of
attacks against broadcasters that began with Vice-President Agnew's Des Moines statement in 1969. The attacks were admittedly
intended to counteract or reverse a media attitude that the
Administration saw as anti-Nixon and that most broadcasters saw
as an attempt to maintain objectivity in the face of increasing
political pressures.

Apart from the Administration's hostility to broadcast journalists, which had expressed itself in proposed legislation and executive action (notably the vetoing of the bill proposing long-term
funding of public TV) as well as outspoken criticism, there were the
other continuing governmental threats. They included the shutting
off of access by government agencies, the possibility of subpoenas
and contempt charges, the uncertainty of the application of the
First Amendment to broadcast journalism. More ambiguous in
their effect on broadcast journalism were a flood of license
challenges frequently connected with news and public affairs, and
the Fairness Doctrine, which more and more special pleaders liked
to invoke as justification for their contention that in a "controversial" story every damaging fact had to be matched by a favorable
one.

There were several attempts by broadcasters during the year to
explain their predicament to the public at documentary length.
None was more complete or lucid than KPIX San Francisco's
"And Now the News," one of a series of hour-long Expanded
Eyewitness News programs in prime time, which dealt expertly
with important local subjects and their national implications.
Among the subjects were urban rapid transit, mental hospitals and
their alternatives, and land use.

Unfortunately, after a season of local documentaries that
equaled any in the nation, KPIX could still complain of lack of
sponsor support and low ratings.

The most successful attack from Washington remained that
nebulous and yet potent one against the broadcaster's credibility.
The endless accusations of bias and lack of balance were effective

enough to loose a stream of invective against the networks from officials and the public which seemed to label all bad news incredible. More than one news director saw his effectiveness decline in an inverse ratio to the realism of his reporting. On a national level, William Paley, the head of CBS, canceled all analysis following presidential speeches, ostensibly to avoid the slightest appearance of unfairness.

Despite the most rugged twelve months in its history, public TV still was responsible for four out of twenty DuPont-Columbia Awards and Citations. Two were strictly local efforts: KCET Los Angeles' outstanding regular coverage of its black and chicano communities, and KQED San Francisco's "The Great California Land Grab," a production by the station's nightly "Newsroom" giving the lurid local ramifications of a nationwide ecological and economic rip-off.

The other two PTV productions singled out by the jurors were broadcast coast-to-coast: Elizabeth Drew's admirable series of interview-portraits for NPACT, "Thirty Minutes With . . . ," TV interrogation at its most informed and incisive, and Craig Gilbert's mind-boggling exercise in cinema verité for WNET/13, "An American Family," which set new limits to what a TV producer could ask for from an American audience in the way of patience and sympathy.

Public tolerance of nonpolitical foibles of their fellow Americans was tested more frequently than ever during the year. "An American Family" exposed the viewer in a uniquely intimate way to such taboos as homosexuality and marital infidelity. Sexual aberrations were explored unflinchingly and without the slightest indication of passing judgment by several stations, including WNBC, New York, and WKYC, Cleveland, whose Montage series again demonstrated that local news staffs were not only capable of making a single high-quality documentary but could keep on making them through a full season. WTTG-TV Washington's series on transsexuals, which ran for a full week in both its evening and midday newscasts, was a virtuoso exercise in making the social outcast interesting if not attractive. More appealing was NPACT's hour-long treatment of the disabled, which gave a new insight into the engaging toughness of a minority knowing no racial, chrono-logical, or sexual boundaries.

Robert Northshield took another blameless minority, the or-phaned and abandoned children of the Vietnamese war, and made an NBC-TV essay, "The Sins of the Fathers," which established him as the medium's unquestioned poet of the youthful innocent adrift in a violent and cruel grown-up world.

A local station, WITI-TV, Milwaukee, did a remarkably thorough and humane exploration of a nationwide problem relating to the war: "Post Vietnam Syndrome," a form of psychic trauma that in Wisconsin as elsewhere in the country had led to violence and misery for many veterans and their families.

Perhaps the most successful example of drawing the totally rejected to the average American viewer's attention was "Death of a Sideshow" (KGW-TV, Portland, Oregon), ninety prime-time minutes on the inhabitants of the local skid row, one of the grimmest in the country. Before the program was over the viewer had some understanding not only of Portland's lost men, but also of one of the nation's handsomest cities and where it might be heading. A one-shot, mostly done on its own time over a period of sixteen months by the station's tiny, fully occupied news staff, the program demonstrated what a small, hard-pressed news staff with a small budget could do to discomfit and inform its audience.

Viewer comments phoned in during the broadcast ranged from "They are exploiting these people. . . . This is terrible" to "This is what TV should be about. . . . It should be rerun and put on national TV."

There was other evidence that public indifference to the troubling and unpleasant on TV might be moderating. With no attempt to jolly up their fare, the network newscasts appeared to be winning back the viewer who, according to statistics, had been drifting away from them during the past few years. The reversal of this disturbing trend could be interpreted as a vote of confidence and indication of a heightened popular concern about the things taking place in the nation and the world.

It could also reflect the steadily growing popularity of the adjacent local newscasts, which, according to a study made for the American Broadcasting Company, now outrated network news in eight out of ten of the top TV markets. In some cities the evening news was the single most viewed program on the TV schedule.

The success of newscasting might have been expected to bolster conventional documentaries, thanks to greater profits flowing back to the news and public affairs operation. In many cases it had the opposite effect. More than one news director rationalized that the growing audiences for newscasts justified breaking up major stories in order to get them before much larger groups than a conventional documentary would ever reach.

Mini-documentaries scattered in 5-minute segments over a week of newscasts, according to this line of reasoning, could command many times the number of viewers that a half-hour or hour-long prime-time program could. As more and more talent capable of producing first-rate documentaries was developed in stations across the country, witnessed by this year's phenomenal crop of full-scale, first-class projects, the mini-documentary became more and more prevalent.

Some examples of the mini-documentary format from network and local producers during the year were first rate, adding substance to what all too often had to be a superficial and breakneck summary of the day's news. Two series on the energy crisis on "The CBS Morning News" and "The CBS Evening News" did a fine job on a subject that dominated TV throughout the year. Equally exhaustive local explorations on the same subject were produced as regular documentaries by WMAQ-TV, Chicago, and KRON-TV, San Francisco.

Another "CBS Morning News" series took a difficult subject, banks, and managed to make it interesting in short takes over a series of days. However, the best examples of the split-news story remained the "CBS Evening News" crucial two-part treatment of Watergate in October 1972 (six months before the televised hearings began) and its devastating three-part essay on the Russian wheat deal. Both were delivered in segments much longer than the usual mini-documentary, probed deeply, and demanded strict attention from the viewer.

Among the best local examples of this form of TV journalism, which was growing in popularity and expertness, were two series on WCCO-TV, Minneapolis, one dealing with death in unflinching detail, the other with private security guards in the Twin Cities area. Other successful instances were WTOP-TV Washington's series on builders and land speculators around the nation's Capital and two extremely vivid series on food preparation and serving, one by WMAL-TV, Washington, and the other by WTVJ, Miami.

Still, for full impact, the mini-documentary series had to wait on the reediting and consecutive presentation as full documentaries that many of the best of them received. An outstanding example was Geraldo Rivera's "The Littlest Junkie—A Children's Story," a potent and painful essay on the effect of heroin addiction on unborn children, which first appeared in short segments on WABC-TV New York's evening newscast. As a half-hour documentary in prime time, it drew the highest rating for a news special in New York TV history.

Such mini-documentaries undoubtedly added quality and substance to the newscast addicted to the 45-second film clip. However, the presentation of serialized news stories as an alternative rather than a valuable supplement to a schedule of full-scale documentaries was alarming to anyone truly concerned for the quality and stature of broadcast journalism. Here the example of radio, where documentaries had been reduced to "actualities" and "actualities" to hourly headlines, all in the name of pleasing the audience, was an edifying and grim one.

Radio was almost, but not quite, a journalistic desert. Most major markets seemed to have at least one station capable of producing a decent newscast or documentary, whether they did so or not. Some smaller markets frequently did better. Radio station WJBO of Baton Rouge, Louisiana, had an outstanding record in investigative reporting last year, which included uncovering several local government scandals involving bribery and fraud and led to indictments as well as a $4.5 million suit for slander.

In the field of broadcast editorials, no one's record surpassed that of KNX, Los Angeles, which not only spoke out eloquently on important community issues, but reached out to bring in voices in the community who might not agree but could speak with equal authority and conviction on matters of controversy and concern. The result was one of the nation's most effective broadcasting forums.

The TV documentary, the form that remained the most demanding and rewarding in the repertoire of all journalism, was under attack on grounds other than its ability to gain and hold a maximum audience. A midwestern news director wrote:

> It is tough to get local firms to sponsor a news program when the content of that program tends to criticize the local establishment. But the "local establishment," political and otherwise, must be kept under careful scrutiny, and in our market other media seem to have abdicated that responsibility in favor of dollars.

PTV stations had allied problems. One reported:

> As a public television station, KQED does not have any "sponsors." The station does seek underwriting. Such underwriting has been somewhat harder to get in recent years. Many firms give as the reason—or excuse—the station's news program, "Newsroom," and its allegedly liberal stance. It is quite possible that administrative criticism has made it possi-

ble for some corporations to feel vindicated in turning down KQED's funding requests.

If advertisers in many markets lined up for newscasts, and one-third of the stations reporting to the Survey claimed increased advertising in the news, they still shied away from documentaries.

Sponsors also continued to try to influence news reporting in all forms by threatening to withdraw support when the news displeased them. More instances than ever were reported this year, including attempts at court injunctions and million-dollar lawsuits, all of them unsuccessful, most of them related to the increasing amount of consumer reporting on the air.

The ambivalence of broadcast newsmen's feelings toward the men who paid the bills (or at least channeled the public's money in their direction) was vividly witnessed—on air, coast-to-coast—by CBS News' "You and the Commercial." In sixty carefully balanced minutes (without commercial interruption) the program asked searching questions about the motives and manners of TV's principal backers, the advertisers of America. The result was not only an exceptionally well-made, entertaining, and illuminating program, but possibly the bravest network documentary of the year.

There was little competition in bravery. Despite the fact that networks and local stations reported their highest income since 1969, when a business recession and the withdrawal of cigarette advertising temporarily reduced broadcasters' profits, slashed budgets and schedules were not reinstated in many instances, at least so far as documentaries were concerned. Even the increased profits that the overall news and public affairs operations were undoubtedly bringing in were not likely to benefit the man who wanted space for treating an important idea at appropriate length.

In the expanding world of local news, 31 percent of the stations reported an increase during the year in budget for newscasts, only 14 percent for documentaries. As for staff, 25 percent had added to their personnel for newscasts, 8 percent for documentaries. Investigative journalism, encouraged by the example of Watergate, did well this year, with 15 percent of the stations reporting increased budgets and 8 percent more staff. In many instances this was the station's first specific commitment to this type of reporting.

WTIC, Hartford, not only gave full backing to a team of expert young investigative reporters, but allowed them a generous amount of air time as well. Probably the most distinguished of the excellent documentaries resulting was "The Nine-Year-Old in Norfolk Prison," an inquiry into the justice of the conviction of a mentally retarded twenty-eight-year-old black man for a brutal murder. Under their persistent examination, the evidence slowly eroded and a vivid picture of legal haste and callousness emerged. The investigators, John Sablón, black, and Brad Davis, white, did similarly searching and interesting jobs on such diverse subjects as cancer remissions and the reconstruction of the last months of a young drug addict who was shot in a Hartford back alley during an unsuccessful robbery.

The stations owned and operated by the networks continued to do a number of first-rate documentary essays put on the air by local news staffs. The fact that they were probably the best-heeled in the nation did not detract from the excellence of the product, which included WBBM-TV Chicago's "The Rape of Paulette" (CBS), an unflinching look at the crime of rape, which enlisted the cooperation of a number of attractive and articulate women who had been victims of particularly brutal attacks. A DuPont citation was voted to Bill Leonard and WRC-TV, Washington (NBC), for "Families on the Road to Somewhere," a program that was obviously intended as an antidote to the negative picture of American family life presented by other highly effective TV documentaries in the recent past and which succeeded in presenting its case without being sentimental or simplistic. Another citation went to William Turque and WNBC-TV, New York, for "Saturday Night at Fort Apache," his fly-on-the-wall treatment of the activities of one New York City police precinct on a typically violent weekend. It was proof of how close to the big city's gut a TV reporter and cameraman can get.

Broadcast groups had a less distinguished record during the year. A consistent top performer in the documentary field, Group W was making disturbing noises about disbanding its winning team, the Urban America Unit, which this year again earned a DuPont–Columbia Award for ". . . And the Rich Shall Inherit the Earth," its definitive treatment of the growth of the big agricultural conglomerate and the tragically rapid disappearance of the small family farm in America. The program's selection and presentation of illustrative detail to tell its sad story was impeccable, the obvious result of an unbeatable combination of experience and concern.

Documentary production outside both network and local stations was represented with distinction this year by two documentaries from World Horizon Films, an arm of the Catholic Missionary Order of Maryknoll. Both were the work of Father Donald Casey, M.M. One, "The Healer," dealing with the natives of the altiplano of Peru, was magnificent both in its photography and its ability to convey the sense of a civilization totally removed from the average North American viewer. "Campamento" was a successful effort to view, from the inside out, a working-class suburb, since decimated by the junta, of Santiago, Chile. It was an example of high-quality documentary-making and a historical record of prime importance.

Another documentary important because of its timing and the thoroughness and objectivity with which it looked at a neglected subject was ABC's "Chile: Experiment in Red," aired just six weeks before the coup. Viewers were given a remarkably clear picture of a country that turned out to be on the verge of chaos.

Despite the talent at their disposal and such instances of individual excellence, the networks were not unusually generous in the documentary field.

Except for Watergate, national public TV, the pacesetter in hard-hitting and controversial public affairs programming in the recent past, had much less to boast about, thanks to a variety of pressures.

The commercial networks, which did yeoman service in their coverage of Watergate and added a respectable number of late night hours to consider important breaking stories, could not bring themselves to put many serious or controversial documentaries in prime time, the real proof of TV's dedication to informing its audience. At the end of the season, "First Tuesday," one of the two network magazine shows responsible for giving broad attention to big stories at a reasonable hour, was canceled, leaving CBS' exemplary "60 Minutes" alone in the field. Still, the CBS series, which contained some of the most consistently adult journalism on the air, was not allotted a regular prime-time slot and was subject to long blackouts to accommodate more profitable and popular programming. This meant that nowhere on the commercial networks' mid-evening schedule could the American public find a weekly spot devoted to news and public affairs.

This fact made it all the more remarkable and praiseworthy that with so little encouragement from the loci of power—the government, the sponsor, the management—an increasing number of top caliber news and public affairs programs kept getting on the air.

There were two possible explanations for this mystery: the persistence, courage, and increasing skill of broadcast journalists as individuals and as a profession, and the growing ability among a supposedly apathetic and restless American public to sit still and pay attention.

—MARVIN BARRETT

The Alfred I. duPont-Columbia University Awards, 1972–1973

ARTHUR HOLCH AND ABC NEWS, for "Chile: Experiment in Red"

IRV DRASNIN AND CBS NEWS, for "You and the Commercial"

ROBERT NORTHSHIELD AND NBC NEWS, for "The Sins of the Fathers"

DICK HUBERT AND GROUP W, for ". . . And the Rich Shall Inherit the Earth"

WBBM-TV, CHICAGO, for "The Rape of Paulette"

WTIC-TV, HARTFORD, for "The Nine-Year-Old in Norfolk Prison"

KGW-TV, PORTLAND, OREGON, for "Death of a Sideshow"

ELIZABETH DREW AND NPACT, for "Thirty Minutes With . . ."

KNX RADIO, LOS ANGELES, for Editorials on important community issues

DuPont-Columbia Citations, 1972–1973

KCET-TV, LOS ANGELES, for minority coverage

GEORGE T. OSTERKAMP AND KPIX-TV, SAN FRANCISCO, for "And Now the News"

KQED-TV, SAN FRANCISCO, for "The Great California Land Grab"

GERALDO RIVERA AND WABC-TV, NEW YORK, for "The Littlest Junkie: A Children's Story"

WITI-TV, Milwaukee, for **"Post Vietnam Syndrome"**

William Turque and WNBC-TV, New York, for **"Saturday Night at Fort Apache"**

Craig Gilbert and WNET/13, New York, for **"An American Family"**

Bill Leonard and WRC-TV, Washington, D.C., for **"Families on the Road to Somewhere"**

Don Hewitt and CBS News, for **"60 Minutes"**

Rev. Donald J. Casey and World Horizon Films, for **"The Healer" and "Campamento"**

WJBO Radio, Baton Rouge, for **investigative reporting**

First Amendment:
Challenge and Commitment

by Lowell P. Weicker

PROLOGUE

THIS ARTICLE was completed on August 16, 1974. It was due
months earlier. It could have been written months earlier because
nothing has transpired that alters what needs saying.

Neither the president's resignation, the June 23 tape, the House
Judiciary Committee votes on impeachment, nor the defection of
Republican congressional leaders from Richard Nixon's side added
any new dimensions to what we all *knew* about the mangling of the
First Amendment of the Constitution of the United States. The
search for a smoking gun in the sense of freedom of the press had
ended months ago with the discovery of an artillery barrage of
First Amendment abuses. But not being as exciting as tracking a
personality—especially one as prominent as the president of the
United States—the discovery was forgotten by the time the next
morning's newspaper was picked up off the doorstep. Therein lies
Watergate's greatest disaster potential. For Watergate was never so
much the story of Richard Nixon as it is the story of a
governmental and political "Circus Maximus" with Americans, not
Romans, obliged to respond to the pleas of a Constitution in the
dust.

As a people, we are slow to anger and quick to forgiveness. All I
suggest is that this national strength will become a fatal weakness if
forgiveness is made synonymous with forgetfulness.

1973's question was: "What did the president know and when
did he know it?"

1974's question is: "What are we going to do about it?"

"It" is not Richard Nixon. "It" is us and one part of us is—

> Congress shall make no law . . . abridging the freedom of
> speech or of the press; or the right of the people peaceably to
> assemble . . . .

CATALOGUE

When the Long Island newspaper *Newsday* decided to run an in-depth article on Bebe Rebozo, the White House sicced the IRS on the reporter and had his income tax returns audited. An FBI agent was sent to investigate the newspaper's offices. An antitrust suit against the newspaper was recommended. There are even strong indications that the Secret Service kept tabs on reporters while they were in Florida writing the story.

A key prospectus for intimidation of the press was the infamous memorandum from Jeb Magruder to H. R. Haldeman (October 17, 1969) entitled "The Shot-gun versus the Rifle," which laid out the plot for influencing news coverage of the White House. [See Appendix V.]

Among its recommendations was one to "utilize the antitrust division [of the Justice Department] to investigate various media relating to antitrust violations. Even the possible threat of antitrust action, I think, would be effective in changing their views," Magruder declared. The memo, which included twenty-one specific requests from President Nixon to counter stories he personally deemed unfavorable to the Administration, didn't stop at the threat of antitrust actions. Magruder also proposed getting the IRS "to look into the various [press] organizations that we are most concerned about" and to have the FCC officially monitor network news. Such threats, Magruder argued, "will probably turn their approach."

When the late NBC newscaster Chet Huntley wrote a piece in *Life* magazine containing what the White House felt were unfavorable remarks, Lawrence Higby authored a memo suggesting retaliation. It contained these revealing sentiments: "The point behind the whole thing is that we don't care about Huntley—he's leaving anyway. What we are trying to do is tear down the institution. Huntley will go out in a blaze of glory and we should attempt to pop his bubble." [See Appendix I.]

"Tear down the institution." There it is, spelled out with ominous clarity.

One heavy-handed effort to bring broadcasters to heel came in a series of meetings between Charles W. Colson and the chief executives of the three networks. Colson observed in a memo [Appendix VIII] that the executives were "terribly nervous" about the FCC and that "although they tried hard to disguise this, it was obvious. The harder I pressed them (CBS and NBC) the more accommodating, cordial, and almost apologetic they became."

He concluded by saying: "I think we can dampen their ardor for putting on 'loyal opposition' type programs."

One of the most brazen tries at intimidating newsmen involved the FBI investigation of respected CBS news reporter Daniel Schorr. When the fact that he was being probed broke loose, the White House clumsily put out the alibi that Schorr was actually being investigated because he was under consideration for appointment to a high Administration position. Fred Malek assumed the blame for the investigation even though it had been ordered by Haldeman.

Newspapers and reporters uncovering the Watergate story were systematically ridiculed and attacked. Four months after the break-in, for example, the "official White House position" was that articles about Donald Segretti and his dirty tricks operations were "stories based on hearsay, character assassination, innuendo, or guilt by association." Even when those who made such statements had been briefed by Segretti himself to the contrary. When it became impossible for the White House to cover up the truth any longer, its chief spokesman blithely announced this statement was now "inoperative."

The record is replete with incidents showing the news media being exploited by using them to transmit stories known to be improper, misleading, and, in some cases, totally false—this from the same Administration which, when fighting for its life, bitterly denounced news leaks.

On one occasion, Howard Hunt testified he had used confidential FBI files to prepare a derogatory article on Leonard Boudin, an attorney in the Ellsberg case, which information was passed on to the press by Colson.

Haldeman stated in a memo that "we need to get out people to put out the story on the foreign or Communist money that was used in support of demonstrations against the President in 1972. We should tie all 1972 demonstrations to McGovern and thus to the Democrats as part of the peace movement." Even though there was no evidence to support such stories, the memo went on to recommend that "we should let [columnists] Evans and Novak put it out and then be asked about it to make the point that we knew and the president said it was not to be used under any circumstances."

The technique of trying falsely to associate Senator McGovern with Communist money did not stop there. Patrick Buchanan recommended a number of news strategies in the campaign, including "the Ellsberg connections, tying McGovern to him [Ellsberg] and his crime," because "if the country goes to the polls in November scared to death of McGovern, thinking him vaguely anti-American and radical and pro the left-wingers and militants, then they will vote against him—which means for us." Another clear abuse of executive power against the press.

What I characterized as "one of the most cold-blooded memos to come out of the White House" during this period was written by the same Buchanan. It analyzed the pros and cons of a press attack on Dr. Ellsberg. The memo began: "Having considered the matter until the early hours, my view is that there are some dividends to be derived from Project Ellsberg." Personally, he confided: "It would assuredly be psychologically satisfying to cut the innards from Ellsberg."

Buchanan concluded, however, that the Ellsberg issue would not be "turned around in the public mind by a few well-placed leaks." He then stated, to make his position clear: "This is not to argue that the effort is not worthwhile—but that simply we ought not now to start investing major personnel resources in the kind of covert operations not likely to yield any major political dividends to the president."

Buchanan was not inhibited by any such old-fashioned considerations as legality or morality. Just a pragmatic judgment that it wouldn't pay off.

Another example of peddling wrongfully obtained information was Buchanan's testimony about documents surreptitiously taken from the Muskie campaign and photographed by "Fat Jack" Buckley. Buchanan testified that he "did get the material on two occasions, and did recommend that it be sent to columnists Evans and Novak. Evans and Novak did print, on two occasions I believe, material from Muskie's campaign."

The White House also obtained secretly from the Commerce Department information relating to Senator Muskie's apparently legitimate efforts to help the troubled Maine sugar beet industry and leaked that information to the press for political purposes.

Also recommended for press leaking was information from the Department of Defense as to Senator McGovern's personal and confidential war records.

Lastly, the now famous "Hunt cables" were, in effect, an attempt to rewrite history. To rewrite a portion of Vietnam history for unwitting use by the nation's news media.

EPILOGUE

The attacks, strident and surreptitious, on the news media by the Colsons, Agnews, Magruders, Buchanans, Zieglers, Clawsons, and Haldemans are stilled and the press is free, not manipulated. But other persons will have another run at the First Amendment, probably much in the same manner and for the same reasons as set forth in the Catalogue. Whether a John Sirica, Sam Ervin, Bob Woodward, or Carl Bernstein is around is something I'd just as soon not gamble on when we have a government of laws available and not men.

Rather to legislate shield laws, even though Gerry Ford and Jerald terHorst are "nice guys." If the press is to remain independent while the Sixth Amendment (accused's right to witnesses) is to remain operative, then the resolution of a potential Constitutional conflict better be in writing—regardless of who is in the White House.

Rather to legislate congressional oversight of the FBI, CIA, SS, MI, etc., even though Clarence Kelley, William Colby, et al. are "nice guys." If law enforcement and intelligence is to be civilian-controlled, it must be congressionally accountable.

Rather to legislate limitations on access to IRS data, even though Bill Simon and Don Alexander may be "nice guys." If privacy is to be respected by a federal government awesomely equipped to be inquisitive, then it had best be established by law rather than by individual.

I'm not worried about the country overreacting to Watergate. The odds favor no change at all. With what *we now* know, such inaction would make all of us participants in a Constitutional cover-up.

To believe one man's resignation resolved Watergate is to believe in a form of government that is not American democracy. The problems of our democracy can only be resolved by the democracy, and that's us, not just him.

So to work!

The People and the News

by Michael Novak

WHEN AT MY DESK high up on the forty-second floor of the Time-Life building I look out at the other skyscrapers of mid-Manhattan and imagine all the other managers, assistants, lawyers, trustees, officers, and publicists who fly on the same airplanes with me and read the same magazines, *here,* I think, is the culture of the national news. It is not the most populous culture of America. It has little emotional, symbolic connection with the Americas I love best; yet it could have, if we nourished our many possibilities.

During 1973–74, both Theodore H. White and David Halberstam tried to describe why so many of the American people dislike and distrust the national news media. Neither their discussions nor those of others, it seems, have yet hit the mark. The national news media—print and video—are somehow disconnected from large numbers of the American people: agreed. But the nature of this disconnection is difficult to state. The following reflections are an effort to contribute to a more satisfactory connection in the future.

Halberstam describes in *Esquire* (April 1974) a typical accusation against the media: Richard Nixon is a victim "of an Eastern-bred, Eastern-educated elite working for Eastern newspapers and the great networks. They do not like him and never have; they will never give him a fair chance. They are against him because of his ideas . . . because he is too American, too representative of American culture. . . . His vision of America was more accurate than theirs. For that, for being more right about the country, they can never forgive him."

In reply to this accusation, Halberstam argues that the press is not "liberal" in any simple ideological sense; most national reporters, like other Americans, have rather complicated political and social views. Moreover, he notes, most national news reporters are not in fact easterners. (The same issue of *Esquire* carries a long portrait of Dan Rather of Houston.) Chet Huntley, David Brinkley, Harry Reasoner, Walter Cronkite, Eric Sevareid, James Reston,

Tom Wicker, and many other stars of the news were born, bred, and educated in the heart of the country. "Eastern," indeed, is an odd term. To be born in Queens or Newark, in Dorchester or Lackawanna or North Pittsburgh, is not exactly to be "eastern" in the sense intended.

Halberstam goes wrong, however, in arguing that what makes national reporters special is their critical faculty. They are "more skeptical and less reverent than their fellow Americans," he says, but truck drivers and construction workers are quite capable of irreverence; farmers in Iowa and ranchers in Wyoming have been known to be skeptical; some people of Missouri say "show me." It is not that they are eastern, Halberstam then writes of reporters; they are "a product of something more complex, an educational system that is largely eastern (but often not: Oberlin, Stanford, Tulane, Northwestern, Reed), where the *critical facility* [sic] is appreciated, developed, and honed. The ability to sit outside, think, and analyze is appreciated." Here the Harvard-educated Halberstam betrays his own outrageous bias: "Most American universities do not develop the critical faculty; they mass-produce education. . . ." For if you check the school roster from which our national journalists come—Willie Morris, Bill Moyers, James Naughton, Bill Kovach, R. W. Apple, Max Frankel, Frank Mankiewicz, and all the others—the distribution seems quite representative of small colleges, sprawling state universities, Catholic schools, subway campuses—all the varieties of American schools. The point Halberstam seems to be aiming at is quite different from the one he states. A university education changes the class status of reporters. They are not any more cynical or skeptical or critical than ordinary American farmers, workers, or other taxpayers. But they do tend to identify with different objects of reverence, to exhibit a different cognitive style, and to nourish a different vision of the nation's past, present reality, and future. Their interests are different from those of many of their fellow citizens.

Nonetheless, journalists do have a preponderant role in shaping the public universe of discourse. *Their* vision becomes a public fact, in the papers and on television. Other Americans must cling to their own private vision, defending it against media bombardment. In an odd way, national reporters have a majority public power and other citizens feel like various minorities of dissenters.

The media create a public symbolic reality, a mainline mythical world more real than any private world. It is a world in which status is ascribed, narrative position is assigned ("forward-look-ing," "old-fashioned," "timely"), and values are lavishly or faintly praised (the "new" morality, the "old" morality). However realistic and correct a private person may judge his or her own attitudes to be, when these attitudes are not confirmed in the public media they cannot help seeming rather sectarian, narrow, even "uninformed." It is assumed that the media represent some public norm, or at least a mainstream reality—and that those not in tune with it are quaint, out of touch, not "with it," not where "it's at." (What is this "it" that we should be "with"? The action, the front edge, that which makes "news." "It" makes news and news discerns "it." So the media are arbiters of relevance.)

Many professors and intellectuals do not identify with what is represented as reality in the supercultural seven: *The New York Times,* the Washington *Post, Time, Newsweek,* ABC, CBS, and NBC. Many other citizens also do not identify reality with the reports of the supercultural seven. But the supercultural seven *do* create a reality with which all citizens have to deal.

The media, in a word, are instruments of culture as well as of information; of status, position, value preference; of the enforce-ment of a public reality.

It is not, then, that national reporters have more native skepticism than Missouri farmers or more native cynicism than Sicilian longshoremen. It is rather that they are, as Halberstam puts it, "a product" of "something more complex, an educational system," and have the ability to "sit outside." That they are a "product" indicates that they are not quite so individual, not quite so *self*-critical, as Halberstam suggests. And it is not so much an educational system as a class system of which they are the product. That they have the luxury "to sit outside" is mainly the function of their extraordinarily high class position. Who can forget George Herman questioning Senator George McGovern during the Cali-fornia primary of 1972 about the senator's $1,000 "demogrants"? What will the impact of these grants be, Herman asked incredu-lously, on people with ordinary incomes, well, like myself? Let us suppose for simplicity's sake that Herman's income was $25,000 per year. That placed him in the top 5 percent of all Americans. He seemed oblivious to the distance between himself and others. Less than a quarter of American families have an income over $15,000 per year; and the vast majority of families find their income is fixed for the rest of their lives by age thirty-five. National journalists tend to lose touch with the daily economic hardships of a majority of the American people.

National journalists participate in the culture of the upper classes—in the mobile, fluid, national superculture of America's higher circles. Most do not rank as high on scales of status as the landed rich or university professors; they are subject to snubs and slights, too. But from the point of view of those who travel less and earn less and meet no celebrities, national journalists live in the world of glamour, wealth, status, and power. They are no longer representatives of ordinary people.

A national journalist like Tom Wicker, say, outranks most U.S. congressmen, and even a great many U.S. senators, in most social contexts—is better known, has a greater public power, has a certain power *over* "men of power" (just as Rich Morgan has in *Facing the Lions*). The national press represents a far greater social power in a postindustrial society than it used to represent in an agricultural society; for so much of today's marketing and sudden obsolescence depends upon images projected by the media. Not only private careers, even whole industries, depend upon image-making. The makers of images are today stronger than local realities, because outside of the public information systems social ties are weaker than ever before. What the public networks say is true is less and less balanced by effective and organized private networks. Senator Hugh Scott is known to the citizens of Pennsylvania through the media, not through personal contacts. He is what he appears to be. Few public figures are so well known to their constituencies apart from the media that they are invulnerable to fluctuations in media approval.

What people resent in the media, therefore, is not the irreverence of outsiders, not the sharp skeptical minds of innocent, powerless reporters. Quite the opposite. What people resent is the new economic power of the media, the myth-making that erects great new realities. They also resent the arrogance represented so subtly by Halberstam's essay, the arrogance that tells people every day: "We're smarter, better informed, more critical, more skeptical than you. You've been mass-produced; we've been specially produced, custom-made." They also resent the fact that *they* are so often excluded. The news so seldom reflects their point of view, their values, their skepticism.

In the massive publicity about social reforms in the 60's, for example, national reporters seemed to be the true believers, the enthusiasts, even the missionaries. It was ordinary people who were at times (while providing huge voting majorities) more skeptical; and for that they were sometimes chided for being reactionary, stupid, and mean. Concerning school bussing, it was again millions of ordinary people, white and black, who were skeptical and cynical; national reporters tended—and still tend in 1974, although with noticeable wavering—to believe that some great ideal would be realized through so fallible and flawed an instrument. For ordinary people understand the realities of class, pluralism, and institutional racism in America; their key life decisions about where to live are made with these realities in mind. The children of a Polish auto worker, none of whose family has ever gone to college, will experience no class gain if bussed to a school in a black neighborhood. His children will not be going to a better school than the one they are in. Why should people who believe in the possibility of upward mobility surrender to enforced downward mobility? Such people are liable to be more skeptical than David Halberstam and his colleagues—and reasonably resentful of the palpable moralistic innuendos they are made to suffer because they cannot make their stubborn realism go away.

The class bias in which national reporters share is rather well described by Theodore H. White in his chapter "Power Struggle: President versus Press" in *The Making of the President 1972*. White places more stress than seems illuminating on the fact that the great newspapers lumped under the rubric "the Eastern Liberal Press" are family-owned or family-controlled. He says these "newspaper families of the baronial press are the last great aristocracy in American life." His description of their values is revealing:

> . . . a sense of patrician responsibility, a sense of the past, both of their own communities and of their nation, and an invulnerability to common fears, common pressures, the clamor of stockholders and advertisers that weaken the vigor of lesser publishers. They understand power better than most politicians; their families have outlived most political families, locally and nationally; they can make politicians—and, on many occasions, break them.
> . . . They insist on their own concept of honor and style. The families that own the great newspapers of the Liberal Press have the taste, and the purse, for the finest newswriting; they invite from their staffs elegant, muscled, investigative reporting. . . . These families regard their star reporters as almost sacred—as great racing families regard their horses,

horse-handlers and jockeys. Men and women are proud to work for such publishers; their reporters set the style for all other reporters everywhere. . . . They live in a world of their own.

The media are not powerless in America. And the supercultural seven, at least, are thickly tied to the traditional patrician elites of American history. "Power in America today is control of the means of communication," White writes, quoting Arthur Schlesinger, Jr. Ordinary people have every reason to be skeptical of powerful institutions. They are just as likely to be betrayed by broadcast journalism as by any other institution. It seems quite clear that the values and interests of "the opinion industry of Manhattan," the perceptions "of the universities, of the opinion set, of the intellectuals" are not identical to those whose incomes are lower, whose cultures are diverse, whose education is different, whose narrative vision of the United States and whose grasp of the class, racial, and ethnic struggles of our history is different.

There are, then, many critics of the national news apparatus. Many feel that the newsmakers live in a world different from their own. But such critics do not always state accurately what it is they oppose. The following accusations miss the mark:

(1) *The national media lack objectivity.* But suppose national reporters presented conservative views with more sympathy? The problem is not lack of objectivity, distance, or coolness. Every editor and every newsman faces enormous problems of selection. Moreover, news must always be presented in the form of a "story." And to choose the form, narrative line, and point of view for telling a story is not plausibly called an exercise in "objectivity." For the narrator is necessarily part of the story. A story may be more or less fair, complete, accurate to known facts, revealing, illuminating, etc.; one thing it cannot be is "objective," impersonal, read off by some scientific instrument.

When we hear a news story, we can hardly help asking *whose* story it is. (Did it appear in *Human Events*? In *The New York Times*?) Some storytellers we trust; others we do not. Newsmen are supposed to be truthful storytellers. They must meet criteria of truthfulness and reliability. But these criteria derive from the realm of human relations, not from the realm of scientific investigators detached from the objects they study. "Objectivity" describes a scientific ideal; it does not describe what a truthful journalist achieves. Journalism seeks a truth that is neither the truth of science nor the truth of the poet or the novelist. The ideal of truthfulness in journalism needs a new name, a name that accurately reflects journalism's unique necessities. We would like journalists to be able to portray many positions with sympathy and, as it were, from the inside; to be able to put themselves in other persons' positions; to report with insight and accuracy even what they do not like. We don't want them to be "objective" but to be fair and multi-sympathetic.

(2) *The media exhibit an eastern bias.* It is plain that a number of family-owned newspapers and individual television stations in Los Angeles, San Francisco, St. Louis, Louisville, Chicago, and other places share the world view and attitudes incorrectly described as "eastern." The force of the word "eastern" here is not geographical but historical. It points to the continuance of that high civil religion whose roots in American history lie in New England and Virginia: that cultivated patrician respect for law, the individual, due process, moral reform, and the like that represents one among several American civil religions. (I have tried to elaborate this notion in *Choosing Our King.*) Richard Nixon, by contrast, identifies with the more salesmanlike denominational civil religion widespread across Protestant America, intermediate between the high civil religion (Elliot Richardson) and the evangelical civil religion (George Wallace, Lyndon Johnson). The high civil religion of the Northeast is extremely influential in American institutions but represents far fewer citizens than the other major civil religions.

(3) *The media exhibit liberal bias.* The use of "right" and "left" (terms that derive from nineteenth-century French politics) and "conservative" and "liberal" (terms derived from nineteenth-century British politics) are mischievous when applied to American politics. American politics is pluralistic. Several major civil religions are in competition, several different cultures, several different class, racial, and ethnic interests. Almost every person and every group is sometimes "liberal" and sometimes "conservative," and what motivates each is not some pure doctrine either of liberalism or of conservatism. The motivating forces in American politics are almost always group interests.

Our politics is complicated by the fact that each person belongs to more than one group, and that each group is involved in more than one coalition with other groups. American politics is oriented to personal and group interests, and these interests range from economic, material interests to interests of recognition, pride, representation, and (especially among the highly educated and the affluent) to doctrinal or attitudinal interests. These are not necessarily narrow interests. But they are interests.

In some respects, Senators Fulbright and Ervin are "liberal," in others "conservative"; similarly with the American Jewish Congress or the Catholic workingmen in Homestead, Pennsylvania. Few Americans try to be doctrinally pure. Most try to be realistic about their own interests, as they perceive them. National newsmen, too, have interests—interests, for example, in a supercultural rather than subcultural point of view and in the patrician high civil religion of their employers. Both conservative and liberal journalists on the national level have such interests. Indeed, many Americans do not make sharp distinctions between liberal and conservative newsmen so much as between national and local newsmen. Not very many Americans actually live in "superculture"; almost all live in some subculture or other. For this reason the national newsmen, speaking to superculture, are always out of focus in the eyes of many who live in other cultures.

National news reporters fail to make connection with many people because of a structural flaw in the concept of "national news." In order to take a national point of view and to report on events from a national perspective, a more or less national language, style, and point of view have been constructed. While there are some millions of Americans who *do* live in this national superculture, there are many millions who do not, who identify rather with their own cultural or regional history. A large majority of Americans has never been on an airplane. Even a great many colleges and universities tend to reflect local cultural or regional perspectives rather than national perspectives; they are agencies rather of local subculture than of national superculture. Moreover, the national superculture is not, precisely, cosmopolitan, except in flavor. It is true that persons from many subcultures enter into it. But, once there, tendencies they encounter are not so much directed toward gaining insight into and sympathy for the many subcultures of America as toward imagining the vast sprawling set of subcultures as some sort of inferior and homogeneous "middle America." That expression, "middle America," reveals an indifference to diversity that is not truly cosmopolitan.

There is a related structural flaw in the national news. Reporters are commonly sent into subcultures to "report on" what is happening there *from the perspective of* and *with the tastes of* representatives of the national superculture. Seldom does it happen that reporters go into communities in order *to express the perspec-*

tive, the way of life, and *the attitudes of* the members of that community. A vivid example of this difference occurred in the television reports on the riot at Attica. All three contending parties—the prisoners, the townspeople and relatives of the guards, and the families of the prisoners—felt that their own stories had been distorted. How could this be? Reporters, apparently, did not try to tell the three separate sorts of stories, in a full and sympathetic way, but rather to tell a single story. They simplified the story from their own point of view. They did not show it as a conflict among (at least) three separate cultures. Many stories are cut in this Procrustean way.

It would help national reporting, I think, if reporters were given freer rein to do what some of them could already do splendidly: to report *from* various American subcultures *to* the larger world, rather than to report *on* such subcultures from the perspective of the national culture. (This phrase, the "larger world," is not identical with the "national culture." A minority of Americans actually lives in the national culture: the new class that is often airborne, geographically mobile, no longer identified with any region or cultural group, tuned into the technological networks that make little distinction between place or culture. To report from one subculture to "the larger world" is to permit all who live in minority cultures, including the minority that lives in the national culture, to share for a brief moment a distinctive part of American experience.)

What I have in mind are the people in the towns and neighborhoods all across the United States that I visited in the political campaigns of 1970 and 1972: I recall faces in Jeannette and Central City, Pennsylvania; the Irish quarter of Manchester, New Hampshire; a school yard in Youngstown, Ohio; a motel in Laramie, Wyoming; a Spanish-surname festival in Albuquerque, New Mexico; a lodge in Sioux Falls, South Dakota. Seldom does one see these people again, ever, on television or hear again their accents and their surprisingly complicated views. They are not smooth and slick like the actors on TV or reduced to a slogan or a single sentiment in a sidewalk "opinion sample." One wonders, indeed, whose world *is* represented on television? It is no one's world. It is a fantasy. A report on no place.

Charles Kuralt, it is true, keeps a "journal" on the unusual character, the colorful angle of vision, the extraordinary ordinary person. And this is a help, like drops of water in a desert. But a larger strategy is needed. News programs, as "reports on America," should confirm in image what is true in reality: the diversity and concrete complexity of this land. The medium, one would think, would prosper from attention to nuance and concrete difference. It would gain in novelty and variety. Above all, it would gain in credibility—not that credibility that comes from "not telling untruths" (almost abstract) but that credibility that comes from reflecting back the actual concrete texture of American diversity.

National reporters would have to be allowed to present themselves in rather new postures. Tom Wicker, for example, has often reflected on the complicated vision of self and world that is the heritage of the born southerner; yet somehow, in his reporting, one gains the impression of a southerner trying to prove to his readers that he is at least as liberal as they. One does not often gain the impression that the distinctive experience of the South, whether liberal or conservative, has truth and wisdom to it that need no apology. Willie Morris describes well the pressures of New York: The national culture makes Uncle Toms of local boys. It ought, instead, to recognize that those who can put into words a distinctive local culture are an invaluable resource. Reporters now must prove their aptitude for grasping the national point of view. The new criterion would be whether they can represent local points of view so accurately that local people say: "That's how I feel."

This new skill can be learned. Anthropologists and others have to attempt it all the time, the practice of "participant observation." Some are better at it than others; there are standards of excellence.

Some examples might be useful, even though some of them do not bear directly on the news. We hear much of the waning of "the Protestant work ethic." Even without benefit of Protestantism, cultures like the Japanese, the Sicilian, and the Polish have a centuries-old work ethic. Each of these approaches to work is different, has different roots and consequences. When Richard Nixon wanted to suggest that a decision had been difficult, he revealed that he had punished himself, driven himself, stayed up all night, snacked on cottage cheese and ketchup, etc. When President Kennedy was engaged in a difficult decision, he often showed himself playing touch football or wading at the beach—playing. One cultural symbol is that worthiness comes from work; another, that worthiness comes from grace. Both men might *work* equally hard; but the governing symbol was quite different. Similarly, there is the cultural symbol of purity and integrity in politics—Eisenhower wanted Nixon to be "as clean as a hound's tooth"—and the cultural symbol of loyalty: Kennedy did not pretend to be purer than he was; he expected a certain amount of dirtiness in politics. (His response to Nixon, during the Great Debates, on Harry Truman's profanity illustrated the difference whimsically.)

Imagine taking a film crew into five different neighborhoods in Toledo, Ohio, in order to film five different families' response to death. Or filming the kitchens in five different homes, showing in how many different ways a kitchen functions in different cultures. Or filming five weddings, or births, or graduations. Such ritual occasions exemplify quite different conceptions of life.

Similarly on occasions of social conflict. A high proportion of political conflict in the United States is group conflict and arises not only out of conflicting material interests—income, jobs, neighborhoods, scholarships, etc.—but also out of conflicting cultural perceptions. Matters would be simpler if what was at stake were simply a straightforward competition over the distribution of goods. Instead, perceptions are almost always in conflict, too. Imagine an Italian-American neighborhood in Brooklyn, whose families have lived there with remarkable stability ever since their first arrival in America about 1910. When their neighborhood school is obliged to admit black students from nearby areas, what are the real economic interests of this community and what are its actual perceptions? It is not likely that the neighborhood views the in-migration of blacks as a signal of improved services and long-range stability or as a portent of upward mobility for their own children. What that is good will probably now happen to their community? On their arrival in the United States, Italian-Americans were being paid *less* than black workers doing comparable work. They were not responsible for, and do not feel guilty for, the three centuries of slavery suffered by blacks; indeed, they themselves have been freed from the institutions of serfdom in Sicily about the same number of decades as blacks. They tend to be cynical about the superior morality affected by leaders of the New York City establishment, who speak so eloquently about civil rights, equality, and opportunity; for the *price* for the mistreatment of blacks is usually not exacted from the establishment that benefited from it. Who pays the price? The newer immigrants. And yet the community has many resources for coping with black in-migration. Its preference for staying put is one such resource. Its deep-reliance upon family networks is another. Its shops, cafés, stores, and special character are a third. Its hardheaded realism and distrust of moralism are a fourth.

There is, in short, a way of reporting on such a community

locked in such a struggle that gives the viewer a sense of the very real tentacles and loose ends of the story. Who are the blacks who are moving in? Are they successful, reasonably affluent blacks looking for a stable, integrated neighborhood? Or poorer blacks, less well off than the Italian-Americans? What have their family trajectories been like these past three or four generations? In what ways are their values and life-styles similar, or dissimilar, to those of the community they are entering? What are their perceptions, aspirations, fears? Do they perceive their future neighbors as "whites" or as "Italian-Americans"? Are their perceptions of Italian-Americans accurate, and have the Italian-Americans an accurate perception of them?

It may not be the case that city planners or city officials have a nuanced sense of the different ecology of integration in different neighborhoods. It may be that official, legal, and moral statements made about the situation only inflame matters because they are disconnected from the community and seem to emanate from foreign and unaffected powers. (These may seem, indeed, rather like the feudal powers of Sicily.)

The point is that it is not enough for a national newsman to sample opinion from two or three citizens. The cultural ecology of our cities must be explained, and the secrets of communal living brought to the surface. Integration can and does proceed under certain circumstances. What are they? How can integration be rewarded, so that communities desire it? Why should they be punished for it by a decline in services, as at present? Integration is one of the greatest and most complex dramas of American history; it is occurring in every major city of the land, and television has yet to explore its cultural ecology. Where it has not simplified, the television news has appeared merely to moralize. As at Attica, so almost everywhere, both black and white workers feel that their point of view has never yet been aired on the news in the full context of their own experience.

What I have here tried to suggest about one neighborhood might be said of virtually every neighborhood in every American city. The newspapers and the broadcast journalists seldom render the realities of a city's neighborhoods. The major metropolitan organs proceed as if they were reporting on a more or less homogenized melting pot with a "citywide" perspective. But a majority of the citizens in any neighborhood almost certainly do not maintain a citywide perspective in their daily lives. This is why so many Americans feel that the media leave them out, forget them, do not notice them. When they do appear in a news item, it is ordinarily in the grossest of clichés: a "tight-knit ethnic neighborhood, with row after row of neat homes, where men and women work hard to make ends meet. . . ." These clichés should be banned.

It never seems to occur to journalists that even our suburbs are ethnically rather stratified; almost every suburb is predominantly of one ethnic group or another. In such environments, too, cultural history continues to affect perception and judgment. (I write this from Nassau County, in the midst of an Italian-American Republican political machine of awesome suburban strength.) The outward style of life may seem American and assimilated; the internal landscape of convictions and attitudes will usually reveal ancient roots.

Each generation is different from the preceding. Ethnicity is not static. But, even under generational transformation, it is astonishingly resilient. Political issues sometimes described as "conservative" or "liberal" are often of a wholly different order. A Jewish abhorrence of quotas has historical roots which make "liberal" or "conservative" irrelevant categories. The Polish peasant's symbol of status as a free man is ownership of a home; fierce attachment to home has symbolic meanings not remotely suggested by "liberal" or "conservative." An Alabama sharecropper's antagonism to the wealthy and the powerful and the cultured, and his desire to "send them a message" (not, you will notice, a new order of things, just a message) is not properly described as "liberal" or "conservative."

The accusations that the national news is not "objective," has a liberal bias, or a Northeastern bias, are, then, wide of the mark. What really is at stake is that the national news is geared to too high and general a focus. It assumes that there is a national, homogeneous point of view. It does not adequately focus on America's real diversity of soul—a profound diversity of perception and point of view. Thus the national news seems often to be out of focus. Even when it zooms down into a local neighborhood, it almost always gets the story from a point of view foreign to the neighborhood. The problem is not so much the assumption that there is a common national culture; in a certain sense there is. The problem is, rather, the choice of one part of that culture—those who live on a national wavelength, attuned to a national perspective, a kind of overclass—as the vehicle through which all others will be understood. This is where the distortion arises.

One reason there is room for hope is the goodwill of national reporters; they are always in search of new angles, new possibilities. Another is the prospect, from a stronger emotional connection to the many publics of the land, of greater profits. Incentives to do the best job possible are many.

Indeed, since I first wrote in this Survey in 1971 about the absence of ethnic diversity on family television, we have been swamped with "Banacek" and "Kojak" and "Colombo." Of these, two shows have mainly changed the name of the classical detective. But "Kojak" is the first and most brilliant rendition of a Southern European sensibility ever sustained on American television: full of subtlety, nuance, gesture, and exact articulation. Lieutenant Kojak —plainly Greek, despite his Slavic name—observes ethnic and class distinctions with absolute, silent, unadorned precision; so do his subordinates.

And so, if the adventure shows can do it, there are additional grounds to hope that television may open up new depths in the American psyche even on the evening news.

Big Media—Free Press

by Clay T. Whitehead

THE AMERICAN CONSTITUTION is a remarkably optimistic document. For all its checks and balances predicated on the frailties of human nature, the Constitution presumes a populace basically responsible, reasonable, and self-directed. Freedom, to our founding fathers, was not something that flowed from the government to the people because it was good for them; freedom was a limitation on the powers of the government and of other individuals so that individuals could control their own lives and their interactions with one another. In this admittedly bicentarian and perhaps antique view, the character, the values, and the goals of society sprang directly from the people rather than from or even through government.

The First Amendment reflects this view more succinctly than any other part of the Constitution. Freedom of religion, of speech, and of the press assure each individual his right to hold, to express, and to learn ideas, values, and opinions. The First Amendment thereby excludes government from those parts of human endeavor most fundamental to being human and most important to the character of our society.

The right of the press to be free thus reflects a broader philosophy of individual freedom and self-government. Unlike the freedoms of speech and religion, the right of the press to be free of governmental control is a right of institutions rather than an individual right. But it is quite clear that all three of these rights are closely bound up with one another, and that the individual rights are meaningless without the right to organize institutions to disseminate information and opinion among interested individuals. The free press provision in the First Amendment, therefore, was intended to establish the press firmly in the realm of the people and their ideas and to keep it totally apart from the realm of governmental action.

In the prevailing political philosophy of the time, the exclusion of government action from the press was to serve two broader purposes. One of these purposes was the protection of society and of individuals from the too easily abused and potentially despotic power of governmental censorship. The other purpose of a free press was to foster an unimpeded flow of information, ideas, and opinion among the populace. The presumption, largely unchanged in two hundred years, has been that in the absence of governmental restraint such a flow would arise as a matter of course, that each individual would be able to inform himself by picking and choosing among a wide diversity of points of view, and that ideas would gain currency in proportion to their ability to withstand public scrutiny.

How free is the press, and how well have these two purposes been served? Since the time of John Peter Zenger, American journalists, their teachers, and their employers have rallied to defend the freedom of the press from all manner of subtle and blunt attempts at governmental censorship. The press has been a bit hysterical or self-righteous on occasion and has often tried to justify totally irresponsible action on its own part, but then so have the politicians. The public has not always been on the side of the press in these disputes but, as things go in the affairs of the nation, the press has defended itself quite successfully against governmental censorship.

The other purpose of a free press, to assure what has been called a "free marketplace of ideas," has, I think, not fared so well. To be sure, our conventional wisdom still holds that this is a sound concept, but the free marketplace of ideas has been eroded—not by design but, ironically, as an unintended consequence of the importance and the success of our modern press institutions.

It has eroded because today the government is no longer the only institution with significant national power to affirm or repress alternative views of the meaning of national and international events, and because the power to give exposure and currency to ideas and to the interpretation of events is as potent a threat to a democracy as the power to censor. The "press" in this country is no longer a diverse population of independent publishers and pamphleteers. The national press establishment, or the "media" as we now call it, consists largely of a few large and very profitable corporations in the business of buying and disseminating entertainment and information in the form of newspaper articles, magazines, and radio and television broadcasting. For the most part, the content of the media is not paid for directly by the consuming public, but indirectly through the advertisers who use the media to reach the public with their messages. The individual journalist is an employee of one of these corporations or a free lancer who sells his material to them. By combining the economies of scale in distributing information with the power to control what information is distributed, a few large corporations have come to dominate the national media scene. By protecting the free press rights of these corporations, the First Amendment has acted to deny anyone else the right to gain access to these media. As a result of this industry structure, there has arisen a substantial paradox about the rights of the press that are to be protected by the First Amendment, the rights of individuals to have their ideas disseminated, and to whom those respective rights flow.

Such large and powerful institutions inevitably must become the subject of public debate. It is not that there is anything inherently wrong with large corporations in any field of endeavor; but we are beginning to see some of the unintended side effects of the large bureaucratic institutions—corporate, nonprofit, and governmental —that we have established to carry out the work of our increasingly complex society, and some of those side effects are clearly undesirable. Liberals and conservatives alike, although often focusing on different sides of the problem, find more and more fault with these large and bureaucratic institutions, most notably problems of social responsibility and accountability. "Big media," no less than "big government" or "big oil," have accrued significant amounts of power over essential facets of our national life, power that often seems uninterested in the broader implications of its exercise and unresponsive (if not downright antagonistic) to those who seek to point out how it might be better used or better distributed. These problems are not easy in their solution, no matter how zealously the defenders or attackers of institutional power feel the rightness of their cause. We are, after all, working out a new social and economic institutional order at least as difficult as the transition of the industrial revolution that gave rise to the complexity of our society and the corporate institutional structure in the first place.

But having said all that, we come back to the highly concentrated corporate ownership and control of our national mass media establishment, the growing dissatisfaction with the role it is performing, and to the need for some constructive public debate about the matter. It may be a phase we are going through and it may be due in large part to the impact of the national news media themselves, but the fact is that debates today about the social responsibility of large institutions, particularly the large corporations, quickly devolve into calls for government action answered by outraged, cries of infringed freedom. And the debate about the large corporate media is no exception.

Those readers who are tempted at this point to summon forth once more the anti-censorship free press rhetoric have missed the point entirely. The dominating issue of government-media relations today is not censorship, it is the question of the *role* of the big corporate media in our national life and the recourse citizens have, through government processes and otherwise, to influence use of the economic, political, and social power of those large corporations. The media are at the center of our collective action and our common awareness, and their rights and responsibilities in a sense constitute the rules for our sharing of information and entertainment among ourselves. Most of the debate then is not so much about freedom of the press as about the role of the media in our national life.

There was considerable argument during the time of the Nixon administration that modern national media corporations had to be large and hold some substantial degree of monopoly power in order to have the independence to counter the power of government. But there was little concern about the corollary principle that any media corporation that powerful would inevitably evoke calls from the public to check that power. In other words, a media establishment with power over what the public sees and hears sufficiently concentrated to check and balance the federal government will itself require governmental check and balance.

The faults of the media are legion, and those that might have been tolerated in a simpler time now give rise to calls for governmental action. Television has become the modern patent medicine show, providing programming that will attract the largest possible audience of eighteen- to forty-nine-year-old middle-class consumers for the sales pitch. Without the opportunity to pay directly for their TV entertainment and information, audiences have little to say about the quality or diversity of TV programming. Television panders violence and sensationalism to young children. The profession of journalism rewards itself through peer acclaim more than through monetary reward, creating considerable incentives toward faddishness and idealistic concern for social change rather than responsiveness to public interests, especially where new firms cannot enter the field to compete. Each of these "problems" is exacerbated by the extreme concentration of control in the national news media, and each has brought forth pressures for governmental correctives.

The centrist tendency of network TV entertainment programming toward the "least offensive program" has called forth a host of FCC program categories deemed good for us, if not of sufficient mass appeal at any given hour to compete with good sensational entertainment. The sensible network and local broadcaster pays his Washington lawyer a considerable fee to know just how much programming of agricultural, public service, religion, local news, and the like he is expected to provide in order to stay in the FCC's good graces and to survive a challenge to his license. The remarkable reluctance of the networks to correct the most abusive children's programming and advertising has led to proposals for a government-maintained violence index and for the prohibition of advertising on programming directed principally toward children (however *that* is determined). The TV newsman who does a gripping documentary finds his network hit with a Fairness Doctrine decision that not enough time was given to whatever the FCC decided was the opposing point of view. And newspapers in Florida found themselves for a while obliged to provide equal space to politicians unhappy with an editorial about them.

Nor can one ignore the Watergate revelations of plans discussed in the White House to abuse the legal powers of the FCC and the Justice Department antitrust division to coerce news coverage favorable to the Nixon administration. Most disturbing, although perfectly legal, was the conversation in the Oval Office about having challenges filed against the Washington Post-Newsweek TV stations. There was a strong suggestion of an abuse of process in that conversation, but the basic proposal of a politically motivated license challenge was well established in communications law by minority groups and liberal-to-radical social activists during the 1960's.

Finally, there was the furor over the blunt public challenge to the professionalism and political neutrality of the journalistic profession by Vice-President Agnew and others. To be sure, much of Agnew's rhetoric was politically self-serving, but it is too much to ask of any politician that he criticize the media for being too favorable to his political philosophy. And it is clear to almost everyone except the journalists that they need this kind of criticism.

Even a highly professional press corps needs some jawboning in the spirit of healthy give and take between politicians and the press. But apart from the unusually thin skin of the media when it comes to criticism, there was another factor behind the violent reaction of the media to Agnew's message. The government, particularly over the decade of the sixties and particularly in broadcasting, had developed in the courts and in the FCC a rather pervasive set of *legal* controls over the media, and the Justice Department had been paying more attention to the anti-competitive concentrations of corporate ownership of the media. Therefore it was implicit in Agnew's message, whether he intended it or not, that the legal controls developed for other political purposes might well be turned to the Administration's political advantage.

As a practical matter, the Nixon administration was sporadic and inept in attempting to use these legal levers over the media to its own advantage, but a more adept Administration more attuned to the political predispositions of the national press corps *could* abuse those legal powers. The greater political danger of extensive bureaucratic control over the media is more from seduction of favorable press coverage than from repression of unfavorable coverage.

Whatever our personal inclinations about the merits of each of these modern media "problems," our political and judicial processes are being forced to deal with them. There are better and worse ways of dealing with the concentration of media power, but you would hardly know it from the public debate. The District of Columbia Court of Appeals, with help from the FCC and the Supreme Court and prompted by social activists, has made a mockery of the First Amendment in broadcasting. The consistent trend has been toward giving the FCC more power and more discretion to second-guess the programming and editorial functions of broadcast stations and networks. Listening to the siren rhetoric of the new populists, the courts have based the legality of this trend on the scarcity of broadcast outlets and the corresponding cost of broadcast time. Great governmental power over the media is necessary, it is argued, to assure that the great power of the few broadcasters will be used to the benefit of the viewers and listeners. A more blatant circumvention of the First Amendment is hard to imagine: it is the viewers' right to see and hear what is worth seeing and hearing, not the broadcasters' free press right that is paramount; and since only the government has the power to enforce the public's right vis-à-vis the broadcaster, the government must have the right to review programming and establish requirements for what the broadcaster shall program if the government is to allow him to stay in business.

The danger here is only in part that such power could be abused politically; it is probably more debilitating in the long run for a democracy to have routine programming decisions heavily determined by an apolitical bureaucracy in Washington. A paternalistic imposition of socially progressive programming is likely to be harder to fight and therefore to have a bigger and more lasting impact on the bias of views readily available to the public.

It is also amazing to see so many print journalists encouraging the extension of federal controls over broadcasting as an expedient way of encouraging socially progressive causes. Seeing some of the more liberal newspapers editorializing in favor of more stringent criteria for license renewals and for maintaining the Fairness Doctrine really gives pause—as if the press functions can or cannot be regulated, based on the use of ink as opposed to electrons—and causes some wonder about the press freedom of those newspapers or magazines that one day are distributed by electronic facsimile.

The Supreme Court rationalization of controls over broadcasting, based as it is on the scarcity of outlets, can be applied as well to daily newspapers in spite of the recent *Tornillo* decision. At some point the court-made laws of print press freedom and of electronic press freedom will have to be reconciled, and no student of the subject can be very sanguine about the outcome.

The Supreme Court has never allowed any one constitutional right to become absolute, and in the area of the First Amendment the Court has tried to balance competing rights and freedoms rather than upholding total press freedom. Journalists and civil libertarians of all political persuasions who believe in a minimal imposition of governmental action of the media, therefore, have a much more complex and difficult task today than those who in the past have defended the press from straightforward censorship. They must be willing to study the structure and performance of the media and their impact on the social order; and they must be thoroughly professional in finding ways to resolve legal battles over press freedom and the roles and responsibilities of the media. In such a debate, waged in public discussions, congressional hearings, and Supreme Court arguments, emotional anti-censorship rhetoric will seem as self-serving and antiquarian as the emotional appeals to rights of private property did coming from the cartels and trusts earlier in this century.

It is easy to see that big government exercising its power over big media to produce the socially most beneficial programming is not the best way of preserving the First Amendment in our modern society. It is much more difficult to see the right way for us as a nation to deal with the extensive concentration of corporate control over our national news sources, but that has become the chief issue of press freedom and of our public policy for the mass media. None of us have the answers, but we must begin to seek them in open and widespread debate. It will not be easy. The journalists will not like being talked about critically; the symbiotic relationship between the politicians and the network managements will be threatened; and the public will wonder even more than today whom to believe. But if our democracy cannot have a debate about the role of the mass media in its national political life, and about how information, entertainment, and opinion are exchanged, then our democracy is in deep trouble.

My personal view is that the most likely approach for preserving the spirit and presumptions of the First Amendment is to eschew extensive bureaucratic controls over the programming of broadcasting—even for the most noble and most pressing social and political objectives. But that means the public must have some direct right, not now recognized in law, to distribute ideas on TV and in print without depending on the whim of the broadcasters or publishers. We have a moderately practical system right now in that most newspapers and magazines will print any political advertisement that is in good taste; and in spite of the inefficiency of the Postal Service, it is not all that difficult to print and circulate your own views directly if there is enough serious interest. But even that recourse is missing in television and radio broadcasting, and indeed broadcasters have fought strenuously and have won in the Supreme Court their right to refuse to carry political advertising. It would be far preferable if broadcasters would voluntarily allow, or be required by law to allow, the public to buy time to distribute ideas (and to solicit funds to support that distribution) just as freely as advertisers can buy time to sell soap. This right would no doubt change the character of TV a bit, but only in the direction of being a more faithful mirror of the interests and concerns of society as a whole. Until the public has that right, there does not seem to be much hope for avoiding the accumulation of more and more special interest programming requirements lobbied through the FCC and the Congress on the basis of who currently has the most political clout.

The real hope for the future, of course, lies in cable television. With its capacity for indefinite expansion of TV channels so that TV programs can be distributed nationwide or neighborhood-wide to whatever extent supply and demand allow, cable promises to be to the electronic mass media what the mails are to the print media. If the cable system owners are denied from the outset a monopoly over the programming carried on their channels, and instead are required like the Postal Service or a delivery service to serve all without discrimination, then we can have a highly competitive TV programming industry with programming produced by diverse sources, sold either to advertisers or directly to the consumer, and delivered at low cost via satellite and cable. We could have university extension courses offered in the home, adding revenues badly needed by our colleges and universities; we could expand greatly the box office for the arts, helping to expand support for the arts in the most direct way possible; and there would be new opportunities for entrepreneurial journalism far beyond the network news format.

Such an electronic media structure would not be perfect, but it clearly would be superior to what we have now. By separating the ownership of the transmission medium from the control of the material that is made available to the public, the concentration of ownership problem would be greatly alleviated, public policy could be directed mainly at assuring equitable and low cost *distribution* of TV programming and other electronic media services rather than at the fairness and social desirability of the *content* of the programming itself. When each individual can choose for himself what programming will come into his home and which of it he chooses to pay for, the rationale for governmental specifications of program offerings will fade greatly.

Cable's promise is twofold: more and better TV fare to choose from, and an escape from the First Amendment dilemma in broadcasting that threatens the freedom of all mass media. But cable's threat is equally real: more competition for the broadcasters and political pressure to "save free TV." Most broadcasters seem more willing to be told by the government what their social responsibility is in order to keep out competition than to tolerate the longer-run freedom that more media outlets would facilitate.

It is one thing to recognize that cable is an important hope for the future and that other changes should be made in the structure of our mass communications media; but we must seriously contemplate whether and how we can get from here to there.

The First Amendment for broadcasting has come to be bent around the 1934 Communications Act and the corporate structure of the television industry, when in fact the opposite should be the case. In broadcast journalism at least, the functions of the press and the government are comingled, and the First Amendment wall of separation between government and press envisaged two hundred years ago has been eroded significantly. The precedent is not healthy, and it will be difficult to change.

The real question of press freedom today, it therefore seems to me, is whether the government regulators and the broadcasting regulatees can be persuaded to loosen the big media, big government grip they have on television programming today—and whether our future journalists will care as much about the well-intentioned bureaucratic erosion of a free press as they have about poorly intentioned attempts at press censorship.

Appendix I

July 16, 1970

SECRET

MEMORANDUM FOR: MR. MAGRUDER
FROM: L. HIGBY

As I indicated to you the other day, we need to get some creative thinking going on an attack on Huntley for his statements in *Life*. One thought that comes to mind is getting all the people to sign a petition calling for the immediate removal of Huntley right now.

The point behind this whole thing is that we don't care about Huntley—he is going to leave anyway. What we are trying to do here is to tear down the institution. Huntley will go out in a blaze of glory and we should attempt to pop his bubble.

Most people won't see *Life* magazine and for that reason I am asking Buchanan to draft a statement for the Vice President to give. We should try to get this statement on television. Obviously there are many other things that we can do, such as getting independent station owners to write NBC saying that they should remove Huntley now; having broadcasting people look into this due to the fact that this is proof of biased journalism, etc.

Let's put a full plan on this and get the thing moving. I'll contact Buchanan and forward copies of my correspondence with him to you so that you will know what the Vice President is doing.

Appendix II

July 17, 1970

CONFIDENTIAL/EYES ONLY

MEMORANDUM FOR: MR. HALDEMAN
                        MR. KLEIN
FROM: JEB S. MAGRUDER

Enclosed is a tentative plan on press objectivity. Please indicate your comments.
  Thank you.

Enclosure

CONFIDENTIAL/EYES ONLY

July 17, 1970

TENTATIVE PLAN
PRESS OBJECTIVITY

Description: In the July 17th issue of *Life* magazine a prominent television newscaster is quoted as making some extremely disparaging remarks about the President. It is understood that the newscaster intends to send a letter to the editor of the magazine claiming he was misquoted and will also send a letter of apology to the President.

Objective: To question the overall objectivity of a television newscaster who has expressed opinionated views in an influential consumer publication while still employed as a supposedly objective television newscaster and to question the motivation for such remarks and the possible breach of professional ethics by allowing such remarks to be published prior to retirement into private life. Further, to extend these questions to cover the professional objectivity and ethics of the whole media and to generate a public re-examination of the role of the media in American life.

Tactics: Since the newscaster enjoys a very favorable public image and will apologize for his remarks, claiming to be misquoted, we should not attempt to discredit him personally. Also, since his remarks were expressed as an individual, we would have difficulty attacking his network directly. The focus of our effort should be to raise the larger question of objectivity and ethics in the media as an institution. To do this, we will have to turn objectivity into an issue and a subject of public debate.

Follow-up: Release the letter of apology to the press along with a gracious reply from the President. —Ziegler

Plant a column with a syndicated columnist which raises the question of objectivity and ethics in the news media. Kevin Phillips could be a good choice. —Klein

Arrange for an article on the subject in a major consumer magazine authored by Stewart Alsop, Buckley, or Kilpatrick. Also, request Hobe Lewis to run a major article. —Klein

Through an academic source, encourage the dean of a leading graduate school of journalism to publicly acknowledge that press objectivity is a serious problem that should be discussed. Also, attempt to arrange an in-depth analysis in a prestigious journal like the *Columbia Journalism Review.* —Klein/Safire

Arrange a seminar on press objectivity with broadcast executives and working newsmen. Attempt to have this televised as a public service. —Klein

Make this issue a major item at the Radio-Television News Directors Convention this Fall and at the next major NAB meeting. —Klein

Ask the Vice President to speak out on this issue. We could point out that the *Life* quote has proved his point. —Buchanan

Have Rogers Morton go on the attack in a news conference. He could tie in the quote with the free-time grants to the Democrats. Also, revive the WETA-Woestendiek affair. Have him charge that the great majority of the working press are Democrats and this colors their presentation of the news. Have him charge that theirs is a political conspiracy in the media to attack this Administration. —Klein/Colson

Have Dean Burch "express concern" about press objectivity in response to a letter from a congressman. —Nofziger

Through independent Hill sources, stimulate nonpartisan congressional questioning of the issue. Place such remarks in the *Record.* —Nofziger

Arrange for an "exposé" to be written by an author such as Earl Mazo or Victor Lasky. Publish in hardcover and paperback. —Klein

Produce a prime-time special, sponsored by private funds, that would examine the question of objectivity and show how TV newsmen can structure the news by innuendo. For instance, use film clips to show how a raised eyebrow or a tone of voice can convey criticism. —Klein/Magruder

Have outside groups petition the FCC and issue public "statements of concern" over press objectivity. —Colson

Generate a massive outpouring of letters-to-the-editor. —Magruder

Life occasionally runs an opposition view column entitled "Guest Privilege." Position an appropriate writer, preferably a professor of journalism, to discuss this issue in that column. —Klein/Safire

Form a blue-ribbon media "watchdog" committee to report to the public on cases of biased reporting. John Cosgrove, a former president of the National Press Club, could set this up. This group could sponsor the TV special mentioned above, conduct a speaking campaign to service groups and colleges, issue press releases, etc. —Magruder

Have a senator or congressman write a public letter to the FCC suggesting the "licensing" of individual newsmen, i.e., the airwaves belong to the public, therefore the public should be protected from the misuse of these airwaves by individual newsmen. —Nofziger

Through contacts in the ASNB and NAB, bring up the question of a "fairness pledge" for members. —Klein

Project Manager—Magruder

Appendix III

The original CBS announcement (June 6, 1973) of the end of "instant analysis"

CBS CHAIRMAN WILLIAM S. PALEY
ANNOUNCES NEW POLICY ON PRESENTATION OF
VIEWS RELATING TO PRESIDENTIAL ADDRESSES

*Within Week After a Presidential Broadcast on
Major Public Policy Issues,
CBS Television and Radio Networks Will Devote
a Special Broadcast to Other Views*

CBS has adopted a new policy providing for presentation of views contrasting to those expressed in Presidential broadcasts "on matters of major policy concerning which there is significant national disagreement," CBS Chairman William S. Paley announced today.

Mr. Paley said that such broadcasts will be scheduled as soon after the President speaks as practicable but generally in no later than a week's time. They will be presented on the CBS Television and Radio Networks, with which some 500 stations throughout the country are affiliated.

"Fundamentally," Mr. Paley said, "this decision is an application of a long-standing CBS policy—a cardinal principle of our news operation since its inception—of providing fair and balanced coverage of public issues. Traditionally, as times have changed, CBS has sought new approaches to serving the public interest through expanding the public dialogue on national issues.

"Recent Presidents," Mr. Paley noted, "have conceived as one of the main functions of the Executive the focusing of national attention on public issues. To accomplish this, they have turned more and more to broadcasting as a means of direct access to the people. This in turn has increased the need for broadcasting to develop new avenues to provide a broad spectrum of significant views and a multiplicity of representative voices on public issues.

"Fulfilling our journalistic responsibilities to present issues objectively and fairly, generally speaking CBS has followed two basic approaches. First, in our regularly scheduled news broadcasts we provide continuous opportunity not only for the views of the Administration whose actions make news, but also for significant differing views. Second, CBS News presents coverage of points at issue on such broadcasts as "Face the Nation," "Spectrum," "60 Minutes," and on documentary and special broadcasts. The new policy, by providing an additional dimension to the coverage of public issues, institutes a third approach."

The main elements of the new CBS policy, which is effective immediately, follow:

1. Whenever the President speaks to the Nation on radio or television on matters of major policy concerning which there is significant national disagreement, CBS will present a broadcast of other viewpoints related to those matters of major policy.

2. The length, format and persons appearing on such broadcast will be determined by CBS News in light of the relevant facts of the Presidential appearance. The broadcast will be scheduled as soon as practicable, but generally no later than one week after the President speaks.

Simultaneously, CBS announced that henceforth CBS News will not provide news analyses immediately after Presidential appearances, nor after broadcasts presenting views contrasting to those expressed in Presidential broadcasts. Such analyses will be scheduled by CBS News during the normal CBS News broadcast schedule.

Appendix IV

Roger Mudd's canceled script, scheduled for CBS Radio on June 7, 1973

THIS IS Roger Mudd reporting, with news and analysis, on the CBS Radio network. When Vice-President Agnew first blasted TV network news—in his famous Des Moines speech, back in 1969— he complained that broadcast presidential speeches were followed by what he called "instant analysis and querulous criticism" from people he said were "hostile critics" on the network news staffs. The analyses by network newsmen immediately following broadcast presidential speeches have been a matter of public controversy ever since. Now, CBS announces it is breaking stride with the other two major networks—and dropping instant analysis.

The apparent consensus within the rank and file at CBS News is that the new policy announcement by CBS Chairman William Paley contains, as they say, "some good news and some bad news." The good news: from now on, there'll be special broadcasts of opposing viewpoints as soon as possible after presidential speeches, when the President has discussed major matters over which there is significant national disagreement.

But for many around CBS, the bad news came in the final brief paragraph of the Paley press release—seemingly tacked on almost as an afterthought. Henceforth, CBS News is discontinuing its own analyses immediately after presidential appearances on the air.

The press release said nothing about *why* the so-called instant analysis was being discontinued. In an interview, Mr. Paley said that for some time, inside the CBS hierarchy, there was discussion of whether the practice would sometimes result in putting a correspondent on the air improperly prepared, right after the President goes off. Apparently, one of those to raise the question first was Eric Sevareid, who felt that he was doing an inferior job when he immediately followed the President on the air, performing without an advance text or briefing. Sevareid of course is one of those most qualified to discuss instant analysis, since he has done so many of them. However, he admits his opposition to instant analysis probably is a minority view among CBS newsmen. So, in all probability, is his evaluation of his own performance.

Newsmen being what they are, the common reflex reaction on the CBS staff was concern that their superiors might have knuckled under, to pressure from the government. When it was put directly to Mr. Paley, he was indignant at the very thought. In fact, he maintained, Vice-President Agnew probably would disapprove of the new system—since it puts the opposition on the air—and still reserves the right of analysis by CBS News—only on regular newscasts, when there's time for more thorough preparation. On the question of pressure, CBS News President Richard Salant provided an interesting footnote: he said he and Eric Sevareid were discussing the pros and cons of abolishing instant analysis as early as 1969—but then dropped the matter after Agnew's Des Moines speech—because abolishing it *then* would certainly have seemed like caving in under pressure. The Agnew speech, then, apparently helped perpetuate the very practice the Vice-President was attacking.

Both NBC and ABC disagree with CBS—and intend to continue with instant analysis following broadcast presidential speeches, when they feel it is warranted. Part of the disagreement may stem from the dual nature of the presidency itself. On one hand, the President is chief of state. And it may seem disrespectful to his office not to let him communicate directly with the people, without some bumptious individual immediately "explaining" his remarks. But on the other hand, the President is also a highly partisan advocate. On occasion, presidents on the air may leave out an inconvenient fact or two, as they plead their causes. Instant analysis afterward by a qualified newsman can supply these pertinent facts—and thus provide a useful perspective for the viewer to evaluate the President's speech. Without such analysis, the whole truth has to go running after the distortion . . . and some unconsulted newsmen here at CBS feel it can never completely catch up. This is Roger Mudd reporting for CBS News.

Appendix V

October 17, 1969

MEMORANDUM FOR: H. R. HALDEMAN
FROM: J. S. MAGRUDER
RE: The Shot-gun versus the Rifle

Yesterday you asked me to give you a talking paper on specific problems we've had in shot-gunning the media and anti-Administration spokesmen on unfair coverage.

I have enclosed from the log approximately 21 requests from the President in the last 30 days requesting specific action relating to what could be considered unfair news coverage. This enclosure only includes actual memos sent out by Ken Cole's office. In the short time that I have been here, I would gather that there have been at least double or triple this many requests made through various other parties to accomplish the same objective.

It is my opinion this continual daily attempt to get to the media or to anti-Administration spokesmen because of specific things they have said is very unfruitful and wasteful of our time. This is not to say that they have not been unfair, without question many situations that have been indicated are correct, but I would question the approach we have taken. When an editor gets continual calls from Herb Klein or Pat Buchanan on a situation that is difficult to document as to unfairness, we are in a very weak area. Particularly when we are talking about interpretation of the news as against factual reporting.

The real problem that faces the Administration is to get to this unfair coverage in such a way that we make major impact on a basis which the networks-newspapers and Congress will react to and begin to look at things somewhat differently. It is my opinion that we should begin concentrated efforts in a number of major areas that will have much more impact on the media and other anti-Administration spokesmen and will do more good in the long run. The following is my suggestion as to how we can achieve this goal:

1. Begin an official monitoring system through the FCC as soon as Dean Burch is officially on board as Chairman. If the monitoring system proves our point, we have then legitimate and legal rights to go to the networks, etc., and make official complaints from the FCC. This will have much more effect than a phone call from Herb Klein or Pat Buchanan.

2. Utilize the antitrust division to investigate various media relating to antitrust violations. Even the possible threat of antitrust action, I think, would be effective in changing their views in the above matter.

3. Utilizing the Internal Revenue Service as a method to look into the various organizations that we are most concerned about. Just a threat of an IRS investigation will probably turn their approach.

4. Begin to show favorites within the media. Since they are basically not on our side let us pick the favorable ones as Kennedy did. I'm not saying we should eliminate the open Administration, but by being open we have not gotten anyone to back us on a consistent basis and many of those who were favorable toward us are now giving it to us at various times, i.e., Ted Lewis, Hugh Sidey.

5. Utilize Republican National Committee for major letter writing efforts of both a class nature and a quantity nature. We have set up a situation at the National Committee that will allow us to do this, and I think by effective letter writing and telegrams we will accomplish our objective rather than again just the shot-gun approach to one specific senator or one specific news broadcaster because of various comments.

I would liken this to the Kennedy Administration in that they had no qualms about using the power available to them to achieve their objectives. On the other hand, we seem to march on tiptoe into the political situation and are unwilling to use the power at hand to achieve our long-term goals, which is eight years of a Republican Administration. I clearly remember Kennedy sending out the FBI men to wake up the steel executives in the middle of the night. It caused an uproar in certain cases but he achieved his goal and the vast majority of the American public was with him. If we convince the President that this is the correct approach, we will find that various support groups will be much more productive and much more cooperative; and at the same time I think we will achieve the goals this Administration has set out to do on a much more meaningful planned basis.

PRESIDENT'S REQUEST

TO	ITEM	DATE
H. Klein Ron Ziegler	President's request that you attack *Life* magazine's editorial accusing the Administration of creating a Coherence Gap. (Log 1366)	September 27
H. Klein	President's request that you contact Howard K. Smith and give him the true record on what the Administration has done. (Log 1367)	September 26
A. Butterfield	Sen. Kennedy's Boston speech alleging that the war in Vietnam remains virtually unchanged. (Log 1292)	September 23
P. Flanigan	Ralph Nader's charge that the President pays little attention to consumer affairs. (Log 1293)	September 24
Dr. Kissinger	Article by Jack Anderson which alleges that some U.S. officers in Vietnam favor Thieu's hard line over the President's moderate policy and are sabotaging the truce efforts. (Log 1281)	September 23
H. Klein	President's request that you inform Walter Trohan about our substantive programs and that you place the blame for inaction on the Democratic Congress. (Log 1246)	September 30

TO	ITEM	DATE
J. Ehrlichman	President's request for a report on possible answers to Evans-Novak charge of an Administration retreat on tax reform. (Log 1224)	September 23
Dr. Kissinger	President's request for a report on Walter Cronkite's comment that the South Vietnamese did not observe the truce resulting from Ho Chi Minh's death. (Log 1154)	September 16
P. Buchanan	President's request that appropriate columnists be informed of the extemporaneous character of Presidential press conferences. (Log 1551)	October 10
H. Klein	President's request that you demand equal time to counter John Chancellor's commentary regarding the Haynsworth nomination. (Log 1559)	October 7
H. Klein	President's request for a report on what action is taken concerning Sen. Muskie's appearance on the "Merv Griffin Show."	October 8
A. Butterfield	President's request for a report on what resulted from our PR efforts following up the Friday press conference. (Log 1496)	October 3
H. Klein	President's request that we have the Chicago *Tribune* hit Senator Percy hard on his ties with the peace group. (Log 1495) CONFIDENTIAL	October 3
H. Klein	President's request for letters-to-the-editor regarding *Newsweek*'s lead article	September 30

TO	ITEM	DATE
	covering the President's U.N. speech. (Log 1443)	
H. Klein	President's request that we counter Ralph Nader's remarks regarding Virginia Knauer accessibility to the President. (Log 1404)	September 29
P. Flanigan	President's request that you take action to counter Dan Rather's allegation that the Hershey move was decided upon because of the moratorium. (Log 1733)	October 17
J. Ehrlichman	President's request that you talk to Ted Lewis concerning the present status of discipline within the Administration. (Log 1699)	October 15
P. Buchanan	President's request for a report on what actions were taken to complain to NBC, *Time,* and *Newsweek* concerning a recent article coverage on the Administration. (Log 1688)	October 14
H. Klein	President's request for letters-to-the-editor of *Newsweek* mentioning the President's tremendous reception in Miss. and last Sat. Miami Dolphin football game. (Log 1627)	October 10
H. Klein	President's request that you take appropriate action to counter biased TV coverage of the Adm. over the summer. (Log 1644) CONFIDENTIAL	October 14
H. Klein	President's request that you ask Rogers Morton to take action to counter Howard K. Smith's remarks concerning the three House seats lost by the GOP this year. (Log 1558)	October 8

Appendix VI

Report by Fred Graham on "World News Roundup," CBS Radio Network, September 22, 1973, 8:00–8:15 A.M.

"CBS NEWS has learned that the plea-bargaining between Vice President Agnew's attorneys and the Justice Department is being conducted, at least officially, by Attorney General Elliot Richardson himself. But the Government's position is being set by Assistant Attorney General Henry Peterson [sic], chief of the Criminal Division, a veteran prosecutor who has taken a tough line. One source has said that the Vice President is offering to resign in exchange for a promise that he will not be prosecuted. But a source close to the negotiations has disclosed that in a plea-bargaining session last Wednesday morning in the Justice Department, Peterson [sic] insisted that he had the evidence to win a conviction on the bribery and kickback charges and that he would insist that Agnew plead guilty at least to a reduced charge. *Peterson [sic] was quoted as saying, "We've got the evidence, we've got it cold."* Richardson was said to have sat in approving silence as Peterson [sic] held out for a guilty plea that could possibly involve a jail sentence for Agnew, depending upon what the judge decided. CBS News could not learn if further meetings had been held since Wednesday or if either side has since shifted its position. [*Italics supplied.*]

Appendix VII
First and Sixth Amendments to the Constitution of the United States

ARTICLE I.
Religious Establishment Prohibited. Freedom of Speech, of the Press, and Right to Petition.

Congress shall make no law respecting an establishment of religion, or prohibiting the free exercise thereof; or abridging the freedom of speech, or of the press; or the right of the people peaceably to assemble and to petition the Government for a redress of grievances.

ARTICLE VI.
Right to Speedy Trial, Witnesses, etc.

In all criminal prosecutions, the accused shall enjoy the right to a speedy and public trial, by an impartial jury of the State and district wherein the crime shall have been committed, which district shall have been previously ascertained by law, and to be informed of the nature and cause of the accusation; to be confronted with the witnesses against him; to have compulsory process for obtaining witnesses in his favor, and to have the Assistance of Counsel for his defense.

Appendix VIII

FYI—EYES ONLY, PLEASE
September 25, 1970

MEMORANDUM FOR H. R. HALDEMAN

The following is a summary of the most pertinent conclusions from my meeting with the three network chief executives.

1. The networks are terribly nervous over the uncertain state of the law, i.e., the recent FCC decisions and the pressures to grant Congress access to TV. They are also apprehensive about us. Although they tried to disguise this, it was obvious. The harder I pressed them (CBS and NBC) the more accommodating, cordial, and almost apologetic they became. Stanton for all his bluster is the most insecure of all.

2. They were startled by how thoroughly we were doing our homework—both from the standpoint of knowledge of the law, as I discussed it, but more importantly, from the way in which we have so thoroughly monitored their coverage and our analysis of it. (Allin's analysis is attached. This was my talking paper and I gave them facts and figures.)

3. There was unanimous agreement that the President's right of access to TV should in no way be restrained. Both CBS and ABC agreed with me that on most occasions the President speaks as President and that there is no obligation for presenting a contrasting point of view under the Fairness Doctrine. (This, by the way, is not the law—the FCC has always ruled that the Fairness Doctrine always applies—and either they don't know that or they are willing to concede us the point.) NBC on the other hand argues that the fairness test must be applied to every Presidential speech, but Goodman is also quick to agree that there are probably instances in which Presidential addresses are not "controversial" under the Fairness Doctrine and, therefore, there is no duty to balance. All agree no one has a right of "reply" and that fairness doesn't mean

answering the President but rather is "issue oriented." This was the most important understanding we came to. What is important is that they know how strongly we feel about this.

4. They are terribly concerned with being able to work out their own policies with respect to balanced coverage and not to have policies imposed on them by either the Commission or the Congress. ABC and CBS said that they felt we could, however, through the FCC, make any policies we wanted to. (This is worrying them all.)

5. To my surprise CBS did not deny that the news had been slanted against us. Paley merely said that every Administration has felt the same way and that we have been slower in coming to them to complain than our predecessors. He, however, ordered Stanton in my presence to review the analysis with me and if the news has not been balanced, to see that the situation is immediately corrected. (Paley is in complete control of CBS—Stanton is almost obsequious in Paley's presence.)

6. CBS does not defend the O'Brien appearance. Paley wanted to make it very clear that it would not happen again and that they would not permit partisan attacks on the President. They are doggedly determined to win their FCC case, however; as a matter of principle, even though they recognize that they made a mistake, they don't want the FCC in the business of correcting their mistakes.

7. ABC and NBC believe that the whole controversy over "answers" to the President can be handled by giving some time regularly to presentations by the Congress—either debates or the State-of-the-Congress-type presentations with both parties in the Congress represented. In this regard ABC will do anything we want. NBC proposes to provide a very limited Congressional coverage once or twice a year and additionally once a year "loyal opposition" type answers to the President's State of the Union address (which has been the practice since 1966). CBS takes quite a different position. Paley's policy is that the Congress cannot be the sole balancing mechanism and that the Democratic leadership in Congress should have time to present Democratic viewpoints on legislation. (On this point, which may become the most critical of all, we can split the networks in a way that will be very much to our advantage.)

Conclusion:
I had to break every meeting. The networks badly want to have

these kinds of discussions which they said they had had with other Administrations but never with ours. They told me anytime we had a complaint about slanted coverage for me to call them directly. Paley said that he would like to come down to Washington and spend time with me anytime that I wanted. In short, they are very much afraid of us and are trying hard to prove they are "good guys."

These meetings had a very salutary effect in letting them know that we are determined to protect the President's position, that we know precisely what is going on from the standpoint of both law and policy and that we are not going to permit them to get away with anything that interferes with the President's ability to communicate.

Paley made the point that he was amazed at how many people agree with the Vice President's criticism of the networks. He also went out of his way to say how much he supports the President, and how popular the President is. When Stanton said twice as many people had seen President Nixon on TV than any other President in a comparable period, Paley said it was because this President is more popular.

The only ornament on Goodman's desk was the Nixon Inaugural Medal. Hagerty said in Goldenson's presence that ABC is "with us." This all adds up to the fact that they are damned nervous and scared and we should continue to take a very tough line, face to face, and in other ways.

As to follow-up, I believe the following is in order:

1. I will review with Stanton and Goodman the substantiation of my assertion to them that their news coverage has been slanted. We will go over it point by point. This will, perhaps, make them even more cautious.

2. There should be a mechanism (through Herb, Ron, or me) every time we believe coverage is slanted whereby we point it out either to the chief executive or to whomever he designates. Each of them invited this and we should do it so they know we are not bluffing.

3. I will pursue with ABC and NBC the possibility of their issuing declarations of policy (one that we find generally favorable as to the President's use of TV). If I can get them to issue such a policy statement, CBS will be backed into an untenable position.

4. I will pursue with Dean Burch the possibility of an interpretive ruling by the FCC on the role of the President when he uses TV, as

soon as we have a majority. I think that this point could be very favorably clarified and it would, of course, have an inhibiting impact on the networks and their professed concern with achieving balance.

5. I would like to continue a friendly but very firm relationship whenever they or we want to talk. I am realistic enough to realize that we probably won't see any obvious improvement in the news coverage, but I think we can dampen their ardor for putting on "loyal opposition" type programs.

I have detailed notes on each meeting if you'd like a more complete report.

Charles W. Colson

Appendix IX
William S. Paley's statement
rescinding the rule
prohibiting instant analysis

November 12, 1973

ON JUNE 6 CBS announced a new policy regarding the presentation of views contrasting to those expressed in all presidential broadcasts "on matters of major policy concerning which there is significant national disagreement." The policy committed CBS to provide time for opposing views by qualified spokesmen as soon after the President's broadcasts as practicable. It is the first such commitment by network television and radio in this country, and we believe it represents an important and constructive step forward. This policy will be continued.

At the time this innovation was announced CBS also announced that news analyses of presidential speeches and of responses to them would be postponed until the next regularly scheduled CBS News broadcasts. This decision was made in the belief that additional time for reflection and research would enhance the analyses.

Since June 6 the nation and the world have witnessed a rapid series of exceptionally newsworthy events. This has made it clear that postponing news analysis under all circumstances may impair a journalistic service of far greater value to the public than we had realized.

Accordingly, hereafter CBS News will provide analyses immediately following appearances of the President and others of public importance, when in its news judgment such service seems desirable and adequate preparation is feasible.

This action is in accord with CBS's long-standing practice of giving new approaches a fair trial, maintaining those that work best in the public interest, and modifying or rejecting those that do not.

Appendix X

Report by the National News Council on President Nixon's Charges Against the Television Networks

ON OCTOBER 26, 1973, at a news conference in the East Room of the White House in Washington, D.C., the President of the United States, Richard M. Nixon, made certain charges against the nation's three major television networks—ABC, CBS, and NBC.

Referring to network newscasts, midway through a conference devoted largely to a discussion of events surrounding the Watergate break-in, the President declared that "I have never heard or seen such outrageous, vicious, distorted reporting in twenty-seven years of public life."

A nationwide television audience estimated at 63,900,000 people, plus a roomful of reporters, heard the President go on to say:

"I'm not blaming anyone for that. Perhaps what happened is that what we did brought it about, and therefore the media decided that they would have to take that particular line.

"But when people are pounded night after night with that kind of frantic, hysterical reporting, it naturally shakes their confidence."

Later during the conference the President was asked: "What is it about the television coverage of you in these past weeks and months that so arouses your anger?"

The President did not specify.

These were serious charges leveled by a President of the United States against the media.

The National News Council, established earlier in 1973 as a nonprofit, independent organization to serve the public interest in preserving freedom of communication and advancing accurate and fair reporting of news, determined on October 30 to review and analyze the President's charges. By a unanimous vote of its fifteen members, the Council decided to ask the President for the specific instances upon which he based his charges.

Speaking on behalf of the Council's nine public members and six members from the media, Roger J. Traynor, chairman, declared that "The charges brought by the President against the media, particularly against the electronic media, are so serious that the National News Council believes they warrant a public airing.

"As an independent body, in a position to make an objective study, we feel that the President's remarks, made publicly before millions of television viewers and reported by the press throughout the world, should be thoroughly investigated."

The chairman, a former Chief Justice of the California Supreme Court, declared that "The Council is undertaking this study as a public service. We believe that the information we develop should be placed on the public record as soon as possible. It is anticipated that the Council's investigation will culminate in a public hearing, and that later its findings will be issued for publication."

On the afternoon of October 30, the Council sent a telegram to Ronald Ziegler, White House press secretary. Signed by its executive director, William B. Arthur, the telegram stated:

> The National News Council today announced that it would investigate charges made by President Nixon in his news conference of October 26 against the television networks for certain news reports and commentaries.
>
> The News Council hereby requests the cooperation of the executive branch in making available to it specific examples of the reporting complained about in order to assist us in our impartial study and analysis of the charges.
>
> Ned Schnurman of the Council staff and I are available to discuss in detail the nature of our investigation and to answer any questions you may have relevant to making this material available to us.

On that same afternoon, the Council hand-delivered to the news divisions of the three television networks letters seeking their cooperation in the study. Addressed to Elmer Lower, president of ABC News, Richard Salant, president of CBS News, and Richard Wald, president of NBC News, the letters, signed by Mr. Arthur, stated:

> The attached news release tells of an action taken by the National News Council today to examine charges made

against the television networks by President Nixon at his news conference of October 26.

I respectfully request your cooperation in making available to the Council for its independent study and analysis of the matter any pertinent transcript or tape aired by [name of network] involving material cited by the President. We would, of course, arrange to do this in a manner most convenient to you.

I welcome an opportunity to discuss this with you further and await your response.

Within a brief period of time, all three network news chiefs informed the Council that they would cooperate in a study of the President's charges if they were given the specific details of the charges. Each of the networks declared that it would make available to the Council transcripts of network newscasts that were designated specifically by the President as being "outrageous, vicious, distorted."

On November 1, Mr. Arthur confirmed, in a telephone call to Mr. Ziegler's office, that the telegram had been received. In that conversation, Ms. Diane Sawyer, administrative assistant to Mr. Ziegler, asked for and was given information about the Council, including a listing of its membership, its funding, its purposes.

Ms. Sawyer informed Mr. Arthur that she would be in touch with him in a day or two.

Receiving no further word from the White House, Mr. Arthur and Mr. Schnurman, associate director of the Council, arranged a meeting on November 6 with Kenneth W. Clawson, deputy director of the White House Office of Communications. The meeting was held in Mr. Clawson's office in the Old Executive Office Building.

Out of this interview came several charges by Mr. Clawson against television network reporting, but he would neither affirm nor deny that they triggered Mr. Nixon's news conference charges. He said that he was not aware of the Council's request to Mr. Ziegler for specific facts to support those charges; that the Council would have to obtain such data from Mr. Ziegler.

The interview consisted largely of a repetition and an elaboration of charges Mr. Clawson had made in interviews with *The New York Times* and *Time* magazine, published on the preceding day. On subsequent publication these charges became known as "The Press Firestorm," a label attributed to Mr. Clawson.

Mr. Arthur and Mr. Schnurman asked Mr. Clawson if he would assist in arranging an immediate interview with Mr. Ziegler, and Mr. Clawson gave them permission to use a White House telephone to call Mr. Ziegler's office.

Mr. Arthur immediately called Mr. Ziegler's office and was advised by Ms. Sawyer that Mr. Ziegler was with the President. She suggested that Mr. Arthur call again at 4:00 P.M. He did so, and Ms. Sawyer said that it would be impossible to see Mr. Ziegler either that day or the next, but that she would get in touch with Mr. Arthur.

Mr. Arthur called Mr. Ziegler's office again on November 9 and November 12, but was unable to arrange a meeting with Mr. Ziegler.

On November 12 the Council, in a meeting in New York, instructed Mr. Arthur to continue his efforts to obtain from the White House specific data in support of the President's charges.

On November 14, Mr. Arthur sent a second telegram to Mr. Ziegler as follows:

> The National News Council urgently requests a reply to our telegram of October 30 asking for specific examples of the television reporting and commentary referred to by President Nixon in his news conference of October 26. The information we seek is to aid us in an objective study and analysis of the charges made by the President at that time.
>
> Ned Schnurman and William Arthur of the Council staff remain available to discuss in detail the nature of our investigation.

There was no response.

In a call to Mr. Clawson's office on Tuesday, November 20, arrangements were made to see Mr. Clawson on Wednesday, November 28.

On Monday, November 26, Mr. Schnurman called Ms. Sawyer to inquire whether he and Mr. Arthur could see Mr. Ziegler while they were in Washington to see Mr. Clawson. Ms. Sawyer said she would call on the following day with an answer.

In two calls on Tuesday afternoon, November 27, to Ms. Sawyer, her secretary responded that Ms. Sawyer was in meetings but would return the call.

Early on Wednesday, November 28, Ms. Sawyer called to report that Mr. Ziegler would see Mr. Arthur and Mr. Schnurman and that the time would be coordinated with the meeting with Mr. Clawson. Because of fog over the Eastern Seaboard, the meeting scheduled for that day with Mr. Clawson was postponed to 11:30 A.M., November 29.

On November 29, Mr. Arthur and Mr. Schnurman met with Mr. Clawson in the office of Deputy White House Press Secretary Gerald L. Warren, who was not present because of illness. Mr. Clawson said that Mr. Ziegler would meet with Mr. Arthur and Mr. Schnurman following that morning's press briefing by Mr. Ziegler.

There was no further interview with Mr. Clawson.

That afternoon, Mr. Arthur and Mr. Schnurman met for approximately twenty-five minutes with Mr. Ziegler and at the outset reiterated their request for specifications of the President's charges against the television networks.

Mr. Ziegler said that the White House could not supply the Council with such a list; that it had neither the time nor the staff to devote to such a project. He declared that it would be inappropriate for the White House to act in concert with the Council in a study of the President's charges.

Mr. Arthur assured Mr. Ziegler that the Council had no intention of "working in concert" with the White House; that the Council simply was seeking specification of the charges.

Mr. Ziegler said that the White House would cooperate if the Council provided examples of what it wanted. He said that he preferred to see a broad-based study of White House-media relationships and suggested that a time span beginning with the Cambodian intrusion to the present would make sense.

He said that the Council should feel free to call him, Pat Buchanan, or Ken Clawson at any time such a study were undertaken.

Among other points that he made were the following:

The President's charges at the October 26 news conference were not just the result of stories after the firing of Special Prosecutor Archibald Cox, but that these stories had triggered his reaction.

He expressed a fear that a superficial, "quickie" study of the record would result in a Council finding that the networks were simply doing their job and that they were really "good boys."

He said that he firmly believes that certain elements of the media are out to get the Nixon Administration.

He said that the genesis of the President's charges encompasses many examples of television reporting, and referred specifically to the CBS interview Walter Cronkite had with Mr. Cox.

"I don't mean to single this one out," he said, referring to Mr. Cronkite's mentioning a trust fund for the President during that interview and at the same time "ignoring an earlier White House denial that such a fund exists."

He referred to the use of Hanoi radio quotations during news broadcasts following the resumption of bombing of North Vietnam on December 18, 1972. This use was in connection, he said, with the President's charge that he had been called a "tyrant, dictator . . ."

The Associated Press, in a dispatch datelined Washington as published in *The New York Times*, among others, reported as follows:

WHITE HOUSE REFUSES
TO JOIN STUDY ON NEWS

Washington, Dec. 8 (AP)—The White House said yesterday that it would be "unable to join in any cooperative research study" regarding the press and news broadcasting as urged by the National News Council.

The council had asked President Nixon's press secretary, Ronald L. Ziegler, for further information and specifics regarding the President's reference at a recent news conference to "vicious, distorted reporting."

Asked if Mr. Ziegler had given a reply to the council's request, Gerald L. Warren, the deputy press secretary, said the White House could not join in the study "because we simply don't have the staff or the time."

The National News Council, which is based in New York, describes itself as a nonprofit organization established to consider public grievances about national news reporting and to study issues involving freedom of the press.

Mr. Arthur and Mr. Schnurman reported to the Council, at a meeting at "Wingspread," Racine, Wisconsin, on December 10, the results of their efforts, since the meeting of the Council on November 12, to identify the specific broadcast items on which the President based his charges. They reported that Mr. Ziegler and Mr. Clawson dwelled at some length in their interviews on six areas of television network reporting:

1. Reporting on Hanoi's charges of Presidential tyranny during the bombing period beginning on December 18, 1972.

2. Reporting in the early fall of 1973 on the President's personal finances.

3. Accusations against the Administration of "manufacturing" the Mideast alert to divert attention from Watergate.

4. The Cox interview and other reporting about an alleged Presidential trust fund.

5. Reporting on the ITT settlement, with alleged unfavorable references to the President.

6. The preponderance of "unfavorable" comments and interviews on network newscasts beginning on Monday evening, October 22, following the firing of Mr. Cox on October 20.

The Council decided that it should continue its efforts to get specific details of the President's charges. Abstracts of network evening newscasts and commentaries surrounding these six listed areas were obtained from the Vanderbilt Television News Archives in Nashville, Tenn. These were to be presented to Mr. Ziegler's office with a request that the White House designate specifically which newscasts were, in the opinion of the President, "outrageous, vicious, distorted."

Requests for a meeting with Mr. Ziegler to present these abstracts were made by telephone to the White House on December 11, 14, 15, 19, 26, and 27.

The following letter was sent by Mr. Arthur to Mr. Ziegler on January 3:

> I am writing to request a response to our continuing attempts to learn of specific instances of "outrageous, vicious and distorted" reporting by the national television networks as described by the President in his October 26 news conference.
>
> Ned Schnurman and I were most grateful for the time you spent with us when we visited with you on November 29. Since that time we have endeavored, through our research, to compile areas that could be the subject for further discussion in an effort to pin down the specifics related to the President's charges. Our efforts to obtain a further meeting with you, or with some member of your staff, were made in phone calls to your administrative assistant, Diane Sawyer. Those calls were placed on December 11, 14, 15, 19, 26 and 27, but none has been returned.
>
> We request a further meeting and await your response so that we may advance our report to the full Council, which meets later this month.

On January 11, Diane Sawyer called to say that her office had received Mr. Arthur's letter of January 3 and that Mr. Ziegler had requested her to report that he had hoped to see Mr. Arthur and Mr. Schnurman, or have Mr. Clawson do so, but that his stay in San Clemente had resulted in a delay. Ms. Sawyer inquired about the date of the next Council meeting and said that she would be in touch with Mr. Arthur within a day or two after the Presidential party returned to Washington.

On January 16, Connie Gerrard of the White House press office called to report that Mr. Ziegler would see Mr. Arthur and Mr. Schnurman on the following day at 3:00 P.M.

On January 17, Mr. Arthur and Mr. Schnurman met with Mr. Ziegler in his office for approximately thirty minutes.

Mr. Arthur opened the conversation by stating that the Council was seeking again to obtain specifications of the President's charges of October 26.

Mr. Ziegler reiterated his earlier assertion that the White House did not wish to get into any "cooperative research venture" with the National News Council. Mr. Arthur again stated that the Council did not wish to get involved in a "cooperative research venture"; that it was, and still is, seeking only the specifications of the President's charges of "outrageous, vicious, distorted" reporting by the networks.

Mr. Ziegler again stated that the White House did not have the time or the staff to prepare such a list.

Mr. Schnurman then advised Mr. Ziegler of the research undertaken by the Council since the previous meeting with him. He gave Mr. Ziegler a copy of the Vanderbilt abstracts of newscasts on subjects the Council had been able to identify as those that Mr. Ziegler and other members of the President's staff asserted were unfairly presented on the networks. He was asked to identify from these abstracts television network newscasts that, in the opinion of the President, were "outrageous, vicious, distorted."

Mr. Ziegler accepted the file of abstracts. He stated that he did not necessarily agree with some of the thoughts that other White House aides had on the subject of network coverage. He said, however, that he did object to what he described as "incomplete" reporting.

At the conclusion of the meeting, Mr. Ziegler said that the abstracts would be studied and that his office would respond with an answer on how far, if at all, it would go in providing the Council with the information it is seeking. He assured Mr. Arthur and Mr.

Schnurman that an answer would be forthcoming before the next scheduled Council meeting, on January 28 in New York City.

As of January 28, no such answer has been received.

CONCLUSION

Through a period of three months, the National News Council has been unable to obtain from the White House specific grounds for the charges made by President Nixon against the television networks during his October 26, 1973, news conference.

Two telegrams, at least fifteen telephone calls and three interviews produced statements by Mr. Ziegler that the White House has neither the time nor the staff to prepare a listing of the instances giving rise to the President's charges.

The National News Council believes that the public needs to know:

What television network news reports were "outrageous"?

What television network news reports were "vicious"?

What television network news reports were "distorted"?

The Council hoped that, in the public interest, it would get answers to these questions.

As a service to the American people in preserving freedom of communication and advancing accurate and fair reporting of news, the Council is prepared to study and analyze such answers and the responses of the networks to them carefully and impartially. In the public interest it would bring to this task the experience of its fifteen members, representing the public and the media, and its six advisers, and would invoke the advice and assistance of other concerned citizens.

It is prepared, as an independent and objective body, to hear both sides in a public hearing and to make public its findings.

It would be difficult, if not futile, however, for the Council to attempt to deduce, from broad and nonspecific charges, the particular actions of the television networks that inspired the President's remarks at his news conference on October 26, 1973. Under the circumstances, the National News Council cannot proceed with the type of study and analysis it contemplated.

We believe it is seriously detrimental to the public interest for the President to leave his harsh criticisms of the television networks unsupported by specific details that could then be evaluated objectively by an impartial body.

Appendix XI

The National News Council's Report on ABC's "Oil: The Policy Crisis"

ABC's documentary is entitled "Oil: The Policy Crisis." Near the outset, Jules Bergman describes its purpose in part as follows:

> . . . this program is a primer on oil and oil policy. It is designed to help understand the current crisis.

According to Mobil's Mr. Schmertz, in his April 9 letter to Mr. Duffy of ABC, ABC had sent Mobil a telegram on March 18, inviting comments on the documentary (which was to be aired March 20). The telegram described the program as "basically a primer on oil, designed to help Americans understand a highly charged and difficult problem," and went on to say that "it has been researched and executed from every conceivable point of view."

After viewing the program, Mr. Schmertz took strenuous exception to it, asserting that the implication of the above remarks was that the program "would be balanced and educational," but that "It was not." He made several general criticisms of the organization and basic thrust of the program, and appended an analysis discussing what a Mobil press release described as thirty-two statements in the program which Mr. Schmertz and his colleagues regarded as "particularly inaccurate or unfair."

The Grievance Committee will not comment on the issue of the precise accuracy or fairness of the individual statements, because we feel that ABC kept well within the bounds of robust opinion journalism in its selection and presentation of material. There are no significantly misleading factual misstatements. Beyond that key test, in an area as complex as oil policy, a one-hour television documentary is bound to omit much that is important. Moreover, ABC was not under any obligation to give a scrupulously balanced presentation in any single program. It could, and did, select certain facts that pointed in one direction and omit others that pointed elsewhere. Its organization of the facts presented, moreover, created one specific editorial impression: namely that government policy on oil has been manipulated over the years by the oil industry itself, to the detriment of the public interest and for its own private profit.

Whether that is true or not is not for this Council to say. It is, however, well within the right of ABC under the First Amendment to say it.

Where ABC did err, however, was in giving the impression indicated in the first two paragraphs above. We believe Mr. Schmertz was correct in assuming, and we believe that viewers generally were also led to assume, that this documentary was striving conscientiously for balance and fairness. In cultivating that impression, ABC was professing adherence to a standard higher than was required of it and higher than it in fact achieved.

It is a mistake, in this Council's opinion, for a television network to contend that a documentary on a controversial subject is necessarily "executed from every conceivable point of view." Such a documentary can be imagined; it might even be produced. But such comprehensiveness is certainly not legally required, and in fact is rarely achieved. Rather, the Council believes that ABC and the other networks should be encouraged to take forthright stands on controversial subjects, promoting their editorial views with vigor and supporting them with such facts as they deem relevant and persuasive. In the interests of credibility, certain standards are of course advisable, and in addition, under the Fairness Doctrine, a reasonable balance of opposing opinions must ultimately be presented. But, short of outright factual misstatements, the interests of free expression are best served by allowing full scope to a variety of views, very definitely including those that are one-sided.

Complaint dismissed.

The following two appendices were part of "Broadcasting in America: The Performance of Network Affiliates in the Top 50 Markets," which was issued May 31, 1973. It was a dissenting opinion to the 1973 Arkansas, Louisiana, and Mississippi license renewals by Nicholas Johnson, who was then serving as a commissioner on the Federal Communications Commission.

Appendix XII

MR. JOHNSON asks the reader, in reviewing the ranking for news and public affairs, to bear a few things in mind: "It is impossible to tell without actual observation . . . whether a station's news operation is of the wire service 'rip and read' variety or whether there are mobile camera units roaming the city to provide original feeds at all hours. Until such information is available, however, we must rely on what the stations are required to tell the Commission quantitatively about their programming operations. For, although a station broadcasting only 8 hours of news in a 140-hour week may in fact be investing more time, expense, and imagination in its production than one airing 14 hours in the same week, the only presumption we can make is the contrary—the more news, the better the potential for public service." Mr. Johnson adds that because of the deficiencies of the data asked for by the FCC on license renewal applications, this ranking fails to take into account at what time of day news and public affairs programs are broadcast. It is based solely on the number of hours of programming presented.—EDITOR

Network affiliates ranked by total hours of News, Public Affairs, and "Other"* in composite

Rank	Call letters	Net. aff.	Mkt. no.	Location	News hours and rank		Pub. affairs hours and rank		Other hours and rank		Composite
1	WPLG	ABC	18	Miami	17.90	9	11.12	7	16.82	12	45.833
2	WMAQ	NBC	3	Chicago	19.98	4	9.10	15	14.00	21	43.083
3	KNBC	NBC	2	Los Angeles	22.00	1	10.03	9	10.78	70	42.817
4	WCBS	CBS	1	New York City	16.13	27	4.10	83	21.72	1	41.950
5	WAGA	CBS	17	Atlanta	17.72	12	4.97	59	18.92	6	41.600
6	KDKA	CBS	9	Pittsburgh	20.20	2	7.13	31	13.50	27	40.833
7	KYW	NBC	4	Philadelphia	18.55	6	11.43	3	10.83	60	40.817
8	KNXT	CBS	2	Los Angeles	17.05	19	4.10	83	19.63	5	40.783
9	WCAU	CBS	4	Philadelphia	16.37	25	3.62	98	20.12	3	40.100
10	WTOP	CBS	10	Washington D.C.	17.12	17	9.92	10	12.52	38	39.550
11	KMOX	CBS	12	St. Louis	16.25	26	4.70	68	18.22	8	39.167
12	WBRC	ABC	38	Birmingham	13.97	54	6.07	39	18.72	7	38.750
13	KPIX	CBS	8	San Francisco	16.62	23	10.72	8	11.37	59	38.700
14	KCRA	NBC	27	Sacramento-Stockton	20.15	3	7.67	20	10.57	77	38.383
15	WRC	NBC	10	Washington D.C.	14.83	41	9.37	13	13.78	23	37.983
16	WBZ	NBC	6	Boston	18.53	7	7.78	19	11.17	65	37.483
17	WNBC	NBC	1	New York City	15.08	39	11.13	6	11.08	66	37.300
18	WBBM	CBS	3	Chicago	14.28	49	5.57	48	17.42	9	37.267
19	WBNS	CBS	28	Columbus	13.60	55	5.60	47	16.87	11	36.067
20	KFMB	CBS	49	San Diego	19.27	5	4.22	80	12.08	46	35.567
21	WBEN	CBS	25	Buffalo	15.90	30	7.45	23	12.05	48	35.400
22	KPRC	NBC	15	Houston	15.80	32	7.32	27	12.03	49	35.150
23	WHNB	NBC	22	Hartford-New Haven	15.20	36	6.27	36	13.55	25	35.017
24	WWL	CBS	31	New Orleans	16.77	20	5.50	49	12.70	36	34.967

* "Other" programming is described by the FCC as all programming not falling in categories of news, public affairs, entertainment, or sports.

Rank	Call letters	Net. aff.	Mkt. no.	Location	News hours and rank		Pub. affairs hours and rank		Other hours and rank		Composite
25	WMAR	CBS	19	Baltimore	15.07	40	6.33	35	13.52	26	34.917
26	WLWI	ABC	14	Indianapolis	8.17	127	6.83	32	19.83	4	34.833
27	WCKT	NBC	18	Miami	14.37	46	7.38	25	12.68	37	34.433
28	WTIC	CBS	22	Hartford-New Haven	13.58	56	5.18	55	15.60	18	34.367
29	KOIN	CBS	26	Portland	14.03	53	3.07	117	17.25	10	34.350
30	KHOU	CBS	15	Houston	14.65	44	8.70	16	10.47	83	33.817
31	WWJ	NBC	5	Detroit	14.80	42	4.75	66	13.95	22	33.500
31	WTVT	CBS	24	Tampa-St. Petersburg	16.77	20	5.22	54	11.52	56	33.500
33	WBAL	NBC	19	Baltimore	14.07	52	4.45	74	14.85	19	33.367
34	KDFW	CBS	11	Dallas-Fort Worth	16.65	22	3.22	113	13.45	28	33.317
35	KGW	NBC	26	Portland	16.48	24	5.73	44	11.05	68	33.267
36	KXTV	CBS	27	Sacramento-Stockton	17.22	16	4.07	89	11.40	58	32.683
37	WOTV	NBC	41	Kalamazoo-Gr Rapids	14.68	43	6.42	34	11.53	55	32.633
38	WFMY	CBS	48	Gnsb-High Pt-Win Sal	12.82	67	3.87	92	15.82	16	32.500
39	WRTV	NBC	14	Indianapolis	12.62	69	7.47	22	12.33	43	32.417
40	WMAL	ABC	10	Washington D.C.	10.43	101	7.67	20	14.25	20	32.350
41	WNAC	ABC	6	Boston	11.43	84	11.17	4	9.38	95	31.983
42	WLWD	NBC	39	Dayton	11.83	74	7.92	18	12.08	46	31.833
43	WJW	CBS	7	Cleveland	11.57	81	3.43	104	16.70	13	31.700
43	WLCY	ABC	24	Tampa-St. Petersburg	8.08	129	7.38	25	16.23	15	31.700
45	WZZM	ABC	41	Kalamazoo-Gr Rapids	6.25	137	4.30	79	21.12	2	31.667
46	WAPI	NBC	38	Birmingham	15.63	33	4.90	60	11.08	66	31.617
47	WJAR	NBC	34	Providence	13.35	63	7.40	24	10.53	79	31.283
48	KING	NBC	16	Seattle-Tacoma	13.48	61	4.50	72	13.25	32	31.233
49	WCPO	CBS	20	Cincinnati	11.27	88	3.28	110	16.52	14	31.067
50	WBAP	NBC	11	Dallas-Fort Worth	15.02	29	7.22	30	7.90	118	31.033

Rank	Call letters	Net. aff.	Mkt. no.	Location	News hours and rank		Pub. affairs hours and rank		Other hours and rank		Composite
51	WFLA	NBC	24	Tampa-St. Petersburg	16.10	28	2.98	119	11.85	52	30.933
52	WBTV	CBS	35	Charlotte	15.13	38	3.30	108	12.40	41	30.833
53	WIIC	NBC	9	Pittsburgh	17.55	13	4.83	62	8.40	110	30.783
54	WAVY	NBC	44	Norf-Newp News-Hamp	13.50	58	8.15	17	9.10	99	30.750
55	WDSU	NBC	31	New Orleans	17.12	17	4.53	71	9.10	99	30.750
56	WSB	NBC	17	Atlanta	17.40	15	4.10	83	9.22	97	30.717
57	WSPA	CBS	40	Gnville-Sptnbg-Ashvi	11.32	87	3.57	100	15.62	17	30.500
58	WSAZ	NBC	33	Charleston-Huntington	14.37	46	5.38	51	10.73	71	30.483
59	WJZ	ABC	19	Baltimore	11.58	79	11.90	2	6.85	133	30.333
60	WTAE	ABC	9	Pittsburgh	11.82	75	9.63	12	8.75	104	30.200
61	WLS	ABC	3	Chicago	9.50	114	7.25	28	13.43	30	30.183
62	WPVI	ABC	4	Philadelphia	9.32	117	9.25	14	11.50	57	30.067
63	WFBC	NBC	40	Gnvile-Sptnbg-Ashvi	11.33	86	7.23	29	11.35	60	29.917
64	KTAR	NBC	45	Phoenix	17.85	10	6.27	36	5.67	140	29.783
65	WISH	CBS	14	Indianapolis	18.42	8	2.50	126	8.67	107	29.583
66	KOMO	ABC	16	Seattle-Tacoma	12.88	66	5.30	53	11.32	61	29.500
66	WLWC	NBC	28	Columbus	9.33	116	9.67	11	10.50	80	29.500
68	KSD	NBC	12	St. Louis	17.47	14	6.05	40	5.98	138	29.500
69	KCMO	CBS	23	Kansas City	11.72	77	3.93	90	13.62	24	29.267
70	KGO	ABC	8	San Francisco	10.05	107	11.15	5	7.80	121	29.000
70	WIOL	CBS	45	Toledo	13.37	62	2.35	133	13.28	31	29.000
72	WDAF	NBC	23	Kansas City	17.75	11	4.18	81	6.88	132	28.817
73	KMGH	CBS	32	Denver	11.58	79	4.32	78	12.82	35	28.717
74	WCCO	CBS	13	Minreapolis-St. Paul	13.50	58	3.88	91	11.20	63	28.583
75	WSOC	NBC	35	Charlotte	13.50	58	4.77	65	10.18	86	28.450
76	KOOL	CBS	45	Phoenix	15.33	34	2.52	125	10.57	77	28.417

Rank	Call letters	Net. aff.	Mkt. no.	Location	News hours and rank		Pub. affairs hours and rank		Other hours and rank		Composite
77	WABC	ABC	1	New York City	10.58	98	5.37	52	12.42	40	28.367
77	WKY	NBC	41	Oklahoma City	14.58	45	5.88	42	7.90	118	28.367
79	KOA	NBC	32	Denver	14.32	48	6.17	38	7.87	120	28.350
80	WMC	NBC	29	Memphis	15.82	31	5.13	57	7.33	127	28.283
81	WTNH	ABC	22	Hartford-New Haven	8.87	121	12.92	1	6.43	136	28.217
82	KWTV	CBS	41	Oklahoma City	12.25	72	3.55	101	12.22	44	28.017
83	KIRO	CBS	16	Seattle-Tacoma	14.23	50	4.40	76	9.15	98	27.783
84	WHAS	CBS	36	Louisville	15.27	35	1.08	143	11.23	62	27.583
85	WAVE	NBC	36	Louisville	11.47	82	4.08	86	12.00	51	27.550
86	WKYC	NBC	7	Cleveland	11.73	76	5.15	56	10.62	75	27.500
87	WTVJ	CBS	18	Miami	12.05	73	5.07	58	10.23	85	27.350
88	WOAI	NBC	45	San Antonio	15.17	37	6.75	33	5.42	141	27.333
89	WHEN	CBS	43	Syracuse	11.37	85	3.73	96	12.17	45	27.267
90	KSL	CBS	50	Salt Lake City	10.57	99	3.77	95	12.92	34	27.250
91	KSTP	NBC	13	Minneapolis-St. Paul	14.10	51	5.62	46	7.33	127	27.050
92	WIMJ	NBC	21	Milwaukee	12.40	71	4.08	86	10.50	80	26.983
93	KFNS	CBS	45	San Antonio	12.82	67	3.10	116	10.72	72	26.633
94	WPRI	CBS	34	Providence	12.98	65	4.70	68	8.10	115	25.783
95	KIRK	ABC	15	Houston	10.97	91	4.85	61	9.82	89	25.633
96	KATU	ABC	26	Portland	10.85	94	2.83	120	11.83	53	25.517
97	WSM	NBC	30	Nashville	13.00	64	4.35	77	8.17	113	25.517
98	WISN	CBS	21	Milwaukee	10.23	104	2.80	121	12.35	42	25.383
99	WJBK	CBS	5	Detroit	10.05	107	3.28	110	12.02	50	25.350
100	WKZO	CBS	41	Kalamazoo-Gr Rapids	8.58	124	3.30	108	13.45	28	25.333
101	WLAC	CBS	30	Nashville	10.83	95	2.33	134	11.83	53	25.000
102	KGTV	NBC	49	San Diego	13.57	57	4.50	72	6.77	134	24.833

Rank	Call letters	Net. aff.	Mkt. no.	Location	News hours and rank		Pub. affairs hours and rank		Other hours and rank		Composite
103	WTEN	CBS	37	Albany-Schenectady-T	10.62	97	3.20	114	10.65	74	24.467
104	KUTV	NBC	50	Salt Lake City	10.32	102	5.98	41	8.12	114	24.417
105	WXII	NBC	48	Gnsb-High Pt-Win Sal	10.88	93	4.45	74	8.93	102	24.267
106	WKBW	ABC	25	Buffalo	8.75	123	5.82	43	9.67	93	24.233
107	WHTN	ABC	33	Charleston-Huntington	10.22	105	3.48	103	10.50	80	24.200
108	WREC	CBS	29	Memphis	11.05	89	4.17	82	8.75	104	23.967
109	WGR	NBC	25	Buffalo	10.50	100	4.63	70	8.45	109	23.583
110	WTEV	ABC	34	Providence	11.63	78	5.65	45	6.22	137	23.500
111	WITI	ABC	21	Milwaukee	9.55	113	3.43	104	10.40	84	23.383
112	WVUE	ABC	31	New Orleans	10.08	106	3.32	107	9.90	87	23.300
113	WSPD	NBC	45	Toledo	9.68	111	2.50	126	11.10	65	23.283
114	WFAA	ABC	11	Dallas-Fort Worth	12.62	69	3.25	112	7.17	131	23.033
115	KABC	ABC	2	Los Angeles	9.75	110	4.83	62	8.38	111	22.967
116	WXYZ	ABC	5	Detroit	10.30	103	3.82	93	8.75	104	22.867
117	WBMG	CBS	38	Birmngham	7.73	132	5.40	50	9.50	94	22.633
118	WLWT	NBC	20	Cincinnati	11.00	90	3.42	106	7.92	117	22.333
119	WAST	ABC	37	Albany-Schenectady-T	9.22	119	3.73	96	9.30	96	22.250
120	KOVR	ABC	27	Sacramento-Stockton	9.57	112	1.80	142	10.67	73	22.033
121	WRGB	NBC	37	Albany-Schenectady-T	11.47	82	3.00	118	7.38	126	21.850
122	KTVK	ABC	45	Phoenix	9.50	114	4.83	62	7.28	129	21.617
123	WHIO	CBS	39	Dayton	8.38	125	2.45	130	10.60	76	21.433
124	KOCO	ABC	41	Oklahoma City	8.00	130	3.58	99	9.70	92	21.283
125	WSIX	ABC	30	Nashville	5.35	141	2.65	122	12.95	33	20.950
126	WQXI	ABC	17	Atlanta	9.22	119	4.08	86	7.22	130	20.517
127	WSYR	NBC	43	Syracuse	9.25	118	3.55	101	7.47	125	20.267
128	KBTV	ABC	32	Denver	9.97	109	3.20	114	6.55	135	19.717

Rank	Call letters	Net. aff.	Mkt. no.	Location	News hours and rank		Pub. affairs hours and rank		Other hours and rank		Composite
129	WCCB	ABC	35	Charlotte	5.08	142	1.90	141	12.52	38	19.500
130	WTVN	ABC	28	Columbus	7.42	133	2.20	136	9.80	90	19.417
131	KSAT	ABC	45	San Antonio	10.95	92	3.80	94	4.27	144	19.017
132	WCHS	CBS	33	Charleston-Huntington	8.85	122	2.00	139	7.97	116	18.817
133	KMBC	ABC	23	Kansas City	7.37	134	2.40	132	8.98	101	18.750
134	WEWS	ABC	7	Cleveland	8.12	128	2.03	137	8.35	112	18.500
135	WVEC	ABC	44	Norf-Newp News-Hamp	10.63	96	2.43	131	5.27	142	18.333
136	KCPX	ABC	50	Salt Lake City	6.00	139	4.75	66	7.53	124	18.283
137	WLOS	ABC	40	Gnville-Sptnbg-Ashvi	8.00	130	2.62	123	7.58	123	18.200
138	WKRC	ABC	20	Cincinnati	5.88	140	2.50	126	9.78	91	18.167
139	WHBQ	ABC	29	Memphis	6.47	136	2.33	134	8.87	103	17.667
140	KTVI	ABC	12	St. Louis	6.15	138	2.55	124	8.67	107	17.367
141	KMSP	ABC	13	Minneapolis-St. Paul	8.20	126	2.03	137	5.68	139	15.917
142	WLKY	ABC	36	Louisville	4.53	143	2.47	129	7.73	122	14.733
143	WNYS	ABC	43	Syracuse	6.55	135	1.93	140	5.12	143	13.600
144	WDHO	ABC	45	Toledo	1.67	144	.83	144	9.90	87	12.400

Appendix XIII

Mr. Johnson says this is an "evaluation of the programming of each of 144 network affiliates in the top 50 markets on the basis of four distinct programming criteria: a combination of news, public affairs, and other programming; local programming; commercialization; and allocation of financial resources to program expenditures." —EDITOR

Network affiliates ranked by composite of all programming criteria

Rank	Call letters	Net. aff.	Mkt. no.	Location	Local	News, pub. affairs and other	Commer.	Financial
1	KPIX	CBS	8	San Francisco	31	13	1	103
2	WJZ	ABC	19	Baltimore	6	59	4	24
3	KING	NBC	16	Seattle-Tacoma	76	48	6	3
4	KDKA	CBS	9	Pittsburgh	4	6	30	57
5	KYW	NBC	4	Philadelphia	2	7	23	123
6	WPLG	ABC	18	Miami	10	1	81	52
7	WMAL	ABC	10	Washington, D.C.	28	40	41	9
8	WTAE	ABC	9	Pittsburgh	52	60	10	15
9	WFMY	CBS	48	Gnsb-High Pt-Win Sal	96	38	2	76
10	KGW	NBC	26	Portland	67	35	49	2

Rank	Call letters	Net. aff.	Mkt. no.	Location	Local	News, pub. affairs and other	Commer.	Financial
11	WWL	CBS	31	New Orleans	7	24	70	31
12	WRC	NBC	10	Washington, D.C.	49	15	101	7
13	WABC	ABC	1	New York City	63	77	49	1
14	KNBC	NBC	2	Los Angeles	3	3	138	35
15	WIIC	NBC	9	Pittsburgh	17	53	101	8
16	WTIC	CBS	22	Hartford-New Haven	68	28	5	110
17	WNAC	ABC	6	Boston	37	41	24	59
18	KATO	ABC	26	Portland	50	96	24	13
19	WHAS	CBS	36	Louisville	35	84	33	20
20	KCRA	NBC	27	Sacramento-Stockton	27	14	70	69
21	KOIN	CBS	26	Portland	84	29	57	12
22	WBNS	CBS	28	Columbus	22	19	81	61
23	KTAR	NBC	45	Phoenix	8	64	63	48
24	KOMO	ABC	16	Seattle-Tacoma	32	66	57	28
25	WLWT	NBC	20	Cincinnati	1	118	129	44
26	WCBS	CBS	1	New York City	75	4	108	27
27	KMOX	CBS	12	St. Louis	59	11	101	36
28	WSM	NBC	30	Nashville	24	97	63	16
29	WKY	NBC	41	Oklahoma City	16	78	36	70
30	WAST	ABC	37	Albany-Schenectady-T	135	119	8	4
31	WSB	NBC	17	Atlanta	5	56	49	116
31	WBZ	NBC	6	Boston	15	16	49	138
33	KSL	CBS	50	Salt Lake City	57	90	88	6
34	WMAR	CBS	19	Baltimore	11	25	78	104
35	WZZM	ABC	41	Kalamazoo-Gr Rapids	112	45	41	14
36	WDSU	NBC	31	New Orleans	20	55	81	55
37	WRTV	NBC	14	Indianapolis	65	39	36	64

Rank	Call letters	Net. aff.	Mkt. no.	Location	Local	News, pub. affairs and other	Commer.	Financial
38	WBEN	CBS	25	Buffalo	55	21	87	80
39	WNBC	NBC	1	New York City	60	17	88	58
40	KNXT	CBS	2	Los Angeles	21	8	121	88
41	KPRC	NBC	15	Houston	29	22	78	94
42	WCPO	CBS	20	Cincinnati	40	49	98	33
43	WMAQ	NBC	3	Chicago	41	2	132	74
44	KOVR	ABC	27	Sacramento-Stockton	134	120	16	5
45	WITI	CBS	21	Milwaukee	72	111	16	41
46	WCAU	CBS	4	Philadelphia	42	9	121	73
47	WSYR	NBC	43	Syracuse	117	127	13	10
48	WDAL	NBC	19	Baltimore	19	33	88	101
49	WBRC	ABC	38	Birmingham	23	12	49	144
50	WPVI	ABC	4	Philadelphia	14	62	112	45
51	WPRI	CBS	34	Providence	115	34	3	113
52	WAPI	NBC	38	Birmingham	126	46	16	63
53	KUTV	NBC	50	Salt Lake City	83	104	63	11
54	KWTV	CBS	41	Oklahoma City	77	82	70	25
55	WTOP	CBS	10	Washington D.C.	79	10	117	50
56	WCKT	NBC	18	Miami	71	27	41	117
57	WSOC	NBC	35	Charlotte	122	75	16	47
58	WOAI	NBC	45	San Antonio	58	88	30	93
59	KSTP	NBC	13	Minneapolis-St. Paul	43	91	57	71
60	WAGA	CBS	17	Atlanta	70	5	121	79
61	WSIX	ABC	30	Nashville	82	125	30	22
62	WOTV	NBC	41	Kalamazoo-Gr Rapids	48	37	106	67
63	WXII	NBC	48	Gnsb-High Pt-Win Sal	118	105	28	21
64	KIRK	ABC	15	Houston	18	95	63	100

Rank	Call letters	Net. aff.	Mkt. no.	Location	Local	News, pub. affairs and other	Commer.	Financial
65	WLWI	ABC	14	Indianapolis	64	26	129	37
66	KSD	NBC	12	St. Louis	36	68	70	108
66	WTVJ	CBS	18	Miami	105	87	33	46
68	KTVI	ABC	12	St. Louis	86	140	24	19
69	WWJ	NBC	5	Detroit	9	31	129	112
70	KHOU	CBS	15	Houston	25	30	108	127
71	WLCY	ABC	24	Tampa-St. Petersburg	61	44	81	96
72	WFBC	NBC	40	Gnville-Sptnbg-Ashvi	104	63	13	130
73	WKBW	ABC	25	Buffalo	78	106	16	109
74	WTMJ	NBC	21	Milwaukee	13	92	106	89
74	WBBM	CBS	3	Chicago	33	18	141	65
76	KGO	ABC	8	San Francisco	94	70	98	30
77	WJW	CBS	7	Cleveland	69	43	101	77
78	KSAT	ABC	45	San Antonio	90	131	28	38
79	WVUE	ABC	31	New Orleans	107	112	41	34
80	WTVT	CBS	24	Tampa-St. Petersburg	80	32	117	51
81	WAVY	NBC	44	Norf-Newp News-Hamp	121	54	36	84
82	WBTV	CBS	35	Charlotte	46	52	88	120
83	WLWD	NBC	39	Dayton	30	42	137	83
84	WCCO	CBS	13	Minneapolis-St. Paul	12	74	139	72
85	WFAA	ABC	11	Dallas-Fort Worth	47	114	70	85
86	WLAC	CBS	30	Nashville	39	101	114	49
87	KCMO	CBS	23	Kansas City	54	69	101	97
88	WTFV	ABC	34	Providence	130	110	41	32
89	WMC	NBC	29	Memphis	38	80	114	92
90	WTEN	CBS	37	Albany-Schenectady-T	110	103	70	39
91	KOCO	ABC	41	Oklahoma City	62	124	81	53

Rank	Call letters	Net. aff.	Mkt. no.	Location	Local	News, pub. affairs and other	Commer.	Financial
92	WLKY	ABC	36	Louisville	136	142	11	23
93	WBAP	NBC	11	Dallas-Fort Worth	132	50	36	115
94	WJAR	NBC	34	Providence	114	47	70	91
95	WTNH	ABC	22	Hartford-New Haven	81	81	57	124
96	KFMB	CBS	49	San Diego	51	20	132	128
97	KTVK	ABC	45	Phoenix	88	122	49	75
98	WTOL	CBS	45	Toledo	87	71	63	122
99	KMGH	CBS	32	Denver	44	73	117	98
100	WDHO	ABC	45	Toledo	139	144	6	29
101	KDFW	CBS	11	Dallas-Fort Worth	26	34	121	141
102	KABC	ABC	2	Los Angeles	123	115	88	17
103	WHNB	NBC	22	Hartford-New Haven	116	23	63	136
104	WISH	CBS	14	Indianapolis	73	65	78	135
105	KXTV	CBS	27	Sacramento-Stockton	101	36	121	66
106	WAVE	NBC	36	Louisville	95	85	88	86
107	WNYS	ABC	43	Syracuse	144	143	8	18
108	WHEN	CBS	43	Syracuse	127	89	88	54
109	KCPX	ABC	50	Salt Lake City	142	136	16	40
110	WHTN	ABC	33	Charleston-Huntington	140	107	16	102
111	WLOS	ABC	40	Gnvlle-Sptnbg-Ashvi	143	137	12	60
112	KGTV	NBC	49	San Diego	111	102	88	62
113	KOA	NBC	32	Denver	56	79	108	132
114	KIRO	CBS	16	Seattle-Tacoma	66	83	108	125
115	WLS	ABC	3	Chicago	53	61	142	68
116	WKYC	NBC	7	Cleveland	113	86	121	43
117	WXYZ	ABC	5	Detroit	89	116	132	26
118	WRGB	NBC	37	Albany-Schenectady-T	100	121	36	129

Rank	Call letters	Net. aff.	Mkt. no.	Location	Local	News, pub. affairs and other	Commer.	Financial
119	WSPD	NBC	45	Toledo	124	113	41	107
120	WKRC	ABC	20	Cincinnati	74	138	33	133
121	WCHS	CBS	33	Charleston-Huntington	85	132	24	140
122	KMSP	ABC	13	Minneapolis-St. Paul	109	141	13	126
123	WGR	NBC	25	Buffalo	141	109	41	81
124	WSAZ	NBC	33	Charleston-Huntington	119	58	70	139
125	WEWS	ABC	7	Cleveland	92	134	98	56
126	WHIO	CBS	39	Dayton	45	123	132	87
127	WFLA	NBC	24	Tampa-St. Petersburg	120	51	132	78
128	WREC	CBS	29	Memphis	131	108	57	114
129	WSPA	CBS	40	Gnville-Sptnbg-Ashvi	103	57	117	121
130	KENS	CBS	45	San Antonio	106	93	81	134
131	WLWC	NBC	28	Columbus	99	67	121	118
132	WISN	CBS	21	Milwaukee	97	98	121	82
133	WJBK	CBS	5	Detroit	93	99	114	106
134	WDAF	NBC	23	Kansas City	34	72	144	131
135	KMBC	ABC	23	Kansas City	102	133	88	90
136	WTVN	ABC	28	Columbus	128	130	63	105
137	WVEC	ABC	44	Norf-Newp News-Hamp	137	135	41	95
138	WKZO	CBS	41	Kalamazoo-Gr Rapids	108	100	88	142
139	WBMG	CBS	38	Birmingham	125	117	49	143
140	KOOL	CBS	45	Phoenix	98	76	140	119
141	WHBQ	ABC	29	Memphis	138	139	49	111
142	KBTV	ABC	32	Denver	91	128	142	42
143	WQXI	ABC	17	Atlanta	129	126	112	99
144	WCCB	ABC	35	Charlotte	133	129	81	137

Some Information About the Alfred I. duPont-Columbia University Awards for 1974–1975

EACH YEAR the awards are based upon research done in conjunction with the annual DuPont-Columbia Survey of Broadcast Journalism. There is no set number of awards, nor are there permanent categories for the awards, which will vary according to evidences of outstanding performance in news and public affairs during the year. Local and network radio, local and network television, as well as syndicated material, will be surveyed.

Although categories for the awards will not be set in advance, concerned parties are encouraged to suggest to the jurors examples of broadcast journalism which they feel are particularly worthy of attention. They are also invited to suggest subjects for research.

Suggestions for those wishing to participate:

1. Any concerned person, group, organization, or broadcast station may bring to the DuPont jury's attention material dealing with performance in broadcast news and public affairs.

2. If such information concerns a specific program, it should include the following particulars: (a) the time, the date, and the station carrying the program, (b) the subject of the program, (c) the reason the program is being singled out. If possible, there should be notification enough in advance of air time to permit jurors to view or hear the program at the time of the original broadcast. In any event, supporting material such as tapes, films, or scripts should be retained as documentation. *However, films, tapes, and other supporting material should not be submitted unless expressly asked for by the Director.*

3. If information submitted concerns long-term performance of an individual, a station, or other institution, names or call letters should be given, as well as a full statement of the reasons for the submission.

4. Nominations may be made throughout the year for programs aired between July 1, 1974, and June 30, 1975. Nominations must be postmarked no later than midnight, July 2, 1975.

5. All materials submitted will become the property of Columbia University.

6. All inquiries and correspondence should be addressed to:

    Director
    The Alfred I. duPont–Columbia University
        Survey and Awards
    Graduate School of Journalism
    Columbia University
    New York, N.Y. 10027

Acknowledgments

DURING THE PAST MONTHS the editor and jurors received generous assistance from a great number of organizations and individuals. Although it is not possible to list all those who have helped in some way, we would particularly like to express our gratitude to the following: the news directors and news men and women from the networks and individual stations who answered questionnaires, furnished tapes and films, and did the real work with which this volume and these awards are concerned. Each year their contribution to the Survey and to a well-informed American public increases.

We would also like to thank the awards and public information departments of the commercial networks and public television.

We are particularly indebted this year to the many members of the American Association of University Women who undertook and carried out an ambitious survey of local broadcast journalism, coast to coast. Under the direction of Ms. Lynne Stitt, they did an astute and painstaking job.

The volume of material this year was unusually heavy and complex, making the reportorial and research task of this year's DuPont Fellow, Zachary Sklar, particularly demanding. His contribution to the final volume was commensurately large. Associate Director Barbara Eddings and her predecessor, Jane Vittengl, supervised the collection of all materials, and Ms. Eddings was in charge of the arrangements for screening more than five hundred separate exhibits submitted for awards, a formidable exercise in logistics. Peggy Brawley again was responsible for the checking and final editing of the manuscript.

Louis Cowan, director of special projects for the Columbia University Graduate School of Journalism, made invaluable contributions to both the Survey and the broader activities of the program upon which it is based.

Again, special mention should be made of the continuing

coverage of broadcast journalism by *Variety, Advertising Age, Broadcasting, Television Digest, The New York Times, The Wall Street Journal,* and *Television/Radio Age,* which furnished the editor, Marvin Barrett, and the jurors with an invaluable record of the subject throughout the year.

As a reading of the text will indicate, much of the most interesting material came from the correspondents now located in over eighty of the major broadcast markets across the country. Their faithful attention to the news activities of their local stations and the resulting comments and recommendations are of great importance to the continuing success of the Survey and Awards.

Index

3 1543 50082 6385

384.554
B274m

743333

DATE DUE

MY 18 '76			
DE 16 '81			
DE 7 '84			

Cressman Library
Cedar Crest College
Allentown, Pa. 18104

DEMCO